To Walt Manca,
My most insightful
student. I wish
you improved
health & best
wishes.

Fondly
[signature]
Aug. 19, 1996

# THE GUERRILLA WARS OF
# CENTRAL AMERICA

# THE GUERRILLA WARS
# OF CENTRAL AMERICA

## NICARAGUA, EL SALVADOR AND GUATEMALA

# Saul Landau

WEIDENFELD AND NICOLSON
LONDON

To Gregory, Valerie, Carmen, Julia, Marie,
Sebastian, Camilo, Nicole, Marisol and Molly

First published in Great Britain in 1993 by

Weidenfeld and Nicolson
The Orion Publishing Group
5 Upper St Martins Lane
London WC2H 9EA

ISBN 0 297 821148

Filmset by Selwood Systems, Midsomer Norton
Printed in Great Britain by
Butler & Tanner Ltd,
Frome & London

# Contents

# Preface

Late in his life, Mao Tse-tung was reportedly asked to evaluate the French Revolution. 'It's too early to tell,' the Chinese revolutionary leader replied. Each generation judges the past anew. What appears heroic in one generation may well seem absurd to the next. Viewed from close range, the 1980s' wars in Central America emerge as a series of bizarre undertakings that occurred in one of those rare transition periods in which history moves from one identifiable era to another – albeit the nature of the future period is far from clear in this case.

Great epocal transformations mean alterations in the quality and quantity of relationships: between town and city; labour force and means of production; people and technology. In transition periods, agencies of history change as well. Thus, guerrilla wars, which from World War II's end onward brought about national independence in several former colonies, appeared to have run their course as means of transforming colonized peoples into viable nations. Yet in the 1960s, 1970s and well into the 1980s, revolutionary patriots in Central America assumed that only armed struggle could free their people from US domination and oligarchical rule. They also believed that once in power they could direct the construction of real nations, ones that could provide not only the basic necessities of life, but also realize the spiritual destiny of the people. With this nineteenth-century ideal the revolutionary nationlists vied for state power, because they saw the nation–state as their agency of change.

In most of Central America in the 1970s and into the mid-1980s, guerrilla warfare appeared to be the only method available to win power, since the oligarchies and their military cohorts had systematically closed the political space. Central American revolutionaries believed that the guerrilla model, used successfully elsewhere, could work for Nicaragua, El Salvador and Guatemala. The Chinese communists had 'liberated' their nation through a combination of guerrilla and regular warfare; Fidel Castro led some 2,000 Cuban guerrillas to rout the 50,000-man army of Dictator Fulgencio Batista and spark a revolution that rid Cuba of US influence; Algerians drove out the French; and Vietnamese warriors fought both the French and the Americans to reunite their long-colonized land.

In the post World War II era, guerrilla war became an established method to win sovereignty and social justice for Third World peoples. By the late 1980s, geopolitical changes made the axioms of guerrilla war dubious. What means the Third World poor will fashion to transform their impossible conditions of life and work is still unknown. What is certain is that the oppressed will find ways to redress their grievances and revolt against those who grind them down.

I have used shorthand expressions like the United States (or US) to refer to a small group of decision-makers in Washington, who claim the name for the entire population. In fact, throughout the decade of wars in Central America the majority of US citizens steadfastly refused to learn the difference between 'friends' and 'enemies' in the region.

The completion of this book owes a great deal to several scholars who helped me research, think and craft the final product. Angela Blake, Micah Fink, Jim O'Connor, Patrick Steele, Julia Sweig and William Thackeray all contributed imagination, energy and grubby detail work. I am grateful to them.

The Institute for Policy Studies also facilitated the writing of this book by encouraging me and providing support on every level.

November 1992

# Chronology

|        | In September, an FSLN-led insurrection in major towns in the north is put down with massive repression and bombing by National Guard. |
|--------|---|
| 1979 | In April the US cuts off Somoza following the televised murder by a National Guard lieutenant of ABC newsman Bill Stewart. |

In September, an FSLN-led insurrection in major towns in the north is put down with massive repression and bombing by National Guard.

1979    In April the US cuts off Somoza following the televised murder by a National Guard lieutenant of ABC newsman Bill Stewart.

Somoza flees on 17 July. The National Guard surrenders on 19 July.

Government of National Reconstruction, led by the Sandinistas, takes power.

1981    In December, President Reagan authorizes a CIA covert action against Nicaragua, of a force of 500 men to 'interdict' alleged arms traffic from Nicaragua to rebels in El Salvador. In December Nicaraguans report raids by *contrarevolucionarios* (Contras) on the northern border.

1982    Former Sandinista official, Eden Pastora, forms a Contra organization based in Costa Rica, thus opening a two-front guerrilla war against the Sandinistas.

1984    In January, Contras take credit for mining Nicaraguan harbours. An investigation determines that the mining was done by the CIA. In May an assassination attempt at La Penca, on the Costa Rican–Nicaraguan border, wounds Pastora and leaves several journalists dead and wounded. The perpetrator escapes. The CIA is suspected.

1985    Nicaraguan government's law suit against the United States for committing aggression is taken up by the International Court of Justice at The Hague. The Court decides in favour of the Sandinistas. In elections, Sandinistas win over 60 per cent of the vote for parliamentary seats. The United States refuses to recognize the election results; most other countries accept the vote as valid. Congress cuts off aid to the Contras, but national security officials led by Robert MacFarlane and Colonel Oliver North continue to fund the Contras from money derived from surreptitious arms sales to Iran.

1986–89    In the summer of 1986 a Contra company infiltrates into the northern city of Esteli, but is forced to retreat under a Sandinista counteroffensive. Battles rage on many fronts, with the Contras still unable to take and hold a piece of Nicaraguan territory. War casualties, including civilians, number some 30,000. Damage exceeds $14 billion.

1990    Sandinistas lose national election. Violeta Chamorro, widow of the slain Pedro Joaquin Chamorro, backed by the United States, wins the election for president. Washington immediately stops the Contra war.

## El Salvador

1927    Farabundo Marti, a young communist intellectual and organizer, is banished from Salvador, and joins Augusto Sandino to fight US imperialism in Nicaragua.

1932    Marti and others inspire a peasant uprising. General Maximiliano Hernandez Martinez puts down the rebellion, killing over 20,000 peasants in the process. Marti is among the victims.

1944    Students strike, rioting in capital, and an attempted coup against Hernandez Martinez begins a movement for democratic rule.

1969    In June, El Salvador engages in so-called Soccer War with Honduras – Salvadoran air force bombs Tegucigalpa airport. War ends after five weeks, with 2,000 dead.

1969–71    First revolutionary guerrilla organizations form, including groups that later join together in the Farabundo Marti Front for National Liberation. Cayetano Carpio, Joaquin Villalobos and Shafik Handal emerge as young leaders.

1972      Jose Napoleon Duarte, a Christian Democrat, and Guillermo Ungo, a Socialist, are elected President and Vice-President but the military denies them their offices.

1975      Roque Dalton, Salvador's best known revolutionary poet, is assassinated by members of a rival political sect.

1977      Another fraudulent election of an unpopular general is followed by demonstrations and a state of seige.

1978      Over 100 people 'disappear' as the result of activities of members of the armed forces out of uniform. These groups later become known as death squads.

1979      In October, to prevent a Nicaraguan-style revolution, reformist Colonels Adolfo Majano and Jaime Abdul Guttierrez lead a successful coup against the ruling military regime. The United States offers full support.

1980      Death Squads and military units kill more than 1,000 people. Demonstrations become frequent. Armed clashes take place between revolutionaries and the military.

     March 24 Archbishop Oscar Romero is shot to death while conducting a mass in a chapel in San Salvador.

     May 12 Colonel Majano loses his dominant position in the ruling junta when the Salvadoran officers' corps names conservative Colonel Gutierrez as Armed Forces Commander.

     October 10 Several revolutionary groups form the Farabundo Marti National Liberation Front (FMLN) to wage armed struggle against the government.

     November 27 Six leaders of the Revolutionary Democratic Front, the civilian wing of the rebels, are found dead, victims of death squads.

     December 2 Three American nuns and a lay worker are abducted, raped and murdered. US Ambassador Robert White accuses the Salvadoran security forces of the crime. He calls cashiered Major Roberto D'Aubuisson, who is thought to be the leader of the death squads, a 'psychopathic killer'.

1981      January 10 FMLN rebels attack military installations in San Salvador and Santa Ana in a 'final offensive', and appeal for a nationwide strike. Offensive and strike fail to bring down the government. The Salvadoran military undertakes its own offensive to wipe out the rebels. It also fails.

     On August 28 Mexico and France recognize the FDR/FMLN as a legitimate 'representative political force'. Nine Latin American governments accuse the two countries of interfering in Salvadoran internal affairs and favouring the 'subversive extremes'.

1981–82      Major US military presence is established, with 55 advisers and hundreds of millions of dollars in military aid.

1981–83      FMLN cripples parts of the Salvadoran economy. US estimates FMLN sabotage as high as $1 billion. Victims of death squads and army massacres reach 30,000.

1984–86      Salvadoran armed forces and FMLN reach state of dynamic equilibrium, neither side able to gain overriding strategic advantage. The death toll mounts to over 50,000.

1987      The FMLN and the government hold a peace conference, which results in much publicity and little peace.

| 1989 | Duarte serves out his term, and dies of cancer 23 February 1990. A right wing government led by President Alfredo Cristiani replaces the Christian Democrats. |
| 1991 | Guillermo Ungo, director of the FDR and Duarte's running mate in 1972, dies in Mexico of a stroke. |
| 1992 | After multiple rounds of negotiations under UN auspices, the FMLN and the Salvadoran government announce a Peace Accord, promising a cease fire by the end of January 1992. The estimate of war dead is 80,000, most of them civilians. |

## GUATEMALA

| 1920 | US troops land 'to protect American interests' against insurgents for 18 days. |
| 1932 | Dictator Jorge Ubico orders raids on Communist Party headquarters, executes most of Guatemala's communists. |
| 1944 | Demonstrations in the streets lead to removal of Ubico and election of Juan Jose Arevalo, first democratically elected Guatemalan president. |
| 1951 | Jacobo Arbenz elected president, begins agrarian reform, including expropriation of some of the vast uncultivated acreage of the United Fruit Company. |
| 1954 | The government of Guatemala is overthrown by a CIA inspired coup, aided by the United Fruit Company. The Arbenz government is replaced by the CIA's colonel, Castillo Armas, who begins to reverse the reforms of the Arevalo and Arbenz periods. |
| 1957 | Castillo Armas is murdered and Col. Ydigoras Fuentes succeeds him after 'winning' an electoral farce. |
| 1961 | Ydigoras Fuentes offers Guatemalan territory to the CIA as a base to train Cuban exiles planning to invade Cuba and overthrow the government of Fidel Castro. |
| 1962 | Former army officers Marco Antonio Yon Sosa and Luis Augusto Turcios Lima form guerrilla fronts and declare war on the government. |
| 1966 | Julio Cesar Mendez Montenegro is elected president and provides a civilian façade for a US-backed counterinsurgency program to wipe out the guerrillas. |
| 1969 | After suffering military setbacks, guerrilla leader Yon Sosa gives himself up to a Mexican military post and is murdered. |
| 1970 | Oil discovered in Guatemala. |
| 1974 | Fraud and corruption dominate election of General Kjell Langerud over rival military candidate Efrain Rios Montt. |
| 1970–75 | 15,000 Guatemalens 'disappear' as a result of counterinsurgency strategy. Hundreds of thousands become refugees as the military depopulates 'guerrilla dominated' areas. |
| 1975 | Mario Payeras and a group of guerrillas assassinate Luis Arenas Barrera, the 'Jaguar of Ixcan'. |
| 1978 | General Romeo Lucas Garcia elected; less than one-third of the electorate vote, and only half of that for him. |
| 1982 | In February, Guatemalan National Revolutionary Unity (URNG) party formed. 23 March Rios Montt leads a military coup of junior officers against corruption in the military; vows to respect human rights and pursue the war against the subversives. |

1983     Death squads claim more than 200 victims monthly.

8 August A coup overthrows Rios Montt and replaces him with a traditional military government.

1985     International opinion and the Guatemalan middle class successfully pressure for an end to military rule. Christian Democrat, Vinicio Cerezo is elected president, but the military continue to exterminate the Indian peasantry under the pretext of fighting 'subversion'.

1986–89     The revolutionaries change tactics and begin to use newly found political space for organizing in the cities and countryside. The military continues to dispossess and kill Indian peasants.

1990     Myrna Mack, Guatemalan anthropologist who was organizing to protect the rights of the poor, is murdered. Death squads are suspected.

1990–91     UN request peace talks commence between the government and revolutionary organizations. Little progress is reported.

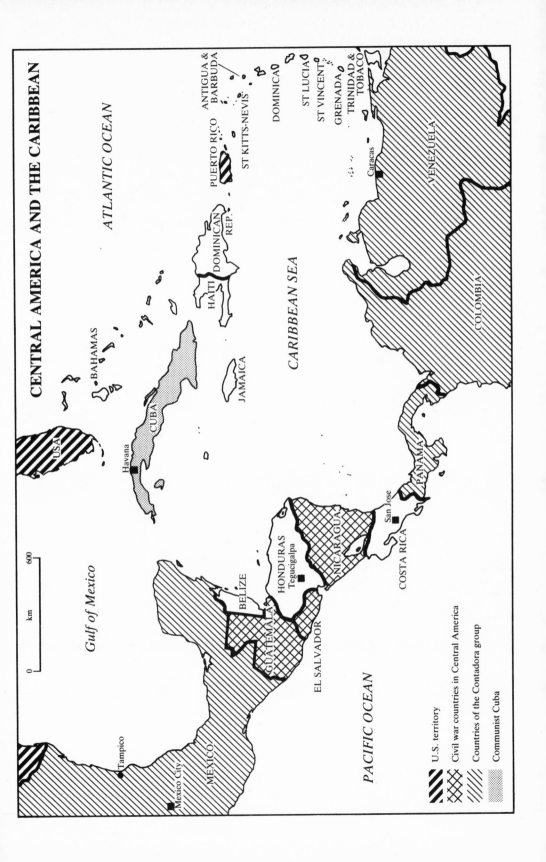

# CENTRAL AMERICA AND THE CARIBBEAN

ATLANTIC OCEAN

Gulf of Mexico

0 ─ 600
km

CARIBBEAN SEA

PACIFIC OCEAN

USA

Tampico
Mexico City
MEXICO

Havana
CUBA
BAHAMAS

JAMAICA

HAITI
DOMINICAN REP.

PUERTO RICO

ST KITTS-NEVIS

ANTIGUA & BARBUDA

DOMINICA

ST LUCIA
ST VINCENT
GRENADA
TRINIDAD & TOBAGO

BELIZE

GUATEMALA
EL SALVADOR
HONDURAS
Tegucigalpa

NICARAGUA

COSTA RICA
San Jose

PANAMA

Caracas
VENEZUELA

COLOMBIA

U.S. territory

Civil war countries in Central America

Countries of the Contadora group

Communist Cuba

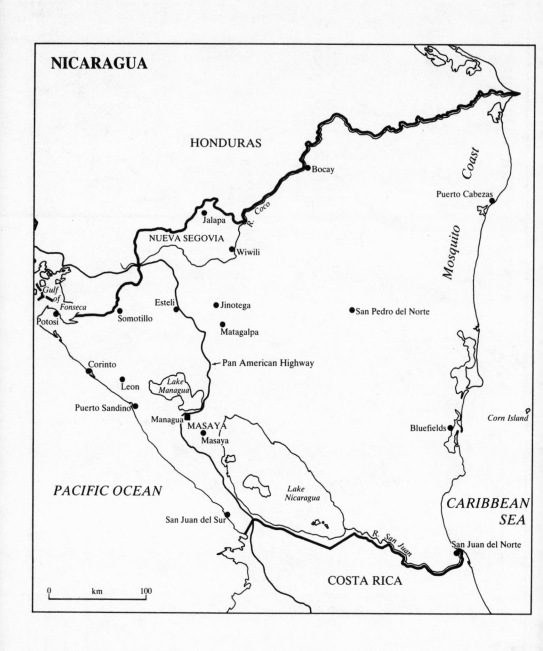

**NICARAGUA**

HONDURAS

Bocay

Puerto Cabezas

*R. Coco*

Jalapa

NUEVA SEGOVIA

Wiwili

*Mosquito Coast*

*Gulf of Fonseca*

Esteli

Jinotega

San Pedro del Norte

Potosi

Somotillo

Matagalpa

Corinto

Pan American Highway

*Lake Managua*

Leon

Puerto Sandino

Managua

MASAYA

Masaya

Bluefields

*Corn Island*

*PACIFIC OCEAN*

*Lake Nicaragua*

*CARIBBEAN SEA*

San Juan del Sur

*R. San Juan*

San Juan del Norte

COSTA RICA

0     km     100

EL SALVADOR

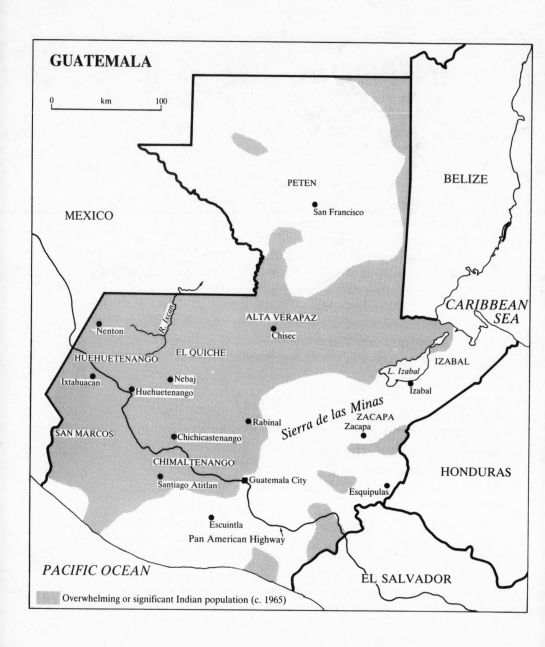

GUATEMALA

0    km    100

MEXICO

PETEN

San Francisco

BELIZE

CARIBBEAN
SEA

ALTA VERAPAZ

Nenton          Chisec

*R. Ixcan*

HUEHUETENANGO

EL QUICHE

IZABAL

*L. Izabal*

Ixtahuacan          Nebaj

Izabal

Huehuetenango

*Sierra de las Minas*

ZACAPA

Rabinal

Zacapa

SAN MARCOS

Chichicastenango

CHIMALTENANGO

HONDURAS

Santiago Atitlan          Guatemala City

Esquipulas

Escuintla

Pan American Highway

PACIFIC OCEAN

EL SALVADOR

Overwhelming or significant Indian population (c. 1965)

# INTRODUCTION: THE ROOTS OF CENTRAL AMERICA'S WARS

"Virtually every study of the region, including the [1984] Kissinger Commission Report, has concluded that the revolutions of Central America primarily have been caused by decades of poverty, bloody repression, and frustrated efforts at bringing about political reform".
James Lemoyne, *New York Times Magazine*, 5 April 1989.

## The United States: One Cause of Central America's Wars

'Central America is certainly in America,' one sage ventured, 'but is it central?' This sarcasm was provoked by the amount of money and emotional rhetoric members of the Reagan administration were expending on a region which, by the mid-1980s, could scarcely claim any US investment. Compared to Europe, Japan, the Middle East, or even South Korea, Central America barely registered in Washington's trade and commerce indices.

Strategically, the Caribbean, seen by President Theodore Roosevelt as a vital American lake, has become extremely well fortified. US fleets operate in both the Atlantic and Pacific Oceans, independent of the Panama Canal – the giant aircraft carriers and battleships are too large to pass through; even the US commercial fleet made little use of the canal by the mid-1980s. The United States maintains bases in Guantanamo, Cuba, throughout Panama and at Vieques, Puerto Rico, in addition to the fortified port facilities offered by US cities on the Gulf of Mexico. US military aircraft can reach the most remote point in the

Caribbean in less than an hour. There is no area in the world more secure militarily.

Similarly, Central America does not fit into the center of US economic strategy. Miami's location, on the Caribbean Sea, serves American investors well as a base for commercial travel and hemispheric banking. The problem was that in the 1980s US investors were not pouring funds into Central America, but into more lucrative places.

Nevertheless, in 1981, the United States' Ambassador to the United Nations, Jeane Kirkpatrick, pronounced Central America 'the most important place in the world'. For her, the region symbolized a larger struggle, between that evil empire, the Soviet Union, seen as the backer of all the 'terrorist, guerrilla movements' in Central America, and the forces of 'democracy', embodied in the very fabric of US policy, as well as by 'our friends' in the Third World.

Ironically, except for the week of the Cuban Missile Crisis in 1962, the Soviet Union has neither possessed nor sought bases or investment opportunities in the area. Fidel Castro convinced Soviet Premier Nikita Khrushchev that without a clear deterrent the United States would invade Cuba and destroy its revolution. Khrushchev gambled and ordered the installation of medium-range missiles and bombers that could easily reach US territory. Before the weapons were battle-ready, however, President Kennedy responded by placing a naval quarantine on Soviet ships. The Soviets backed down and withdrew the missiles and airplanes. When the facts became known, two decades later, it turned out that Khrushchev only possessed four inter-continental ballistic missiles to the United States' sixty. The 'Missile Gap', which Kennedy had dramatized during his election campaign in 1960, existed, but that missile deficit was on the Soviet side.

The Kennedy–Khrushchev Accords, as the negotiated settlement became known after October 1962, reaffirmed the Caribbean and Central America as a US sphere of influence – except for Cuba. The Soviets were allowed to maintain a division of troops on the island, but no 'strategic' weapons. The men in the Kremlin learned from the Missile Crisis that, though their intention was to protect the Cuban Revolution, the United States would interpret as provocation any military moves in territories located near US borders. The facts, however, showed the reverse. For more than thirty years Strategic Air Command bombers with nuclear payloads flew round-the-clock missions up to the edge of Soviet air space. Nevertheless, maintaining a Soviet division in Cuba and establishing a listening post there 'proved' to the Cold Warriors that the Soviets were indeed aggressive in their intentions toward the United States in its own arena.

Soviet marines have never invaded Central America – under any pretext. Nor did the Kremlin leaders ever consider such adventurism. Under Moscow's orders Central American communist parties have been less than revolutionary, measured by Castro's standards. By 1986, moreover, Soviet leaders made it clear that they had little interest in confronting the United States in Central America – or anywhere else in the world. They opposed Cuban leader Fidel Castro's policy of 'exporting' revolution by means of armed struggle throughout Latin America. The Soviets saw themselves as 'stuck' with historical obligations to maintain significant levels of aid to Cuba.

Compared to the amounts given to Cuba, which was ruled by a Communist Party and integrated into the socialist bloc economic plan, the Sandinistas received minimal aid from 1980 to 1990. Soviet officials swore that they had no intention of cultivating Nicaragua with a view to creating 'another Cuba'.

For Mrs Kirkpatrick and the other Reagan ideologues such statements meant nothing. Who could trust the Devil's word? She pointed to Soviet military and energy aid to the Nicaraguan government as proof of Moscow's imperialist intentions. Soviet Foreign Ministry spokesmen insisted that their offer of weapons and oil was only to help the ruling Sandinistas defend their sovereignty, a modest gesture designed to maintain their reputation as defenders of newly independent nations.

Mrs Kirkpatrick persisted in blaming Moscow, dismissing even the possibility that Central American armed resistance to corrupt regimes could have had its roots in the social inequities that had prevailed in most of the region. 'Because the miseries of traditional life are familiar,' Kirkpatrick wrote, 'they are bearable to ordinary people who, growing up in the society, learn to cope and therefore accept the fact that wealth, power, status and other resources favor an affluent few while traditional autocrats maintain the masses in misery.' Massachusetts' Institute of Technology's Professor Noam Chomsky characterized this overtly ideological justification for continued US backing for repressive right-wing oligarchies as a medieval view of human beings: those that are capable of feeling pain, as a result of social inequities; and Mrs Kirkpatrick's 'lower orders [who] feel no pain'.

Only the most callous reactionaries agreed with the Kirkpatrick view that 'our lack of concern is quite proper; indeed quite decent and moral'. Even the godfather of modern realpolitik, Henry Kissinger, who chaired a Central America policy commission for President Reagan, accepted the social root theory of guerrilla war in Central America. Indeed, conservative Latin Americans saw Mrs Kirkpatrick's projection of Soviet bases in Nicaragua as remote at best.

United States' and not Soviet intervention in Latin American affairs for over a hundred years is one of the two root causes of the current series of wars in one of the continent's poorest areas. Ironically, the conflicts in Nicaragua, El Salvador and Guatemala provoked Latin American leaders to take unprecedentedly bold initiatives, including the formulation of a Central American Peace Plan, not because of a Soviet threat, but because they feared that US leaders would once again send troops south of the Rio Grande, which would provoke instability throughout the region.

The division of wealth in the Central American nations followed a colonial pattern – despite the development of a small middle class during the nineteenth century – one that impelled labor, peasant and student leaders to see revolution as the only way to achieve social justice. Beginning with the Spanish conquest in the sixteenth century, a few dozen families amassed the lion's share of Central America's patrimony. By the late nineteenth century, coffee and bananas began to replace traditional crops. The result was that production for agricultural exports suffocated the local market economy. The oligarchs redrew their estates into plantation-size units.

Local elites welcomed foreign fruit companies into Guatemala and Honduras, and displayed an eagerness to share the land with them in return for military protection from the United States against revolution. Together with the United Fruit Company and other outside investors, the ruling elite forced the peasantry into a landless and seasonal labor force. They dispossessed families, many of them Indians, from communal lands and thus set the stage for a classic class confrontation.

There were periodic uprisings, followed by brutal repression. US gunboats and marines became part and parcel of the repression formula, and local struggles for social justice fused gradually with a nationalist sentiment, fueled by resentment against the United States.

By the 1960s, one global ideology linked national liberation, anti-imperial and social justice movements throughout the Third World: Marxism–Leninism. The local oligarchy and their allies, the police and military, were the logical targets of reformers and revolutionaries. Police and military officials, most of them trained by US military professionals, responded to ruling elites, not to law or reason. When the local agencies of repression failed to stop reform or revolution, for a century and a half the United States used its own forces to dominate the territory south of the Rio Grande. From 1800 until the 1930s, according to the State Department, the president dispatched armed forces on more than seventy occasions to Latin America and the Caribbean.

## Brief History of US Interventions

In 1823, President James Monroe's Secretary of State, John Quincy Adams, enunciated an ambitious and audacious strategy, which became known as the Monroe Doctrine. Lacking a mighty economy or formidable navy, the United States nonetheless staked out the entire hemisphere as its domain, warning potential European colonizers to stay away. The United States steadily drove the native Indians, British, French, Russians and Spanish from their North American lands, colonies and possessions; US troops also made periodic landings in Latin America. Initially part of a pirate-pursuing policy, US presidents quickly set a precedent for landing marines on foreign soil for less laudable reasons.

In the 1830s US expeditions landed in Argentina, Peru and Mexico on missions unrelated to pirates. Two were designed to suppress revolution; the incursion into Mexico was related to the Texas 'war for independence'. In 1848 the United States took more than half of Mexican territory, which later became the states of Texas, Arizona, New Mexico, California, Colorado and Nevada. In the 1850s, US forces landed in Nicaragua (three times), Uruguay (twice), Argentina, Panama, Paraguay and Mexico – mostly, according to a State Department document, 'to protect US property interests during a revolution'.

Over the next three decades the State Department established a pattern. US forces intervened in Colombia, Mexico, Panama, Uruguay, Haiti and Argentina. The Washington policy elite avoided using the word 'empire' in explaining the reasons for dispatching US troops abroad. Americans had a 'mission'; indeed, a manifest destiny to dominate the hemisphere. Since colonial times American intellectuals had spun versions of 'our' unique responsibilities, or even divine assignments to bring 'our' order to the less fortunate of the world. By 1890, US leaders faced the issue openly: what kind of empire would best serve US interests? An old-fashioned colonial-style or a new informal empire, which would be less costly and preserve the façade of democracy?

The consensus emerged for the Open Door approach. In a series of unilateral proclamations, called the Open Door Notes, Secretary of State John Hay announced US intentions of entering areas of the world to which European powers had already laid claim. By the early 1900s the Platt Amendment forced the supposedly independent Cubans to allow the US to intervene in Cuba at will, while the Roosevelt Corollary to the Monroe Doctrine established the Caribbean as a US lake. In the Caribbean islands and Central American nations, the Americans allied themselves with local oligarchs, not European colonial administrations. By pushing for nominally republican forms of government, Washington policy makers, often indistinguishable from entrepreneurs, deflected the issue of any real American commitment to democracy. The fragile republican façades fell apart periodically; whenever the populace pressed for real democracy, marines landed to restore them. As long as the cost in money, and dead US marines, remained low, the interventionist consensus held.

From the late 1890s through the early 1930s US presidents routinely dispatched marines and naval forces to Central America and the Caribbean under the rubric of 'safeguarding American lives and property'. Often the impressive shadow cast by the immense US battleship over the capital was sufficient to intimidate a reformist coalition. On other occasions US forces actually used their superior weapons and training against Central American and Caribbean revolutionaries. The beneficiaries of these actions for the first decades of the century were several US corporations and banks, which dominated the Central American export economies. They commanded a cheap labor force, had access to resources and enjoyed the police protection of the US government should rebellion break out. Marine General Smedley Butler reflected bitterly on his thirty-three years in the Marine Corps, leading US invasion forces throughout the region:

During [my military career] I spent most of my time being a high-class muscles man for Big Business, for Wall Street, and for the bankers. In short I was a racketeer for capitalism... I helped make Haiti and Cuba a decent place for the National City Bank to collect revenues... I helped purify Nicaragua for the international house of Brown Brothers in 1909–1912. I brought light to the Dominican Republic for American sugar interests in 1916. I helped make Honduras 'right' for American fruit companies in 1903.

When Franklin Roosevelt won the 1932 election and announced that the United States would change its behavior and begin to act like a good neighbor toward Latin America, optimists in Central America such as Costa Rica's 'Pepe' Figueras, Venezuela's Romulo Betancourt and Puerto Rico's Luis Muñoz Marin believed that the United States might finally respect Latin American sovereignty. The Roosevelt camp proclaimed that the days of 'gun-boat' and 'dollar' diplomacy had evolved into the new era of respect for the poorer nations to the south. Indeed, Rexford Tugwell, one of Roosevelt's 'Kitchen Cabinet', wrote the Puerto Rican Constitution.

But most of the local armed forces and police already had sufficient training by US forces to repress democracy, without the aid of US troops. Both local oligarchs and US investors understood that whatever language the policy people used mattered little to their 'bottom line': revolutionary challenges to their interests would not be permitted to survive. When local forces could not 'handle' protests or rebellions, as insurrection grew in Cuba in 1933, for example, the president dispatched an emissary, along with a large war ship, to convince members of Cuba's armed forces and political leadership that the United States looked with disfavor on their activities.

If persuasion and a show of force failed, the marines came, and, in Nicaragua and Haiti, they stayed as occupying armies well into the 1930s, even as President Woodrow Wilson piously proclaimed his commitment to self-determination. The US government glossed over the gross injustice built into its relations with Latin America with glib rhetoric about republican forms of government.

But history does run on an even course, and in the late 1930s events in Europe and the Pacific brought about a second world war, a shift of geopolitical power and the prevalence of democracy and human rights as internationally accepted guidelines for governance. President Roosevelt, seeking global support for the war effort against fascism, announced his doctrine of the 'four freedoms' – the basis of the modern human rights language – as the cause of all humanity. With the signing of the United Nations Charter, Latin American reformers and even some revolutionaries took inspiration, believing that a new, non-imperialist order could dawn.

It was revolutionary that a US president supported the notion that small nations should have the same rights as large ones to self-determination. In fact, in the post World War II era the United States inherited the empires of the decaying powers – especially of its allies. American control did not mean the end of the formal imperial structures, but, as the liberation-minded Third World nations quickly learned, formal independence did not signify genuine sovereignty.

When a modest experiment in self-determination was tried in Guatemala (1944–54), it was crushed with the same ruthlessness that Washington had historically shown toward independence in its 'back yard'. The CIA carried out a coup in Guatemala, installing a self-perpetuating pro-American gang of military criminals who have held power for almost forty years, using the murder of hundreds of thousands of Guatemalans as their reproductive mechanism.

By the 1950s, the cooperative tone of Rooseveltian wartime rhetoric had changed to a Cold War confrontational discourse. Attention and resources were directed at a global enemy, lest the 'free world' be ground under the mighty red boot.

Washington strategists automatically included Central America as part of 'the free world', although Central Americans had no freedom to pursue their own political destiny. Anti-Soviet ideology justified CIA covert activists who overthrew regimes to 'fight communist subversion', not to 'restore order'.

Not until the triumph of Fidel Castro and his guerrillas in Cuba, in 1959, did Washington face a challenge to its continuing domination. And Castro, Cuba's revolutionary leader, immediately offered his island experiment to the rest of the Third World as a model that could be used for more than token independence. Indeed, African and Latin American liberation movements found inspiration in the Cuban example. Castro proved that revolutionaries need not be inhibited by the old axiom: 'revolution can be made with or without, but never against the army.' The Cuban model illustrated, Castro boasted, that all of Latin America could successfully follow the Cuban road to national liberation.

Latin American oligarchs panicked as events in Cuba unfolded. By 1960 the Soviet Union began to replace the United States as Cuba's most important supplier – and friend. US national security planners saw Cuba as a highly inflammable element, which, unchecked, would spread communism – now interchangeable with revolution. President Eisenhower ordered the CIA to repeat its 'success' in Guatemala on the island nation just ninety miles from the US shore.

Presidents Eisenhower and Kennedy mandated the CIA to recruit, train and launch an exile invasion of the island. The agency's plan envisioned an uprising of anti-Castro elements to take place precisely at the time that the armed Cuban exiles invaded the island. The Bay of Pigs 'fiasco' in April 1961 pushed President Kennedy to admit that the

CIA could not 'get the job done'. As US national security officials plotted to assassinate Castro and invade Cuba, the history of the hemisphere – and the world – was altered. Soviet Premier Nikita Khrushchev installed medium-range nuclear missiles and stationed medium-range bombers in Cuba to 'deter' a US invasion.

The Soviet Union became a player in the Western Hemisphere as the October 1962 Missile Crisis brought the world to the brink of nuclear war. Inadvertently, it also opened a new era of US – Latin American relations. After the confrontation over Cuba, people throughout the world understood that regional crises – even in the Caribbean, which the United States traditionally claimed as exclusive domain – could escalate into global nuclear encounters.

The Missile Crisis produced the Kennedy–Khrushchev Accord, in which the United States pledged not to invade Cuba in return for Soviet missile withdrawal and a promise never to reinstall 'offensive' weapons on the island. To counter the challenge of revolution posed by Cuba, the United States developed two contradictory programs: the Alliance for Progress and counterinsurgency. The alliance offered a capitalist alternative to Castro's revolutionary formula. By pouring development funds into Latin America and promoting political democracy to coincide with the introduction of technology, a healthy development was supposed to occur.

In case that combination failed to deflect the revolutionary cutting edge, US Special Forces would be on hand to train and equip with modern weapons the age-old foes of democratic development: the military and the police. Central American patriots, inspired by Kennedy's promises and money that began to flow from Washington, believed that they could build functioning republics with the help of the liberals up north.

Inside the Kennedy policy apparatus, proponents of these contradictory forces vied for dominance. Some, like General Edward Lansdale, one of the president's favorites, attempted to combine the alliance and counterinsurgency approaches. To capture hearts and minds required spending on social programs and teaching Third-World nations (like South Vietnam) how to build US-style institutions. The communist enemy, on the other hand, had to be met simultaneously with devastating force, whether in his guerrilla lair or underground urban hideout.

President Johnson's dispatch of troops to the Dominican Republic in 1965 destroyed any illusions held by Latin Americans about the United States' respect for their sovereignty. In Bolivia, in October

1967, US-trained rangers captured the Argentine revolutionary physician Ernesto 'Che' Guevara and his band of Cuban and Bolivian guerrillas, thus destroying Castro's most strategic attempt to build a Cuba-style revolution in the Andes. Throughout the continent, US police and military advisers worked with torturers, murderers and fascists to repress not only revolution, but all forms of democracy. By the end of the 1960s dictatorships prevailed in Latin America. The alliance, along with the Kennedy dream of spreading the liberal US order to the Third World, was dead.

However, the counterinsurgency advocates claimed that their formula did work to prevent the spread of revolution. They could not make such claims in Vietnam, since the US military did not defeat the Vietnamese communists, and, in part, because the US public became fiercely divided by the war. Without a consensus to pursue a military mission, or simply to withdraw US troops from Southeast Asia, Lyndon Johnson lost his mandate and his will to govern. His policies had defeated revolution in the Western Hemisphere, except for Cuba. But the resistance to the Vietnam War that developed inside the United States endured after the war ended and became known as the Vietnam Syndrome: the animated public response against the Vietnam War was extended to include any protracted military engagement; for policy makers it meant a reluctance to commit US troops to foreign adventures.

## The Vietnam Syndrome and Low-intensity Conflict

The Vietnam War demonstrated to the world the limits of US power. The determination of the Vietnamese communists and the social discord produced by the 'war at home' diminished the presidential option of deploying troops abroad, so that by the time Nicaraguan revolutionaries threatened to overthrow the regime of Anastasio Somoza, Jimmy Carter saw little advantage in trying to seek public support for a US military expedition. Faced with revolutionaries in power in Cuba, Grenada and Nicaragua, and threats of radical guerrilla triumphs in El Salvador and Guatemala, the US national security neo-logicians reworked older policies and coined a novel addition to the list of bloodless bureaucratic euphemisms: Low Intensity Conflict (LIC).

Low-intensity war was designed to bypass the issue of US troops in Third World wars. While avoiding the appearance of direct military intervention, LIC experts argued, the United States could finance, train and advise local forces committed to a US notion of order. These low-intensity conflicts could be financed year after year with small appropriations from Congress. American TV viewers would see no ugly body bags returning home, nor witness the kinds of incident that first bred the Vietnam Syndrome. What LIC required was a continuing propaganda war against communists, terrorists and, later, drug traffickers, all of which provided the appropriate crisis atmosphere to allow the LIC experts to introduce their jargon into the national security vocabulary.

LIC intellectuals elaborated the finer points of this new form of imperialism into a doctrine, if not an actual literary trend, in certain avant-garde anti-communist political circles. LIC professionals, trained in counterinsurgency war in the 1960s, emerged to provide the doctrine with a sophisticated language and a means to market the idea to the public and to Congress. In the 1980s, Central America became a military and political testing ground for the doctrine. While the justification for interventions took on Cold War language, the actual behavior remained remarkably similar to the past.

After World War II, however, the United States did enjoy world-wide hegemony as the cultural, economic and military superpower. It imposed an ethos of anti-communism as the official justification for most of its post World War II interventions. This new 'free world' discourse did not convince skeptical Latin Americans, however, who saw US policy as a long string of morally unjustifiable interference.

Each US incursion was etched into the Latin American political consciousness; just as American policy-makers dismissed the historical record with literary snaps of the finger. 'Perhaps over the years we should have intervened less, or intervened more, or intervened differently,' Henry Kissinger wrote in his commission report on Central America in 1984. He was articulating the sensibilities of a superpower policy-maker. Kissinger assumed that the United States had the prerogative to intervene, and the Cold War provided ideological justification for such action during a particular period of history.

American global power and its definition of the world within the Cold War framework forced international dimensions on to all regional conflicts, or civil wars. The Iran–Iraq and Iraq–Kuwait conflicts threatened global oil shipments, disputes in Southeast Asia and southern Africa related to rival big power politics, geopolitical alignments and resource accessibility. By the mid-1980s, the continuing struggles for independence and social justice in Central America and the US response to them had evoked concern throughout the Western Hemisphere and

Europe. Indeed, the first Latin American initiative in recent history, Contadora, formed by Mexico, Panama, Colombia and Venezuela, grew directly out of fears that conflicts in Nicaragua and El Salvador could have a severe impact on the rest of Latin America. European nations offered support for these efforts, despite Washington's displeasure with their 'meddling'.

The wars being fought in a few tiny nations engaged the entire political world. Although Nicaragua and El Salvador had no strategic importance or economic weight, the national security elite involved countries as distant as Saudi Arabia, Israel and China in covert arms deals. The US obsession with the Sandinistas caused a major political scandal (Iran–Contra) and placed Nicaragua on the stage of world history. The World Court, major multilateral financial institutions, the OAS and the UN all became involved in the Latin American region. Refugee populations mushroomed well beyond the borders of conflict and the ecological costs of these regional struggles have spread to other areas.

In the following chapters about Nicaraguan, Salvadoran and Guatemalan revolution and counter-revolution, the reader should bear in mind that in the era of the Global Village the causes and effects of what were once isolated and regional affairs reach the far corners of the world. The nationalist quest for the self-realization of each people continues to drive Third World revolutionaries, despite the unpropitious circumstances they face in the late twentieth century. The story of Central American wars is about the attempts of patriots to fulfill the visions of those who began the liberation and independence processes more than a century before. They were aided by courageous and principled individuals inside the United States, whose words and deeds made it impossible for President Reagan to forge a consensus for direct US intervention. In doing so they joined the revolutionaries of Central America as actors on the world stage, even though the ideals of independence for which so many have fought and died are a far cry from being realized.

# 2

# NICARAGUA

*"History repeats itself;*
*first as tragedy,*
*then again as farce."*
K. Marx, *18th Brumaire*

## The Monroe Doctrine and the Marines

In 1821, Nicaragua, along with Costa Rica, El Salvador, Honduras and Guatemala, declared independence from Spain. Two years later, Nicaragua joined the United Provinces of Central America, an entity formed by Spain, which lasted until 1838, when it broke down into the Central American republics. Since then Nicaraguan governments have called themselves independent, an overstatement frequently made by other Latin American nations as well. Independence from Spain and Portugal was achieved with relative ease by most of Latin America, since both empires were declining in strength throughout the nineteenth century. The United States, an emerging empire, was not bound by the traditional rules that Europe had fashioned to carve out colonies from the nations and peoples of Asia, Africa and Latin America.

The Monroe Doctrine of 1823 was a unilateral assertion by the fledgling government of the United States warning Europe not to plan any further colonization in the Western Hemisphere: Washington, the doctrine asserted, planned to exercise control over the destiny of the hemisphere, and would brook no interference from across the ocean.

Although the United States was hardly a global power in the 1850s, the US president had no qualms about dispatching troops to Nicaragua in 1853, 'to protect American lives and interests during political disturbances'.

In 1854, President Franklin Pierce authorized US naval forces to destroy the town of San Juan del Norte 'to avenge an insult to the American Minister to Nicaragua'. Nicaragua had granted permission for the building of a transport line to carry passengers between the Pacific and Atlantic Oceans, thus creating competition for the line owned by Cornelius Vanderbilt. The US minister had investments in the Vanderbilt's transport monopoly along the San Juan River and through Lake Nicaragua. US vengeance for Nicaragua's impudence took the form of burning down the entire town of San Juan del Norte. Pierce agreed with Vanderbilt that competition was a threat to the transport monopoly, and therefore hostile to the interests of the United States. As the smoke rose from San Juan, Vanderbilt felt secure that no future 'threats' against his holdings would be forthcoming from the supposedly sovereign governments in that part of the world.

In 1856, US adventurer William Walker and a gang of fifty-eight mercenaries, tied to Vanderbilt's rivals, arrived in Nicaragua to help the local Liberal Party in its political dispute with the Conservatives. What happened was one of the most bizarre events in American history. Walker led a *coup d'état* and declared himself president of Nicaragua. Vanderbilt, never one to run away from financing violence against his enemies, helped turn the tide against Walker, who resigned, fled and was subsequently shot in Honduras in the midst of mounting another plot to retake Nicaragua. This action took place during the course of two years.

The fact that an American entrepreneur could induce the US government to act against a supposedly sovereign state, and that a US filibusterer, as Walker was then known, could invade and take over a country, left an indelible impression on Nicaraguans – one that was passed on to future generations.

In the United States, however, few members of succeeding eras even learned about the exploits of Walker or the arson-minded marines. From 1890 to 1899 US forces invaded Nicaragua three more times. In 1896 marines attacked Corinto to 'protect American interests during political unrest'; in 1898 US troops landed at San Juan del Sur; in 1899 they were in action in Bluefields and San Juan del Norte, all under the rubric of 'protecting American lives and bridges'. Nicaraguans should have understood by this time that people in Washington, not Managua, would control their destiny.

Nevertheless, some Nicaraguans took sovereignty seriously. In the early 1900s Nicaraguan President Jose Santos Zelaya (who assumed dictatorial powers) committed a bold and, as it turned out, rather imprudent act. This crusty authoritarian nationalist refused to cede to the United States exclusive rights to build a canal, which would have included US control of a strip of Nicaraguan territory. Instead, he invited European and Japanese concerns to aid in building an interoceanic link to connect the Pacific and Atlantic Oceans. He also asked the Bank of England – not a New York bank – for a loan.

US Secretary of State Philander C. Knox took umbrage. Highly conscious of the Monroe Doctrine and the Roosevelt Corrolary to that document, which asserted US 'international police power' in the hemisphere, Knox branded Zelaya's moves as opening the door to 'European infiltration'. He angrily denounced the Nicaraguan president for even daring to think about entering into financial transactions with any but US banks. Knox's subsequent demands on the Nicaraguan government belied even the thinnest respect for its sovereignty: a ninety-nine year lease for a naval base on the Gulf of Fonseca and permanent access rights for a canal through Nicaragua. In words that presaged Reagan administration rhetoric some seventy years later, Philander Knox, in 1909, accused Zelaya of 'keeping Central America in tension and turmoil'.

The stubborn Zelaya, taking seriously the fiction of Nicaraguan independence, refused to accede to Knox's commands. The US government retaliated by destabilizing his regime. During the course of subverting Zelaya's government, two US secret agents were caught *in flagrante delicto* trying to dynamite Nicaraguan bridges. Zelaya ordered them to be tried. Despite US protestations, they were convicted and shot. Knox used the incident to sever diplomatic relations and send marines to Bluefields.

Knox's plan worked. As was the case in subsequent episodes of destablization, the government and the private sector cooperated. United Fruit Company donated $1 million toward the overthrow of the Zelaya government. Zelaya was forced into exile and replaced by Adolfo Diaz who, obedient to Washington's commands, canceled concessions to non-US firms and opened the door to the exaggerated claims of US banks, which then transferred to their own coffers more than half of Nicaragua's national bank assets. In 1914, as the Panama Canal opened to ships crossing between the Atlantic and Pacific, President Diaz made an offer to the United States: $3 million in exchange for 'rights in perpetuity' to any land needed to build a canal through the San Juan route in southern Nicaragua. The $3 million was handled by US-appointed commissioners to repay foreign loans, mostly to US banks, so that a mere pittance actually found its way into the Nicaraguan Treasury. The canal was never built, but the United States acquired a renewable lease for a naval base on the Corn Islands and on the Gulf of Fonseca.

# A Man called Sandino

From 1912 until 1926 US marines remained in Nicaragua as Diaz could not sustain a viable coalition, the minimum basis for governing. Rebellions and revolts broke out and the marines were engaged sporadically in a series of small internal wars. In 1925 the US forces withdrew, but within a year Nicaragua had returned to a state of instability. Having once interfered in Nicaraguan politics, the United States were committed to return until a stable pro-American alternative emerged. They resurrected Diaz but, this time, the opposition was not only willing, but able to withstand the hitherto invincible US marines, thanks to the leadership of a man called Sandino.

On 19 May 1895 Augusto Calderon Sandino, owner of a medium-sized farm in the village of Niquinohomo, in the department of Masaya, gave his illegitimate son his first and last name (the Cesar was attributed to him later, probably by his followers). Until the boy reached adolescence, the elder Sandino took no responsibility for either young Augusto or his mother. The boy suffered the pains of accompanying his mother to a debtor's prison as a young boy. His father later took him into his own household, paid for his education and gave him administrative responsibilities. The young Sandino, now trained and formally educated, quickly acquired business skills and parcels of land, but in 1920 he became involved in the killing of a local politician and fled Nicaragua.

Over the next few years, Sandino worked in Honduras for a US sugar company, in Guatemala as a laborer for United Fruit Company and then in Mexico, where he labored for a US-owned oil company. In Tampico, Sandino ingested not only the nationalism and radicalism that were rife in Mexico, but the anti-Yankeeism that grew up as a logical by-product of continuous US military intervention in the nations to the south of the Rio Grande. Sandino returned to Nicaragua specifically to protest against US intervention; indeed, he wrote, 'as a Nicaraguan I had the duty to protest'.

In October 1926, while working as a payroll clerk at a US-owned gold mine in Nicaragua, Augusto Cesar Sandino organized twenty-nine of his co-workers into a military force and attacked a government garrison. The assault failed, but Sandino, undeterred, raised money, bought better arms and launched a war not only to unseat the US-backed government, but also against the occupying marines. After five years, despite superior technology and formal military training, the US forces could neither capture nor destroy the 'guerrillas', as they came to be known, who rode through the northern mountains raiding US outposts and carrying out a war of sabotage against US interests. The local peasantry provided them with food and shelter, so that Sandino's guerrillas could operate in a manner Mao Tse-tung would later describe as 'fish in water'.

Inside the United States the traditional anti-interventionist current erupted into a movement after Carleton Beals, a US reporter, published a series of articles on Sandino and the war. Carried in *The Nation*, Beals's account contradicted US government claims that Sandino was either a bandit or a Bolshevik, and presented an admiring portrait of a Nicaraguan patriot. Beals also raised the question of whether the Marines could actually win a guerrilla war in Nicaragua.

Since America historically rejected the British or French colonial models, and long-term occupation of Nicaragua certainly smacked of 'colonialism', the marines borrowed a tactic from European imperial strategy. They began, in the 1920s, to train a local 'National Guard', one which could, and eventually did, replace them as the national gendarmarie. In 1933, Congress refused to appropriate money for the continuation of the US expeditionary force, and the marines came home. This did not mean that Washington lacked a long-term strategy for Nicaragua. The National Guard was ready and willing to take over the marines' role of preserving Washington's form of law and order.

With the occupying forces gone, Sandino ended his war, unaware that the departure of the marines did not signal disinterest on the part of Washington. The US government, which had labeled him alternately a bandit and a communist, saw Sandino as a man who had successfully challenged the very premise of US hegemony in the Caribbean Basin. As he made his way, unaccompanied by body guards, to attend a 'truce' dinner in 1934, he was assassinated, an act which marked the end of the first phase of Nicaragua's war for independence.

Sandino had accepted the withdrawal of the marines at face value, as a step toward working out a Nicaraguan political solution. The dinner invitation issued by the head of the Nicaraguan provisional government, with US complicity, was intended to lure Sandino to his death rather than include him in any solution. The assassins, almost certainly directed by an army sergeant named Somoza, were part of the National Guard, a force that would write its history in the blood of the population for more than forty years.

## The Somoza Dynasty

In the course of preparing the Nicaraguan National Guard to assume the monopoly of armed force in the country, the marines discovered a suitable leader. He was an army sergeant, who had proven himself loyal and obedient to US wishes; a man without the slightest tinge of Nicaraguan nationalism and whose understanding of patriotism was acquiescence to US orders. Such obeisance also made Sergeant Anastasio Somoza wealthy and earned him the rank of first and life-long director of the Guard. Somoza started a dynasty, under which Nicaraguan territory and resources became virtually indistinguishable from the tyrant's personal wealth.

The 1934 murder of Sandino did not lead directly to the resurrection of a guerrilla force. The loss of a charismatic leader proved to be a crippling blow to the guerrilla band, whose members had already struggled for six years. Without the guerrillas to act as a countervailing force, power fell exclusively into the hands of Somoza, through his control of the National Guard. No matter who won subsequent elections, the Somoza family ruled the country. The traditional political parties quickly worked out a *quid pro quo* with the Somoza family, one which resulted in the façade of electoral politics that covered the behind-the-scenes understanding: the Somoza family would exact the equivalent of tithes from the population, and the political elite, whose families shared most of the remainder of the wealth, were sufficiently relieved of their fear of popular insurrection grudgingly to accept the guard's leaders skimming their profits.

The Somozas, father and sons, shared with the generals and colonels the spoils gleaned from the productive and service sectors of the society. While the family and its Pretorian Guard became progressively more rapacious, the US government indicated its satisfaction with the state of affairs in Managua. When Somoza came to Washington for a state visit in 1939, one of President Franklin Roosevelt's advisers, upset at the red carpet treatment being planned for the Nicaraguan strongman, told the president that Somoza was nothing less than a 'son-of-a-bitch'. Roosevelt reportedly smiled and replied: 'Yes, he's a son-of-a-bitch, but he's ours.'

## THE ANTI-SOMOZA STRUGGLE: FROM ASSASSINATION TO GUERRILLA WAR

Somoza demanded subservience in Nicaragua but, in contrast, offered servility to Washington. The Somozas sided with the United States in all international matters. After World War II, the Somozas' voting records in the Organization of American States (OAS) and the United Nations proved their total loyalty to the United States. Indeed, Anastasio Jr graduated from West Point in 1948. His older brother, Luis, attended Louisiana State University, the University of California and the University of Maryland.

Anastasio Sr was assassinated in 1956. The gunman, Rigoberto Lopez, a young poet, wrote a letter to his mother in which he explained that he planned 'to put an end to this tyranny'. Lopez was killed on the spot and Luis Somoza ascended to the presidency. His brother, Anastasio Jr, became leader of the National Guard.

While anti-Somoza activists drew some inspiration from Lopez's courage, the 1959 example of Cuban guerrillas overthrowing a dictator provided concrete guidelines for all Latin American revolutionaries. Fidel Castro challenged the axiom of permanent US hegemony over the region, and initiated revolutionary steps toward social justice. The Cuban Revolution combined indigenous Latin American nationalism with Marxist ideology, providing an appealing and accessible political discourse for other Latin Americans. Moreover, in the early and heady years of triumph, Fidel and his comandantes believed that history could and would repeat itself, that the guerrilla *foco* – mountainous areas which the rural guerrillas could control and use as operational bases – was an appropriate military strategy against unpopular dictatorships throughout the hemisphere. The Cuban experience dispelled the notion that revolutions against the army could never succeed. Fidel and revolutionaries from many nations were certain that the pattern could be repeated in Latin America and throughout the Third World.

National security officials in Washington had precisely the same concern. By 1959 it was no longer a simple matter to send troops into

Cuba. In the early months of the revolution's triumph Castro became something of an ambiguous hero in certain circles. President Eisenhower was ailing, and a year passed before he appointed Vice President Nixon to act as duty officer for a CIA expedition to topple Castro. In 1960, President Kennedy replaced the Republican administration before the CIA could gather and train Cuban exiles in sufficient force for an invasion of Cuba. While not canceling the CIA project, Kennedy demanded something more: a new policy toward Latin America.

What emerged from debates in policy circles among Cold War hawks and dovish liberals was a two-pronged strategy to combat the magnetic appeal of the Cuban Revolution. The soft side featured the creation of an Alliance for Progress that offered hundreds of millions of dollars to 'satisfy the basic needs of the American people for homes, work and land, health and schools'. President Kennedy proposed 'that the American Republics begin on a vast new 10-year plan ... to transform the 1960s into an historic decade of democratic progress'. The funds would seek to bring Latin America into the modern world of production and reform its politics. With an educated and healthy populace, modern roads, highways and telecommunications, the alliance theorists believed democratic development would take place. High technology and new industry combined with new wealth would help alleviate the vast discrepancies between rich and poor. In such a setting, democracy would be better able to evolve.

Running parallel to the alliance, the second prong of Kennedy's strategy was designed to defeat revolutionary activity with police and military force. The US counterinsurgency project supplied Latin America's most repressive forces with some $500 million between 1962 and 1967. It also taught them the most advanced techniques of repression, including scientific torture methods. It was a clear statement that the US national security elite did not trust in the alliance alone as a deterrent to revolution. As Kennedy liberals preached the advantages of democracy for an improved economic climate, US Special Forces personnel trained the most ardent foes of democracy and supplied them with the weapons to destroy not only the revolutionaries, but the Kennedy-style democrats as well. Although alliance funds did help build roads, improve ports and develop infrastructure, counterinsurgency money enlarged the power of the extreme right of Latin America.

The already uneven distribution of resources became still more lopsided. By the early 1970s military dictatorships had unseated elected governments in Chile, Argentina, Brazil, Bolivia, Ecuador, Peru and

Uruguay; throughout Central America, barbaric dictatorships held sway, except in Costa Rica. The Somozas grew fat from alliance funds on the one hand, while on the other nourishing the most bestial qualities of the National Guard with counterinsurgency money and specialists.

Luis Somoza, uncomfortable with occupying the office, stepped down from the presidency in 1963, to make way for a puppet president, who died in 1966. Anastasio Jr, 'Tachito', then named himself president of Nicaragua. Tachito felt comfortable with both the counterinsurgency programs and the alliance. The generous US government provided funds, some of which he diverted to his own accounts. Some were invested in export agriculture enterprises, which caused a shift of labor and land use. Peasants were pushed off the land and converted into agricultural laborers; coffee and cotton replaced traditional crops, such as corn and beans. The economy grew from the mid-1960s into the early 1970s, but the total number of poor increased. Alliance funds stimulated economic expansion, but hardly provoked a redistribution of wealth.

The Kennedy policy destroyed whatever faith Latin American liberals may have retained in American good intentions. By negating the creative aspects of the alliance with the heavy fist of counterinsurgency, the Washington policy elite clearly demonstrated their priorities. Stopping revolution outweighed cultivating democracy. When Lyndon Johnson dispatched 23,000 troops to the Dominican Republic in 1965, to prevent 'another Cuba', Kennedy's pledge of non-intervention was nullified as well. The Dominican invasion and the growing counterinsurgency programs clarified US policy for Latin American patriots. By the late 1960s most had narrowed their choices: revolution or continued subservience to Washington, and the military thugs it supported to ensure US hegemony.

Liberal Washington circles had naively misjudged the nature of their anti-communist allies in Central America. There was a tacit assumption in certain policy circles that because the Latin American rulers had eagerly accepted alliance funds they would also embrace the corresponding democratic ideas and allow freedom to flower. Members of the oligarchy throughout Central America sneered. Their family association with repression and anti-democratic ideology dated back centuries.

The Somozas never quarreled with Washington's insistence that democracy could be purchased with US aid money. They understood that Washington's real message was delivered with counterinsurgency dollars and the US military advisers who taught the National Guard new techniques of repression – some of them learned from experience in Vietnam. The United States trained more members of the Nicaraguan National Guard, measured on a population ratio, than of any other repressive force in the hemisphere.

Anastasio 'Tachito' Somoza did not invest state funds in health, social programs, or schools. 'I don't want educated people,' he candidly admitted. 'I want oxen.' His economic policies, based on personal greed, led to the growth of revolutionary consciousness, especially in the universities. Middle-class students found that Marxist descriptions of class struggle coincided more with Nicaraguan reality than did the tomes distributed by US Embassy staff about the virtues of freedom and the evils of communism. Students and veterans of the Sandino wars had learned the same history, one in which the United States invaded Nicaragua, occupied it and then uncritically supported the avaricious and brutal Somoza dynasty. The Cuban Revolution, on the other hand, offered a model of a just society, as well as the potential means and methods to topple the Somoza dictatorship. Fidel's tiny guerrilla force had defeated the 50,000-man Batista military. But Fidel had made some terrible mistakes before arriving at his successful guerrilla formula, and he made many strategic errors afterwards in his effort to spread the Cuban Revolution to the rest of Latin America.

In 1961, some of Fidel's *barbudos* (bearded guerrilla warriors) joined Nicaraguan revolutionaries to form the Rigoberto Lopez Column, a force to liberate Nicaragua from the yoke of the Somoza dictatorship. Emulating if not imitating the Cuban experience, this handful of romantic Nicaraguan patriots were quickly dispatched when both Honduran and Nicaraguan forces ambushed them at El Chaparral. The survivors fled to Cuba. A similar invasion took place from the south, organized by Pedro Joaquin Chamorro and other business leaders but, despite the Somozas' assurances that Castro was behind both expeditions, the Costa Rica-based invasion had little to do with Fidelismo. Like the Rigoberto Lopez adventure, however, Chamorro also failed to gain a foothold, much less develop a *foco* inside Nicaragua. The National Guard, formed and trained initially by the marines and headed by Tachito, proved a more formidable and less easily demoralized force than Batista's troops.

In 1961, cluster of revolutionary nationalists formed the Sandinista Front for National Liberation – FSLN was the Spanish acronym – and initiated guerrilla warfare on several fronts. Their goal was to liberate their country from the Somoza family and the informal US imperial umbrella. They were all Latin American nationalists, imbued with the vision of Simon Bolivar, fighting for independence and social justice. They drew from Thomas Jefferson's Declaration of Independence and, like most revolutionaries in the twentieth century, also from Marx, Lenin, Mao and Castro. Castro, they believed, had proven that military tyrants, like Batista in Cuba, or Somoza in Nicaragua, could only be ousted through guerrilla war. Niacaragua also had Sandino's tradition as inspiration.

The FSLN founders included Carlos Fonseca, who had participated in the Rigoberto Lopez expedition; Colonel Santos Lopez, a comrade of Sandino's; and student leaders, Tomas Borge and Silvio Mayorga. Three young brothers, Daniel, Humberto and Camilo Ortega, whose father had also fought with Sandino, joined the group and established a front in Bocay, near the Coco River, the stream that marks the Nicaraguan – Honduran border. However, Somoza's troops routed the inexperienced guerrillas before they could begin military operations.

One painful lesson learned was that the Cuban guerrilla experience did not automatically transfer to other Latin American countries. Guerrilla forays from Cuba in the early 1960s to the Dominican Republic, Haiti and Venezuela all failed, as did the 1967 attempt in Bolivia by the master of guerrilla warfare himself, Ernesto 'Che' Guevara. The notion of setting up a *foco* in a remote mountain area and waging war against the local armed forces required particular conditions and circumstances which could not be recreated, any more than the actions of Castro and his men could be repeated in other countries.

Ironically, the Cubans in the Sierra were influenced by Sandino, among others. Fidel used Sandino's 'lessons', learned in fighting guerrilla war against the US marines: Sandino taught that successful guerrilla strategy requires the careful choice of when and where to strike the enemy and the maintenance of rebel forces in constant readiness to move camp, thus rendering them elusive.

From 1962 until 1967, FSLN leaders languished either in prison, or in political isolation from potential supporters in Nicaragua and from the dynamic movement emanating from Cuba. In the mid-1960s, Cuba offered limited support to the FSLN. Thinking that chances of success against the well-trained National Guard were minimal, Castro threw his energies behind the revolutionary expedition led by 'Che' Guevara in Bolivia, as well as guerrilla efforts in Guatemala and Venezuela.

Despite military disappointments, FSLN leaders saw popular discontent growing. In 1966 Nicaraguan agricultural production suffered from poor weather conditions. Unable to make a living from farming, rural workers flooded into the cities. The poor and a growing middle class provided a political base for conservative Fernando Aguero to challenge Somoza power. In 1967 the Conservative Party announced his candidacy and staged rallies in the major cities.

Predictably, Somoza ordered the National Guard to repress what appeared to be a challenge to his lifetime ownership of the presidency. Accordingly, National Guard officers, using the methods with which they felt comfortable, brutally ended public rallies and shut down the newspapers and radio stations that had dared attack the Somoza dynasty. Street battles ensued, and in the town of Pancasan, a violent clash took place between members of the FSLN, who joined the anti-Somoza forces, and the Guard. Silvio Mayorga fell in the fight and Pancasan became a historic site.

After the repression, Somoza won the presidency hands down, but anti-Somoza forces had learned an important lesson from this failure: the peaceful or electoral road to dislodge the tyranny was unworkable. Armed revolution, the FSLN method, became attractive to more of the discontented population.

From the late 1960s into the early 1970s the FSLN began to 'finance' their movement. Taking a leaf from the notebook of the Uruguayan urban guerrillas, the Tupamaros, they 'liberated' funds from banks, 'collected' fares from wealthy travelers and 'redistributed' some of the people's funds by kidnapping wealthy Somocistas for ransom. But Somoza and the National Guard were not easily intimidated. Together, the Somoza family and the officer corps had accumulated an immense stake in land, labor and natural resources; in manufacturing, fishing and agriculture; in the ability to direct state funds into personal enterprises. Somoza encouraged Guard officers to participate in the national looting, providing ample incentive to deal aggressively with the fledgling revolutionaries.

In 1969, as the revolutionary leaders began to feel optimistic about success, the Guard ambushed a guerrilla column, killing five. The surprise attack demonstrated that no matter how advanced their social thinking and how avid their revolutionary optimism, there was no substitute for military training and experience – areas in which the National Guard excelled.

# The War Begins with an Earthquake at Christmas

In 1972 nature intervened in Nicaraguan politics. Two days before Christmas, just after the church bells had tolled the midnight hour, the earth moved under downtown Managua. Registering 6.3 on the Richter scale, the quake cracked the foundations of banks, hospitals, hotels, embassies and private homes. Large chunks of buildings fell into the streets; after-shocks brought about an even greater level of panic than the initial jolt and the ensuing blaze. When the tremors ceased, between 12,000 and 20,000 were dead; some half a million homeless; 75 per cent of the edifices of Managua destroyed, starvation, disease and chaos reigned.

People and governments throughout the world poured relief aid into Nicaragua. But instead of distributing the aid, and putting the reconstruction loans and donations toward rebuilding the city, Somoza and the top officials of the National Guard, simply stole a large share of what had been contributed. Somoza, his family and friends used the earthquake to maximize profits on their existing properties. Even the bricks bought by the government to rebuild the destroyed highways that ringed the city came from a Somoza-owned factory. The unabashed greed displayed by Tachito and his clique undermined the implicit acceptance of Somoza family rule.

The business community of Nicaragua, who had previously tolerated the skimming by Somoza and the Guard, reacted emotionally to the quality and quantity of looting by the already engorged military elite: the earthquake was a human tragedy of immense scale; the behavior of Nicaragua's rulers confronting the suffering and death of their own people was inexcusable. The downfall of the Somoza dynasty became possible because the earthquake and its aftermath revealed the true character of Roosevelt's 'son-of-a-bitch'.

After the quake and a rigged election in 1974, FSLN *focos* began to grow. Peasants joined students and newly militant Catholics who believed that revolution was the only path to Christ's justice. The Liberation Theology movement was a boon to the Sandinistas, many of whom were Catholics. Priests, nuns and even some bishops began to form Christian based communities in the 1960s to teach the poor that political struggle for their rights was quite compatible with, and indeed necessary for, the achievement of the just world envisioned by Christ. For centuries the Catholic hierarchy had been willing accomplices to the greed and caprices of the oligarchies and military, but by the 1970s significant numbers were sewing the seeds to reverse their historically infamous role.

FSLN organizers began building support networks throughout worker and peasant communities, often in partnership with priests and nuns, some of whom actually became FSLN organizers. However, the ferocity and unity of the National Guard loomed as a formidable obstacle to revolution, and the United States continued to back Somoza through his worst excesses. Tachito had friends in key committee posts in Congress, and amongst the national security elite. By 1973, even Fidel Castro was not optimistic about the possibilities for successful armed struggle in Nicaragua.

However, on Christmas eve 1974, the FSLN pulled off a stunt that gained them world-wide publicity and bolstered morale in their own ranks to an unprecedented level. A commando team gate-crashed a banquet hosted by a leading Somoza supporter. Some of the guests who were taken hostage included diplomats and government officials. Somoza suffered the humiliation of having to pay $5 million in ransom, release Sandinista political prisoners and guarantee the rebels safe passage out of the country.

Somoza, not one to suffer humiliation quietly, struck back with a brutality that even the most jaded Nicaraguans did not expect. For the next five years, raids, roundups, tortures and murders defined the behavior of the National Guard. The method paid dividends. Carlos Fonseca, one of the FSLN founders, was captured and killed. Guard officers delivered his bloody head to Somoza as proof.

The electrifying success of the Christmas banquet raid faded quickly and the FSLN fell prey to ideological splits over how best to wage guerrilla war, and with whom to ally. In the mid-1970s three factions emerged, each training its own cadre and launching ideological polemics against the others.

The proletarian tendency, headed by Jaime Wheelock, accused the Fonseca–Borge led Prolonged Popular Struggle faction of seeking 'support in the peasantry and urban petit-bourgeoisie rather than in ... mass struggle'. The Terceristas 'represent the most retrograde positions of the petit-bourgeoisie. ... They resort to tactics of terror and putschist adventurism'. The Proletarian tendency tirelessly cited Lenin in its attacks on the other groupings, and insisted on the vanguard role of the working class.

Fonseca and Borge believed that a Viet Cong style organization that could endure a long guerrilla war, with many fronts, would depend upon peasant cooperation. They replied to Wheelock's polemics in kind. Of the three FSLN factions only the Terceristas, headed by Daniel Ortega, posited the idea that a broad, multi-class alliance was necessary to defeat the regime. They appealed for an alliance with all 'democratic' sectors, largely ignoring the rigid class analysis of the others. In 1976 the FSLN had less than one hundred combatants. The low numbers were less important than the devastating lack of unity.

In March 1979, the leaders of the factions finally conceded that their ideological divisions were impeding the revolutionary struggle, and they accepted an invitation to attend a meeting in Cuba. Castro acted both as conciliator and adviser and brought the three into accord – under a Tercerista model.

What Castro taught was his own model. His 1959 insurrectionary success, after two years of guerrilla war, was based on a broad anti-Batista coalition. The July 26th Movement in Cuba included old politicos and their machines, *ad hoc* groups inspired by Batista atrocities, non-Communist Party revolutionaries, special interest sectors, patriots of assorted stripes and finally even the communists themselves. Castro's doctrine, before the guerrilla army won power, allowed each group to see the revolutionary struggle through its prism. Later, Castro made clear the direction of the revolutionary government; but during the insurrection he courted and wooed any faction that could broaden his efforts and add strength and resources to the movement. Members of the anti-Batista coalition tacitly agreed that Fidel was commander in chief of the uprising. After his victory, Fidel faced his challengers with a monopoly over the means of violence.

The Cuban experience, however, taught important lessons to the counterrevolutionaries as well. The National Guard did not make the same tactical mistakes as Batista's army, but Somoza remained ineducable when it came to curbing his greed, or limiting the Guard's brutality. As a result of these vices a steady supply of angry fresh recruits joined the anti-Somoza cause.

The counterinsurgency experts in Washington learned from the Cuban experience as well, but were unable to convince President Jimmy Carter that human rights should not become a factor in determining US policy toward its traditional spheres of control. Carter, because it was a matter of faith, made human rights a leitmotif of his foreign policy.

Somoza was confused by Carter's apparent sincerity on the human rights issue. His family had been installed in power by President Franklin Roosevelt, the man who also had made human rights the center piece of US policy in his Four Freedoms address during World War II. But Roosevelt had never bothered the Somoza clan with complaints about human rights violations. After all, forty-five years of anti-communist obedience should have counted for more than a few cases of maltreating radical trouble makers.

When Somoza finally realized that Carter was serious, he found himself in an impossible position. To lift martial law for the purpose of continuing to receive US aid and legitimation would also mean allowing the FSLN to have the necessary space to organize throughout the country. To abide by Carter's principles would require Somoza to leash and muzzle the National Guard; to remove from it the very instruments by which it had succeeded in terrorizing the population.

Somoza paid lip service to human rights, hoping that it would appease the US ambassador, while at the same time he ordered the Guard to wipe out Sandinista influence in the poor *barrios* and the Christian based communities where the priests and nuns were applying their revolutionary theology. However, the ambassador did not turn the other way in 1977 and 1978 as Guardi members murdered, tortured, raped and looted their way through the *barrios* and rural areas. US officials denounced the abuses, threatened to cut off aid, and eventually did so in 1978. Subsequently writing from exile in Paraguay in the 1980s, Somoza charged: 'Our nation was truly delivered into the hands of the Marxist enemy by President Jimmy Carter and his administration. I was betrayed by a longstanding and trusted ally.' Somoza had a point. Having labeled the FSLN communists, and received encouragement and support from right-wing friends in the US military and in Congress for forty years, Somoza could not believe that the United States would allow the 'communists' to triumph.

But Carter believed he had a mandate to restore US credibility after the stains left by the Vietnam War and the revelations of CIA shenanigans – including its support for corrupt and brutal dictators. The era of world politics had passed when American presidents could with impunity maintain the Somozas of the Third World as reliable clients.

Since Somoza had no desire to transform himself and his Praetorian Guard into anything that could conceivably qualify as democracy, he chose more repression. He thought that by increasing the level of brutality the Guard could cow the populace back into obedience. He was wrong. The more brutal the Guard's behavior, the more resistant the populace grew. As Guard units marched through the *barrios*, or randomly shot poor teenagers and middle-class youth, fear turned to outrage. People who for decades had accepted the savageries of the Guard could tolerate no more.

Inside Nicaragua and in the United States, the anti-Somoza forces coalesced. Illiterate peasants and local merchants in Nicaragua found themselves allied in the struggle against Somoza with exiled dish washers in Houston and University of California students. Some became guerrillas, while others served as lobbyists, pamphleteers, or fund raisers in Washington. A group of well-known professionals and business executives formed 'Los Doce', a group of twelve reasonable and responsible moderates who appealed to middle-class opinion throughout the world to join in with money and moral support to oust the dictator and his hated Guard.

In January 1978, an event occurred that galvanized the fragmented anti-Somoza opposition. Pedro Joaquin Chamorro, the dynamic editor of *La Prensa*, Managua's leading daily, was assassinated. The popular Chamorro had openly published demands for Somoza's removal, and called for broad national unity. Although lacking direct proof, most Nicaraguans assumed Tachito had ordered the slaying. Chamorro, hardly a leftist, had criticized the FSLN's radical rhetoric, but the Sandinistas, nevertheless, joined other anti-Somoza elements, including labor unions, in organizing mass protests, strikes and demonstrations in response to Chamorro's murder. By mid-1978 the Church had added its weight to the growing demand that Somoza resign.

The US government was in the throes of a decisive policy debate. President Carter faced a choice: Somoza, a flagrant rights violator; or the FSLN, regarded in intelligence and diplomatic circles as communists, or, at best, independent leftists friendly to Castro.

'Another Cuba' in Central America was deemed unacceptable, but the continuation of Somoza rule appeared dubious. National Security Adviser, Zbigniew Brzinski, feared that by applying human rights criteria to Nicaragua, the United States would strengthen the revolutionaries. Since the Guard was loyal to Somoza, not the Nicaraguan Constitution, Tachito's removal would lead to its disintegration, Brzinksi believed. The only armed force then remaining would be the FSLN. The human rights activists inside the administration downplayed the Sandinista threat and emphasized to the president the importance of maintaining consistency on human rights. Carter compromised between the competing ideological wings of his administration.

Reversing nearly a century of tradition, President Carter asked Somoza to step down as a way of ending the civil war, while retaining intact the National Guard, whose loyalties should logically turn from Somoza to its next benefactor, the United States. It was not an act of idealism, but rather a realistic judgment on the part of the president. US intelligence reports agreed that the tide had turned in Nicaragua and that the dictator's days were numbered. But Carter's decision came too late for the national security apparatus to save the Guard. The action on the battlefields had ensured the Sandinistas their rightful place as heads of state.

The battlefield included the very center of government in Managua. On 23 August 1978, eleven months before Somoza fled and the Guard collapsed, Sandinista soldiers dressed in Guard uniforms arrived in army trucks at both entrances of the National Palace, where Somoza's legislature convened. Using their best imitation of Guardi officer speech, they deceived the troops stationed at the doors and other posts. Once inside, the Sandinistas held captive Somoza's friends, allies and even family members. For Tachito it was supremely humiliating.

A demoralized Somoza yielded to the Sandinistas' demands for the release of the Nicaraguan glitterati: $500,000 in exchange for safe conduct from the palace to the airport, where the captors would be flown to Cuba, plus the release of fifty-nine political prisoners. Even National Guard officers winced when Somoza caved in. Morale sank for a short time.

To revive the fighting spirit of his men, Somoza ordered unprecedentedly vicious levels of reprisals against the revolutionaries. Inspired by their palace victory, the Sandinistas called for uprisings. In Matagalpa, according to the Nicaraguan press, 'armed youths in rebellion' took over thirty city blocks. The Guard responded with artillery, armored vehicles and heavy machine-gun fire to retake the neighborhood. On 27 August the Catholic Church called upon Somoza to resign as 'the only way to end the current political violence'.

In the final days of August the depressed Tachito regained the ruthlessness that had made him the scourge of the nation. He purged Guard officers who had criticized his weakness in bargaining with the rebels. Charged and found guilty of conspiring to overthrow the government were eighty-five Guardsmen, including twelve officers. As for the 'communists and subversives', his name for all revolutionaries, Somoza told his generals to show no mercy. Sandinistas or suspected sympathizers were rounded up, tortured, interrogated and then killed. The Guard carried out fishing expeditions in the *barrios*, targeting especially the youth. Thousands of men and women were arrested and shot simply because they were young. Instead of submitting, the public were spurred to uncontainable rage.

While the human rights advocates and the national security hawks debated policy in Washington, the Guard's ferocity claimed the attention of the world's media. And the Sandinistas, feeling the public pulse, struck. On 7 September 1978 guerrilla units descended from the mountains to launch a major offensive, attacking and holding parts of five major cities. Several thousand Sandinistas took part in the offensive, sending the Guard reeling. *Los muchachos* (teenagers and children) spearheaded the *barrio* insurrections.

In Leon, Grenada, Diriamba, Chinandega, Matagalpa and Managua, the *muchachos* joined the uniformed guerrillas. They fought with weapons stolen from the Guard, sticks, stones and home-crafted Molotov cocktails. Faced with the wrath of the people, the Guard did not flee, but counterattacked with artillery and aerial bombing. When the smoke finally cleared and the Guard regained control, the bodies of young boys and girls were strewn across the makeshift barricades and trenches. Commercial and residential areas, schools and churches, looked like Coventry after days of Axis bombing during World War II. Those edifices that remained structurally intact bore the scars of bullets and shells.

The neighborhood of Monimbo, in the city of Masaya, rose up and with home-made weapons and rocks held off the heavily armed troops, then suffered the retaliation. 'We fought against the Guard to save our lives,' recalled Ernesto Rodriguez Zelaya, a Monimbo mechanic. 'We realized that after the [Guard's] "mopping up" operation life wasn't worth anything. Whoever stayed home would be killed! It was easier for us to grab a rifle and fight with the *muchachos* than stay home where we would be just a target for the Guard. So it was the repression that made us fight, because we didn't want to die.'

In February 1978, Monimbo residents rose again, fought with unbelievable courage, using paving stones from Somoza's own factory as weapons, and then faced the renewed vengeance of the Guard. But even after the continued bombing and shelling of the area, the Monimbo dwellers refused to submit. The Guard could not regain control.

The behavior of the Monimbo populace dramatized a larger reality, one that even jaded members of US intelligence could not escape: the vast majority of Nicaraguans were prepared to endure immense pain and suffering to rid themselves of the Somoza family and their Guard.

Tachito understood the people's loathing and responded accordingly. He ordered his air force to bomb and strafe guerrilla-held cities. Even after the FSLN had retreated, the air force continued to bomb, to ensure that the populace would get the message. When the bodies were counted, the Red Cross announced that over five thousand had perished from Esteli, Masaya and Leon alone. A further 10,000 were missing; 15,000 were wounded; 30,000 were homeless. Refugees poured into improvised camps just across the frontiers.

By May 1979 Somoza and his generals decided that the situation looked bleak, and that if they were to reassume control of Nicaragua, Masaya was the strategic place to begin. On 9 June the National Guard began intensive bombing and strafing of Monimbo, 'the pissed off barrio', as it became known. Following the bombing, a column of Sherman tanks led Guard foot soldiers through the Sandinista controlled neighborhoods to retake portions of Masaya.

The guerrillas beat a strategic retreat, but returned unexpectedly three days later and retook most of the city. For two weeks the battle raged, block by block. 'The Guard didn't push us out,' a Sandinista officer reported, 'because they didn't receive reinforcements, nor did we take them out since we didn't have any ammunition.'

On 24 June Guard officers and men abandoned their Masaya command post, using hundreds of political prisoners as a shield to cover their retreat. The Sandinistas were in undisputed control of the city, twenty miles south of Managua. Somoza spent his days in the bunker, built on top of a Managua hill overlooking the Intercontinental Hotel. One June evening he met members of the media in an 'off the record' session. One reporter, nevertheless, recorded the conversation. Why was he bombing his own people, destroying Nicaraguan property, he was asked. 'What do you know about underdevelopment?' he slurred, showing the effects of a day of drinking. 'My people are a bunch of lazy, stupid, underdeveloped assholes.'

In late June, Tachito ordered his bombers to drop 500 pounders on densely populated Managua neighborhoods. The Sandinistas, who had taken the poor barrios from the Guard, immediately retreated to Masaya, but the muchachos who survived the bombings continued to snipe at and ambush the Guard in the capital. The US ambassador demanded that Somoza resign, hoping that it was still not too late to save the Guard, except for its most notorious officers. Apart from unwavering support from the Israeli government – of which Somoza had been a loyal supporter – and a few cohorts among the remaining Latin American dictators, Tachito was isolated.

He knew the war was over, but nevertheless ordered his air force to continue bombing. His family had stolen hundreds of millions of dollars from the Nicaraguan people, and Tachito expressed his attitude toward his victims as if to make a final statement that would etch into Nicaraguan memory the essence of the cruelty that had characterized the forty-five years of Somoza clan rule.

On 17 July the Somoza family fled to Miami, Florida. Without Somoza's presence, there was nothing to hold the Guard together. Overwhelmed and demoralized, the once invincible National Guard collapsed. Some units surrendered to FSLN commanders, others fled as one or in ragtag fashion to borders north and south. On 19 July the Sandinistas held state power.

The Nicaragua Revolution triumphed, like the Cuban one twenty years earlier, not just because of the Sandinistas' astute military strategy and tactics employed, or the mistakes of the National Guard. A peculiar conjuncture of events and times also created a setting on which the decisive battles were fought. In Washington, the human rights element in the administration temporarily obstructed national security interventionists; Costa Rica provided unusual levels of help for the Sandinistas, thanks to Somoza's 'bad neighbor' policy toward the San Jose regime; in Cuba, a Solomon-like Fidel Castro persuaded the rival factions of the FSLN to bury their ideological differences and unify.

The revolution could not have triumphed without the ambivalence of President Carter, just as its subsequent programs could not be realized without a similar kind of vacillation from the Reagan administration. The Sandinistas captured world opinion, an intangible factor that nevertheless wove its way through White House thinking and mass media concepts and images. Somoza had made fundamental errors in judgment. His tactics had alienated even the wealthy, who had for decades accepted the caprices of his family rule.

The Somozas had accumulated more than $500 million during their dynastic rule. They possessed one fifth of Nicaragua's arable land and more than one hundred and fifty businesses. In addition, the family had accounts and assets in the United States and Europe that were believed to be more than double what they owned in Nicaragua. Somoza believed that as long as the United States was interested in maintaining its hegemony, the US government would protect him. Tachito's contempt for his own countrymen and women was so great that it did not occur to him that Nicaraguans could play a role in determining the fate of their nation.

The Sandinista triumph on 19 July 1979 came on the heels of a shift in US policy, as well as a shift in world opinion, an increase in Latin American independence, a temporary thaw in the Cold War and the FSLN's ability to persuade mass media of the justness of their cause. Their victory was also made possible because of the US failure in Vietnam, the ensuing scandals over CIA assassinations and the agency's intervention in Chile.

All of the external factors that worked against not only armed US intervention, but actual support of Somoza, would not have added up to victory, however, without the Sandinistas' accomplishments on the battlefield, without their mobilization of the population into support units for the warriors, and indeed auxiliary fighting forces. The *muchachos* in the *barrio* and the seasoned guerrillas in the hills, the makers of homemade bombs in the cities and the young peasant boys and girls who aided the mountain rebels – all merit credit for the successful revolution.

## From Victory to the Contra War to the Aid Cut–off

### THE CONTEXT

On 19 July 1979, hundreds of thousands of jubilant Managuans greeted the Sandinista rebels, clad in their mismatched uniforms, clutching their rifles of different manufacture. The young men, sprouting unkempt beards; the young women, well groomed, and also wearing uniforms, congregated around the cathedral. Priests and nuns celebrated alongside avid Marxist-Leninists. A marriage of religion and rebellion blended into 'la mistica Sandinista', the magical elan that had helped the population transcend its fears and overcome the fierce and brutal dictatorship.

The forward march of revolution seemed inevitable throughout the Third World. In the mid-1970s, African countries broke free from the crumbling Portuguese Empire and joined the ranks of Third World socialism. Ethiopian military officers staged a coup that ousted the emperor and declared their nation to be revolutionary Marxist–Leninist. Black liberation forces in Zimbabwe drove out the white British-made government.

In Asia, in the wake of the US defeat, Vietnam and Laos become part of the Soviet bloc. Cambodia experienced the horrors of revolutionary extremism. Afghan communists staged a successful coup and also joined the ranks of Third World socialist revolution. The most dramatic event from the point of view of US power occurred in 1978, when the Shah of Iran fled into exile to escape the force of Moslem revolutionaries. Arguably the most reliable US supporter in the Third World, next to Somoza, the Shah and his secret police were overpowered by Moslem revolutionary fervor. The United States thus lost an important ideological ally in a major strategic area – and feared the loss of others.

In the Caribbean Basin, the Cuban Revolution appeared stronger than ever, its emissaries traveling with revolutionary messages throughout the region. In neighboring Jamaica, Prime Minister Michael Manley emerged after his electoral victory in 1972 as an English-language articulator of Third World grievances and demands for a new world economic order. In the Non-Aligned Nations meetings anti-imperialist oratory went unchallenged by the United States and Western Europe. The tide of Third World revolution appeared to be overwhelming the great financial and industrial powers of the north.

The profile cut by the Sandinistas caused some despair, but little confusion among US national security managers. The inner councils of the National Security Council and CIA placed the new revolutionary government inside the enemy camp, and thus as a target for future attack. An aggressive grand strategy, whose origins developed before Reagan won office, became evident in Jimmy Carter's turn to the right in foreign policy.

By 1979 the United States began a major arms buildup corresponding with the removal of the 'doves' from key positions. Andrew Young resigned as UN ambassador and detente-minded Secretary of State Cyrus Vance resigned in early 1980. The hawkish National Security Adviser Zbigniew Brzinski prevailed, but not before the Sandinistas had consolidated power in Nicaragua.

The 1980 Republican campaign rhetoric commanded the political high ground. A renewed anti-communism would fuel the foreign policy of the next administration. Statements such as the bellicose Santa Fe Document from the right wing of the Republican Party and missives from the American Security Council set a framework for the national debate so that the Democrats felt forced to react, to prove that they too could be tough on the communists.

Republican advice to the US public was unequivocal: the Sandinistas are communists, who understand only the messages of force and will.

35

The public were inundated with right-wing propaganda, which paraded a series of impending horrors before anxious readers and television viewers. There was the specter of Soviet bases, threats to 'vital sea lanes' and Central American nations falling like dominoes to the cancer of terrorism and Soviet-backed guerrillas. The inventions reached absurd proportions when President Reagan declared that the Sandinista armies were only a two-day march from Harlingen, Texas. The residents of Harlingen laughed when the TV reporters interviewed them, but neither a sense of humor nor truth were built into the new grand strategy.

By employing aggressive tactics on several fronts, so the argument developed, the Soviets' international gains of the 1970s could be reversed, and Moscow forced into retreat, if not outright surrender. The United States should seek to spend them to death in an arms race, out– propagandize them through clever media campaigns, and attack them at their weakest point internationally, by harassing their Third World allies and clients.

Central America was a prime area for the policy test. The United States made efforts to ensure the defeat of the guerrillas by employing low-intensity conflict in El Salvador and Nicaragua – seen as the newest and potentially most vulnerable clients in the Soviet stable. In fact, the Soviets had made no commitments to Nicaragua after the Sandinistas took power. Not until several years later did the Soviets start supplying arms and fuel, after the United States persuaded or coerced other nations not to sell weapons or extend fuel credits to the Sandinistas.

As part of the global offensive against the Soviet Union the Nicaraguan Revolution would be assaulted, along with guerrillas in El Salvador and Guatemala, and Caribbean governments from Cuba through Jamaica and Grenada. The US policy elite that engineered what became nearly a decade-long war with the Sandinista government established a multi-fronted effort to destabilize the new regime. The intention was to bring down the government and replace it with one that fitted more comfortably into Washington's notion of propriety in Latin America or, minimally, to make the revolution an example of what people would have to suffer, rather than what benefits they would achieve by rebellion.

Since the Washington national security elite understood that there was no public consensus for the use of US troops in the region, they decided on other tactics to put pressure on the revolution by forcing the Sandinistas to assume a permanent war posture. By creating a rival military unit, whose activities would be reinforced by virtually omnipresent US military maneuvers, the attention of revolution was thus diverted to the battle front, with its resultant costs in lives and resources. The US military loomed as an invasion threat, a psychological war mechanism, making the Sandinistas mobilize large units to deter such a possibility. Meanwhile, the president could dismiss such suggestions as utter nonsense and reassure Congress and the media that he was not considering the deployment of US troops in Nicaragua.

On the economic and political sides ample precedents existed for CIA-run 'destabilization' campaigns. In 1970, President Nixon had ordered CIA Director Richard Helms to make Chile's economy 'scream'. Eleven years later, under the direction of William Casey, the mission was repeated against Nicaragua. US economic strangulation intensified the difficulties faced by the fledgling Sandinista government. The United States would cut off aid, credit, loans and even trade and commerce. Further, US officials pressured the directors of the World Bank and the Inter American Development Bank to find pretenses to delay and then deny Nicaragua access to those vast storehouses of finance. Indeed, Secretary of State George Shultz wrote a letter to the director of the World Bank demanding that on strictly political grounds no loans be granted to Nicaragua, despite the provisions in the bank's charter to exclude politics from loan decisions.

In addition, the US government would wage a propaganda war to go hand-in-hand with the diplomatic offensive. After Reagan won the election of 1980 the State Department began an energetic campaign to paint the Sandinistas with the stark red color of villainy. They would be shown alternately as bandits and revolutionaries, liars and aggressors. Together, these militant tactics to fight revolution on all fronts became known as The Reagan Doctrine.

## THE CREATION OF THE COUNTERREVOLUTION

The counterrevolution began just as the revolution triumphed in July 1979 when a veteran US covert operator arrived in Managua. 'Bill', in his early forties, had seen 'special' combat action in Vietnam and a host of other wars and revolutions. Several journalists thought he worked for Somoza; others claimed he was an Agency operative or on special assignment from the Israeli government.

Someone had hired Bill to carry out a 'Mission Impossible'. On 19 July 1979, just at the height of chaos and celebration, when Nicaraguans were delirious with the knowledge that Somoza and his hated Guard had been ousted and youngsters in ragtag uniforms carried guns almost as large as themselves, Bill radioed the control tower at the newly named Augusto Cesar Sandino airport for permission to land. He told them he was flying in on a Red Cross mission. Bill had painted his rented jet and wore a Red Cross uniform. He smiled benignly at the young Sandinistas who had recently taken control of the airport and caught a cab to the Guatemalan Embassy. Before the Sandinistas could organize any meaningful security, Bill had managed to load the empty plane in which he had arrived with seventy former officers of the National Guard, disguised as refugees, and flown them to Miami. Within two years, some of them became officers for the Contras.

In 1980 Colonel Enrique Bermudez, a Somoza officer with strong ties to Washington, founded the 15th of September Legion. This loose grouping of former Guard officers and NCOs was the official beginning of the Contra – short for *contrarevolucionarios* or counterrevolutionaries. In August 1981 the legion merged with the Nicaraguan Democratic Union (UDN), a lobbying organization of ex-patriots living in Florida, to form the Nicaraguan Democratic Force (FDN) – the main Contra organization. Bermudez emerged as military chief, the real power, with UDN head, Jose Francisco Cardenal, as political spokesman. By 1981 Cardenal was also on the CIA payroll and had to share authority with Aristides Sanchez, a Somoza crony. One of the conditions for US money to UDN was that they coalesce with the former National Guard contingent. Lt General Vernon Walters, former Deputy Director of the CIA, accomplished the civilian-military mergers as well as the incorporation of Argentine military officials as trainers and advisers.

In the south of Nicaragua, and north at the Honduran border, bands of Guardia escaped the wrath of the Sandinistas, and of the local populace, who had been ravaged over decades by the Guard's venal whims and caprices. One former Guard sergeant, nicknamed 'Suicida', maintained his squad intact, hijacked a boat, kidnapped its captain and brought his men to El Salvador.

It is not easy, even for the fabled CIA, to organize an army. The formation of the Contras began with the escape of the National Guard officers and NCOs. The official funding came in the autumn of 1981, when CIA Director William Casey convinced President Reagan to sign a national security authorization requesting $19 million under the pretext of 'interdicting' arms being sent from Nicaragua to the rebels in El Salvador. Even before the official launching of the war against Nicaragua, the agency had asked extreme right-wing Argentine officers to begin the training and planning for a military takeover of Nicaragua.

With that interdiction money Casey's agents began to operate. They paid the Argentine officers and, by late 1981, Suicida and his Contra units went on a campaign of killing, torturing, raping and kidnapping peasants near the Honduran border. Since the Sandinistas were unprepared for the onslaught of a right-wing guerrilla force, the newly formed squads went virtually unopposed. Commander Suicida became the leader of the most famous, or infamous, of the early Contra units.

The Sandinistas underestimated the significance of the early Contra incursions, using poorly equipped border patrol units to combat them. Revolutionary fervor was still high when the Contras first struck in isolated sectors of the north. The comandantes that directed the Sandinista Front did not devote serious consideration to them. Even when they discovered evidence of CIA involvement in the Contra operations, the FSLN did not undertake heavy mobilization or even tough counter-guerrilla measures. This hiatus between the launching of the Contra and the Sandinista response allowed the CIA's forces to overcome early problems and mount a military effort that eventually tied up thousands of troops, and cost up to 30,000 lives.

During their first two years, however, Sandinista leaders directed their main efforts toward assessing what foreign and domestic policy pursuits would allow them to be benefactors of western aid, friends with the Soviets and leading members of the non-aligned movement. But foreign policy was not the focus of Nicaraguan energy. So much had to be done with so few resources, and the memory of 50,000 casualties in the prolonged war against Somoza lay heavily on the new government and on the populace.

In 1979 and 1980 the last thing Nicaraguans wanted was war with the United States, although they could not erase the anti-Yankeeism feeling that had guided the FSLN and linked it with Sandino and heroes before him. The ideology permeated public discourse and worked its way into the schools and the popular churches. But the working-class peasant base of Sandinista policy did not sit well with the business class that had supported the removal of Somoza and formed a temporary alliance with the FSLN. By 1981 most had left the coalition, resigned from their posts and formed an internal opposition around the newspaper, *La Prensa*, and the office of Bishop (later Cardinal) Obando y Bravo. Some of them fled the country for the United States; others joined the Contra.

In late 1981 and early 1982 Suicida and his gang of teenagers, poor peasant youth and psychotic killers acted as marauders in the sparsely populated areas of the north and northwest. Typically, the Contra bands descended on lightly defended villages, overcame the local militia and then assembled the residents in the square. With women and children watching, the Contras murdered those villagers associated with the government. Party members, militia, teachers and peasants who belonged to government-sponsored co–ops were the usual victims.

Several incidents in 1982 demonstrate the nature of the Contra war in the area. In San Pedro del Norte on the Honduran border, about twenty miles east of Somotillo, a Contra group, composed of mostly ex-National Guardsmen, entered the village after neutralizing the lightly armed militia. The surviving militia members, according to the townspeople, had pieces of their bodies hacked off and their throats cut. The able-bodied men and boys were kidnapped to carry arms or to be trained as future combatants.

One woman whose son was killed defending the militia post described a Contra group entering her house and destroying her TV. 'They chanted slogans like "with God and patriotism we will defeat communism".' The woman's husband never returned. Krill, Judas Iscariot, and The Dead Man were names that Suicida's men gave themselves. They sacked San Francisco del Norte, killing fifteen young men, kidnapping others and stealing a quantity of booty. In the northwest region Suicida and his band along with other roaming Contra units wreaked havoc. Underarmed border patrol outposts were overwhelmed, farms attacked, buildings destroyed. The Contras often raped the women and took prisoner those men who had not been killed in combat.

When some of these activities came to light, the CIA adopted a façade of ignorance and denial. The agency established a variety of fronts to cover its role in launching the war against the Sandinistas. It employed foreign advisers and technicians, set up a series of proprietaries in Honduras and Florida to deal with payroll and supplies, distribution and accounting for some of the money that Congress had reluctantly appropriated to 'interdict arms deliveries to the Salvadoran rebels'.

But the CIA had a difficult time controlling the 'excesses' of Contra commanders like Suicida, as well as in weaving together the diverse anti-Sandinista groups into anything resembling a unified fighting force. Part of the problem came with the attempt to integrate Miskito Indians into the Contra command. Following its practice elsewhere, the agency sought to recruit discontented indigenous groups. In northeastern Nicaragua, it found the Miskitos, a hybrid people descended originally from the Caribs, mostly wiped out in the years following Columbus's landing. Overzealous Sandinista reform programs that ignored the important realities of Miskito life and culture helped create an environment in which recruiting counterrevolutionaries became possible.

Somoza had largely ignored the Atlantic coast region. Transportation by road from Managua was difficult if not impossible for much of the year. The value of the resources was limited and without the lure of wealth the Somozas remained uninterested. The idealistic revolutionaries, however, wanted to compensate for the centuries of neglect suffered by the non-Spanish peoples of Puerto Cabezas and other Atlantic coast settlements. They originated processes that not only conflicted with existing Miskito structures and practices, but violated indigenous land-holding patterns and dynamics.

Steadman Faggoth, one Miskito chosen by the Sandinistas to represent his people, turned out to have been a Somoza supporter. Brooklyn Rivera, a rival of Faggoth, eschewed CIA support and instead sought alliances among groups who advocated self determination for indigenous people. By 1983, CIA-paid recruiters were luring young warriors from their villages, who in turn joined attack parties to challenge Sandinista control over the northeastern area of the country. Defense of the remote region became impossible and the Sandinistas had to organize a forced evacuation from Miskito villages throughout the area northwest of Puerto Cabezas into a region they could defend. The move provoked greater antagonism. The people resented their enforced relocation to resettlement camps, and they hated the war. One result of the war and the relocation was the shooting down by Contras of a helicopter carrying more than seventy Miskitos. All on board died.

In the autumn of 1982 the CIA hired professional sappers who infiltrated from Honduras and destroyed two vital bridges at Rio Negro and Ocotal in northern Nicaragua. Also in 1982 the CIA bought Belgian-made FAL rifles from the Honduran army and delivered them to the Contra soldiers. The CIA arranged to have the Honduran army equipped with new US-made M—16s as a reward. Subsequently, the agency provided Soviet AK—47s for the Contra, as they proved to be better combat weapons.

While Guard officers with headquarters in Tegucigalpa organized a war of infiltration, subversion and sabotage with their Argentine advisers and CIA paymasters, Suicida's men continued to ravage the northwestern area, just below the Honduran border. These were probing actions designed to prepare the way for a larger strategy elaborated by the Argentine and Honduran military staff along with their CIA collaborators. The plan, as Hector Frances, a defecting Argentine officer, later told it, involved opening a military corridor from the Honduran border south, almost half way to Managua, the kind first successfully fashioned in the CIA plot against the Arbenz government of Guatemala in 1954.

By late 1982 the CIA and Argentine advisers agreed that they could take the northern city of Jalapa, and organized over a thousand troops to do so. Once taken Jalapa would serve as the capital of 'Free Nicaragua', the base from which the continuing penetration and takeover of the entire country would occur.

Once having proven themselves able to take and hold a significant piece of land, the Contras could declare themselves to be the legitimate government of Nicaragua, request US military aid and then, with US forces, drive the Sandinistas out of Nicaragua. The plan looked viable on paper, but it failed to take account of two crucial factors: the Contras were not easily to be woven into a smooth and unified force; and the Sandinistas would not panic and run away from a fight against the regrouped Somoza forces as had the members of the civilian government of Jacobo Arbenz in a similar situation in 1954.

In the battle of Jalapa, the CIA distributed mortars to the Contras, who attempted to soften up the defenses before overrunning the city. Some thousand troops surrounded the northern mountainous capital, but each probe of the Sandinista defenses was repulsed decisively. After inflicting heavy casualties on the defenders and townspeople, the Contra troops withdrew to Honduras without accomplishing their objective.

The shooting war had its hostile equivalents at other levels of life. The early coalition with which the Sandinistas brought joyful unity to the nation was rapidly falling apart. Like the Contra, the internal opposition depended upon US support, both moral and financial.

The existing political parties carried over from Somoza times, led by the Liberals and Conservatives in the center and a small Communist Party on the far left. There was also a variety of smaller political groups, each wooing the US government for money. The CIA also looked to infiltrate and manipulate unions not controlled by the Sandinistas and made overtures to professional and business groupings. Owners of large urban and rural enterprises formed associations that proved effective at waging counterrevolution while remaining on the windy side of the law.

As the Contra and the CIA mercenaries destabilized the northern countryside, another guerrilla front emerged in the south, led by Eden Pastora. Pastora broke with the Sandinistas after 1981, and declared his intention to wage revolution elsewhere, but was rejected by the Guatemalan guerrillas – so he returned to do battle against his former comrades.

By the end of 1982 it became clear to the US State Department officials that the Contra would not become a viable force to overthrow the Sandinistas. The Soviets would pour in military aid and ensure the survival of the regime. The Cubans would provide trained military and security advisers. For the politically minded, the Contra represented a threat to consensus, an undermining of the Reagan popularity in other spheres. Assistant Secretary of State for Inter American Affairs Thomas Enders found himself in a strange turf war with CIA and National Security Council officials over who would control the Central American operations.

A Restricted Interagency Group (RIG) met regularly, supposedly to coordinate the various policy lines. In fact, RIG became an inter-office rivalry session, with more deception than veracity on the agenda. William Casey's CIA representative had clear instructions to obscure rather than clarify to the State Department. His ally, Lt Col. Oliver North from the National Security Council, adopted the Contra cause with religious fervor.

Enders, a conservative Ivy League graduate, concluded that the Contras could not overthrow the Sandinistas, and, indeed, would cause domestic controversy and international embarrassment. He went to Reagan in late 1982 to try to force clarity from a White House that appeared more concerned with maintaining a tough image than with reality. Enders later recounted that he had presented to the president the conclusion that the Contras could not win power in Nicaragua, and that it was necessary for the State Department to enter into tough negotiations with the Sandinistas, or have the Defense Department begin to prepare a US military intervention to unseat them.

At the mention of the word troops Reagan became upset. 'Now don't get me into trouble, Tom,' he told Enders. 'I don't want to hear that word. I know you'll work something out.' Reagan avoided decisions on policy questions, and so the RIG continued to work as adversarial agencies within a government whose fighting caused confusion throughout the bureaucracy and casualties in Nicaragua.

In 1983 the CIA command decided it needed some dramatic victories to keep its funding alive by proving to Congress that it could succeed.

The Contras, divided, poorly trained, prone to heavy-handed human rights violations, appeared unable to deliver. So, Casey ordered the recruitment of UCLAs, Unilaterally Controlled Latino Assets, to act in the name of the Contra. After blowing up the two northern bridges, Casey's men had a better idea. In September 1983 UCLA frogmen trained in underwater detonation embarked from a CIA mother ship off the coast of Nicaragua. When they reached striking distance, the scuba sappers placed their charges on the oil pipeline off Puerto Sandino.

A month later the UCLAs struck again, this time at the oil refinery at the Pacific coast port of Corinto. Using sea- and air-launched rockets the UCLA destroyed the oil storage tanks. As Corinto burned and the Sandinistas counted their casualties, the CIA instructed the FDN to claim credit for the attack. A subsequent UCLA operation destroyed Sandinista radio facilities at Potosi. The CIA also imposed on the Contras' political front their own man, Adolfo Calero, a long-time CIA agent. CIA field director Duane 'Dewey' Claridge announced policy to the Contra leader, usually through Calero.

In 1983 Congress openly authorized $24 million to the CIA to carry out military and destabilizing activities against the government of Nicaragua. Ignoring the US–Nicaragua Friendship Treaty, which was still in place, as well as the non-interventionist clauses in the OAS and UN Charters and the Rio Treaty, Congress implicitly called on the Agency to deliver a victory with the money. Contras poured into northern Nicaragua in their thousands, and in the south, Pastora's forces sniped at selected targets. The Sandinis'ta casualties grew dramatically, the destruction of property increased, but the Contra forces did not seize and hold a single piece of Nicaraguan territory. At the end of the 1983 offensive most had retreated to the safe haven of Honduras.

## HARBOR MINING AND ASSASINATION MANUALS

The nadir of the US policy was reached when CIA chief Casey decided to achieve a decisive triumph: his UCLAs would mine selected Nicaraguan harbors, and the FDN would claim credit. Without informing members of Congress – even the loyal ones – the underwater mine layers went to work, using CIA-supplied ships and equipment. And, predictably, ships of several nations, including Holland and the Soviet Union, struck the underwater charges. Loss of life and damage to property occurred. The international community refused to believe the excuse that the Contra were responsible. Indeed, Edgar Chamorro, one member of the Contra political directorate, was surprised 'to read that we – the FDN – were taking credit for having mined the harbors'. Chamorro had been awakened at 2.00 a.m. on the morning of 5 January 1984 by the CIA deputy station chief in Tegucigalpa, a man known as George. 'George told me to rush to our clandestine radio station and read this announcement before the Sandinistas broke the news. The truth is that we played no role in the mining of the harbors.'

The Contra also played no role in another scandal that the media grabbed: the printing and distribution of a field manual that called for the assassination of Sandinista civilian leaders as well as offering diagrams on how to be a model terrorist. 'There is an essential infrastructure that any government needs to function,' a passage from the CIA manual stated, 'which can easily be disabled and even paralyzed without the use of armaments or costly and advanced equipment.' This passage, from *Freedom Fighters Manual*, offered comicbook-style illustrations on how to damage office machinery, destroy government vehicles and power lines, set warehouses on fire and make Molotov cocktails.

A second manual, *Psychological Operations in Guerrilla Warfare*, contained the following passage, which the media then sensationalized:

It is possible to neutralize carefully selected and planned targets, such as court judges, magistrates, police and state security officials, etc. For psychological purposes, it is necessary ... to gather together the population affected, so that they will be present, take part in the act, and formulate accusations against the oppressor.

The CIA blamed 'over-zealous officials', but the order to write and distribute these handbooks came from Casey himself. CIA attempts to downplay the book's impact were countered by the facts that were being produced by independent monitoring groups. Dewey Claridge, known as a cowboy operator, admitted to a closed House Intelligence Committee panel that the Contras had murdered 'civilians', including doctors, nurses, teachers and judges. 'After all, this is a war,' Claridge explained.

The problem was that Congress had not declared a war. The Constitution clearly states that Congress alone has authority to do so. In the Nicaraguan case, the president and his CIA associates made the decision to go to war. In May 1984, Congress responded to the ugly reactions produced by the harbor mining and the assassination manual. It also felt pressure from anti-interventionist, human rights and solidarity groups.

Americas' Watch, a leading human rights monitoring group, concluded in its 1985 report that the Contras had systematically engaged in the killing of prisoners and the unarmed, including medical and relief personnel; selective attacks on civilians and indiscriminate attacks; torture and other outrages against personal dignity. Former CIA Director Stansfield Turner characterized the Contras' behavior as 'state-sponsored terrorism'. These opinions on top of the CIA's disdain for Congressional prerogatives forced the issue: Congress voted to cut off aid to the Contra.

The fact that Congress cut off the Contra program did not deter the zealots at CIA and the National Security Council. *Ad hoc* national security bureaucracies once created tend to inspire those working in them to design self-serving arguments to perpetuate themselves. In the case of the Nicaragua operation, the Contra contingent had a powerful ally. President Reagan spent more television time defending his Nicaragua policy than he did explaining US economic or US–Soviet policy. Thanks to this public promotion of the Contras and denigration of the Sandinistas, the CIA briefs, which had initially been prepared to convince Congress to vote money, became converted into virtual articles of faith inside the agencies.

Concerned that the behavior of those whom President Reagan called the 'moral equivalent of our founding fathers' had inspired neither international legitimacy nor Congressional confidence, the CIA's Contra handlers ordered the diverse and warring factions to unify. In June 1985 the CIA pressured the civilian Contra leaders, Cruz, Robelo and Calero – all on the CIA payroll – to erect a public appearance of unity. At a press conference in Miami members of the anti-Somoza wing, Cruz and Robelo, announced a *rapprochement* with the Somocistas, led by Calero. The result was the creation of the Unified Nicaraguan Opposition (UNO). The word 'unified', however, misled only the naive and uninformed.

That the liberal economist Arturo Cruz Porras and the social democratic businessman Alfonso Robelo Callejas could form common cause with the right-wing CIA agent Adolofo Calero Portocarrero, who represented former Somoza colonel Enrique Bermudez Varela, is a tribute to the imagination of CIA script writers. The CIA never allowed Nicaraguans to control the counterrevolution. Strategy and logistics remained in their hands. According to a National Security Council document, 'Honduran, United States and Argentine advisers were to monitor operations, and Mr Pastora and Nicaraguan rebel leaders based in Honduras were to command troops.' In fact, the members of the different groups despised each other personally and politically never achieved a successful union of operations, nor could they agree on a minimal political program.

Calero, a rough looking middle-aged six footer, weighing more than two hundred pounds, thrived on the conspiratorial life of a covert actor. He embodied the characteristics sought by the aging clandestine warriors in Langley, Virginia, CIA headquarters. He could mouth anti-communist rhetoric faster than a circus barker convincing the yokels to buy a ticket. Clandestine war is hardball, Calero understood, a game not suited to human rights devotees and liberal intellectuals. He was neither.

The manager of Coca Cola in Managua since the early 1960s, Calero rose as a leader of the Conservative Party and worked for the CIA. He did not see any contradiction between being a US agent and calling himself a Nicaraguan patriot. Based in Florida after the revolution, he was chosen by his case officers to run the political arm of the FDN. He did so as an old fashioned, Somoza-style politician – with muscle and threat.

As Calero was a rough and coarse warrior, Cruz was a soft and refined technocrat, very much at home at the Inter American Development Bank (IDB), in Washington, where he worked for years as an economist. In 1977, Cruz entered political life by joining the liberal business group, Los Doce, that called for Somoza to resign. He was rewarded, after the revolution, by being named president of the National Bank. For almost a year, 1980–81, Cruz was a member of the junta of the National Reconstruction Government, the front the Sandinistas had erected to maintain the veneer of unity. In March 1981, Daniel Ortega made him ambassador to the United States, a post Cruz held until he resigned in December 1981 in protest at the arrest of his businessman-friend Enrique Dreyfus, on charges of engaging in counterrevolutionary financial activity.

Cruz returned to the IDB, whose directors allowed him to begin discreet activities against the Nicaraguan government. By 1984, the agency had chosen him to run for president of Nicaragua against Ortega. Although he never registered as a candidate and drew only small crowds since he had little name recognition in Nicaragua, Cruz campaigned like a serious contender. His effort was financed by the CIA. His campaign was organized by agency personnel and never strayed from the political battle plan drawn up in Washington. Because of the image-making talent of CIA public relations 'spin doctors', Cruz was seen in Washington and by US Embassy personnel in Managua as the democrat who had the potential charisma to appeal to an internal opposition and rally international opinion. In fact, Cruz was weak and depended heavily on CIA funds, $85,000 a year, to pay off personal debts and maintain an expensive lifestyle.

While Adolfo Calero scoffed at complaints about the Contra's human rights violations, Arturo Cruz acted as if he took them seriously as a good liberal should, and continued to declare himself a human rights devotee. This attitude endeared him to middle-of-the-road members of Congress who were wringing their hands over allocating money for the Contra. With Cruz in a leadership position, or at least as a figurehead, they felt better able to defend themselves against complaints from the human rights community. But Cruz knew the reality of Contra operations, including the facts about Somoza officers controlling the military action. He also knew that violating human rights was etched into their nature.

Alfonso Robelo, a rotund businessman, also joined Los Doce before the revolution and, after 19 July 1979, became a member of the National Reconstruction Government junta. When it became clear that the comandantes would not share power with non-Marxists, and as Sandinista policies veered sharply to the left in 1980, away from business interests, he resigned from the government and became a vocal opponent of the regime. Robelo had serious ideological differences with the Sandinistas, and the comandantes, in their arrogance, made little effort to seek a compromise – a stance some would later regret. In early 1982 he founded ARDE in Costa Rica along with Eden Pastora. His pact with Pastora, like that with the Sandinistas, proved to be short-lived.

Calero, Cruz and Robelo made up the executive committee of UNO. But power inside the Contra lay in the hands of the CIA and their favored military commanders, led by Bermudez and other former National Guard officers. One was Ricardo 'El Chino' Lau, known under Somoza as a cold-blooded assassin and torturer. Lau's speciality was making prisoners talk. Bermudez made him chief of the FDN counterintelligence, a post he held until late 1983, when the CIA ordered Bermudez to improve the image of the FDN. Calero announced that Lau had been removed from counterintelligence.

But the change was only cosmetic. Several journalists reported as late as 1986 that Lau was still at Bermudez's side, chauffeuring him, acting as head of his personal security and behaving as his aide de camp. Bermudez and his top officers, mostly former Guard officials, appeared as an ideal specialty force to suit the political ends of Central America's military establishment. Since Bermudez and his men were 'guests' of Honduras and always in need of money to support their troops and their own personal needs, they were willing and able to carry out dirty tasks, without fear of being easily traced by regular police – who rarely investigated political assassinations anyway – or by official US watchdogs, who were also less than diligent in pursuing killers of suspected left-wingers.

The revelations of FDN activity came in December 1984, when four members of Lau's unit admitted that they had carried out more than a hundred and fifty murders in Guatemala and Honduras at the behest, and in the pay, of the military intelligence services in those two countries. The four Contras said they had engaged in robberies in Tegucigalpa as well. And, they added, Bermudez himself had ordered these actions. A former Salvadoran colonel claimed that Lau, under Bermudez's direction, had participated in the 1980 assassination of Salvadoran Archbishop Romero and had also helped organize death squads in Honduras.

The activities of Bermudez's gang caused problems for the CIA on its southern front. The most troublesome was Eden Pastora, Comandante Cero, the warrior-cum-democrat, who left Managua in search of other guerrilla wars and because he disagreed with the other samurai. Unwanted by the Guatemalan and Salvadoran guerrillas, lectured to by Cuba's Castro on responsibility, Pastora set out on his own, with little but his charismatic reputation to wage a different kind of guerrilla war against his former comrades-in-arms.

His defection was duly noted by CIA Chief Casey, who ordered his Contra operations Chief Duane Claridge to contact Pastora and 'put him on payroll'. Claridge, known to his covert action pals as 'Dewey', who at age forty-nine wore safari suits and a cowboy hat, cut a conspicuous figure when he appeared for clandestine meetings with his agents. A CIA colleague called the flamboyant Claridge 'dumb and dangerous'. But he was Casey's man in Central America. Along with Station Chief Joe Fernandez and his staff in San Jose, Costa Rica, Claridge began recruiting 'talent' from among the agency's assets and contacts.

The flotsam and jetsam of old dirty wars in Latin American and on other continents heard the call and scrambled to find a place for themselves inside the new dirty war, for which funds were flowing. Claridge put Pastora and his men – some five hundred of his former followers – on payroll. The agency's operators in Costa Rica went to

49

work, building a support structure for Pastora: supply lines, air strips, safe houses and the other accoutrements that the CIA knew from vast experience to be required for staging clandestine war against foreign governments.

Strategically, Pastora's presence allowed the CIA to open a two-front war against the Sandinistas. Politically, in the United States and throughout Europe and Latin America, Pastora appealed to liberals and social democrats, people who heretofore had resisted Reagan's pleas for support. Pastora's inclusion in the Contras would provide a democratic if not downright romantic face, and clean up the image of the shabby force as nothing but torturers and murderers. The agency's 'spin doctors' could convert Pastora into 'Mr Human Rights' himself. But there were problems.

The veterans of CIA covert operations knew from experience that liberals with human rights values and dirty war do not mix. They preferred Colonel Bermudez and his sullied gang to prima donnas like Pastora. Bermudez's boys were precisely the kind of thugs needed to terrify a population, for the purpose of overthrowing a government. That was their job, after all.

The goals of building support for the Contras became confusing for the American public: the Contras were supposed to represent democracy yet were bent on destroying the Nicaraguan government by force, because it was totalitarian. The press, of course, played up the schisms and contradictions. Pastora, whom the liberal media adored, continued to refuse to have anything to do with the Somoza officers who headed the Honduran based campaign; Bermudez and his gang were equally unwilling to deal with their former adversary who, if not a communist, certainly had strong pinkish tendencies.

Robelo, on the other hand, was willing to compromise, and he persuaded the majority that the CIA's ultimatum to ARDE – unify with the FDN or have funds cut off – was serious; failure to heed it would mean their extinction. Pastora scoffed at Robelo's 'realism' and insisted that ARDE's appeal lay precisely in its principled refusal to deal with the former Somoza officers. Pastora set forth grandiose fundraising schemes whereby he alone could persuade European and Latin American social democrats to finance ARDE. Then the CIA would come around. He also boasted of his liberal support in the US Congress.

## The La Penca bombing

'Pastora', said a CIA official charged with unifying the Contra, 'is a royal pain in the ass.' The CIA officials who doled out money and weapons to Pastora could control neither his thinking, nor his tongue. He complained that they were not giving him enough money and weapons. His CIA handlers described him as contrary by nature. 'The Reagan Administration', Pastora proclaimed at a San Jose press conference in May 1984, 'wants to return to a Somocista past.' When pressed, he added that 'it is incapable of coming to terms with a democratic revolution and fears anything that is revolutionary.' Pastora accused the CIA of trying to coerce him to work with former Somoza officers. 'Never,' exploded Pastora. One Pastora staff member told two reporters at the time that 'the feeling is we'd be better off having Pastora as a dead hero than a live troublemaker'. Others, not in his group, thought the same.

In late May 1984 Pastora took a boatload of reporters to a jungle hideout on the Costa Rican–Nicaraguan border. Once ashore at a tiny town called La Penca the crowd assembled, the reporters took out their tape recorders, the TV men unloaded their cameras. One man posing as a photographer for a European magazine excused himself, saying he had left something in the launch. It was then the bomb went off. Pastora was injured, and three reporters lay dead. Several more were wounded. The suspected assassin pretended on the boat ride back from the jungle hideout that he had also been injured. By the time the police began to look for him, he had disappeared. The bomber took advantage of the confusion that ensued when the wounded and dead were taken from the boats and rushed to hospitals and morgues to leave Costa Rica.

An investigation carried out by Costa Rican police showed that the attempt to kill Pastora was connected with John Hull, and some non-Americans who were connected to the CIA and the Contras. Although Pastora survived, he never recovered the panache, the spark of charismatic confidence, that had made him both an exciting figure to social democrats and reporters in many countries, and a man who generated political excitement. Instead of using the assassination attempt to try to enhance his image, Pastora remained shaken by the La Penca affair. He lost his following along with his CIA subsidy and retired to become a fisherman in a remote Costa Rican village. The bombing removed Pastora as a thorn in the CIA's side. The more democratic members of the Contra moved toward the leadership of Alfredo Cesar, the former Finance Minister – a man with whom the agency could deal.

THE CONGRESS: A VACILLATING OBSTACLE

Somehow these facts never penetrated the tough skin of Congress. Although claiming to be outraged over Contra atrocities and the CIA's harbor mining ploy, the Democratic majority lacked the confidence and will to confront the administration. They did, however, make clear their distaste for the president's priorities. Reagan strategists had attached a request for Contra funding to a social welfare bill designed to provide jobs for teenagers, and school lunches and food for impoverished children and pregnant women. House Speaker Tip O'Neill said that for Reagan 'it is more important to pay Nicaraguans to kill than to pay Americans to work'. Those priorities continued to prevail: six years later it was revealed that the Bush administration had placed Nicaragua at the head of one of the summit agendas, before the question of German unification or arms control.

Congressional antipathy for the Contras did not deter Colonel North, CIA Chief Casey's coordinator on the project, from conducting a search for other funding. This quest for money independent of Congress ultimately led to the Iran–Contra scandal. But the shenanigans that began with the inception of the war led to a series of bizarre activities – ones that were less than healthy for American democracy.

One such episode was called the Civilian Military Assistance Program, which emerged from the confines of the Old Executive Office Building. Under Casey and North's unofficial auspices, a private group was organized to recruit and pay mercenaries to fly supply and bombing missions for the Contra against targets in Nicaragua. Working with retired officers and NCOs, North helped this combination of fighting zealots and hustlers to swindle wealthy widows and nouveaux riches entrepreneurs, with the understanding that the president himself was behind the effort. North even went so far as to promise large donors a personal visit with Ronald Reagan.

This operation came to light in the late summer of 1984 when the CIA ordered the Contra to attack a Sandinista military instruction center in northern Nicaragua. The agency provided light planes and helicopters equipped with bombs to support the Contra ground forces. The Sandinistas shot down a helicopter and recovered the bodies of two US citizens, both former US Special Forces personnel. Such actions caused more hand wringing in Congress, but the Reagan ideologues argued so forcefully and at times threateningly that the anti-intervention members could not muster a decisive margin to defeat the Contra aid bill. Reagan cloaked each request inside a larger framework of 'fighting communism', 'defending democracy' and protecting US national security against 'Soviet encroachment'. Although most members knew that this was, as one California Congressman described it, 'stale baloney', they lacked the courage to face the possibility of their opponents' charging them with being 'soft on communism' at election time.

Most members of Congress knew enough about the behavior of the Contras to merit a no vote, but Reagan managed to avoid a full-scale Congressional investigation. Ultimately, the issue was too low on most members' priority lists for them to 'go to the wall'. When White House threats and promises inundated their offices, the majority agreed to accept the administration's word that things on the human rights front were 'improving'. Congress as a whole simply lacked the courage to confront President Reagan and demand an end to the atrocities.

## What happened to the revolution?

From 1984 until their electoral defeat in 1990, the Sandinistas tried to implement their revolutionary agenda while fighting the Contras and the United States. Although they prevented the Contras from winning any substantial victories on the military and political fronts, and managed to maintain some international support against Washington's inflammatory avalanche, they could not win the low-intensity war. The steady drain on an already weak and battered economy broke the will of the majority of the people – or at least pushed them to acknowledge the threshold of their suffering.

An exciting literacy campaign and the early spread of education to the remote parts of the country gradually petered out. Teachers were drafted, or, in the outlying areas, intimidated and sometimes killed by the Contra. The amount of funds that could be allocated to education shrank, as did the money that went to health care.

The Sandinista leaders continued to talk a language that appealed to the working and peasant classes, but they needed foreign exchange, and could ill afford a serious drop in agricultural production. So, their economic policies began to favor the very classes against whom they had made the revolution. To keep the cattle ranchers and large cotton producers from sabotaging production, selling their products over the border to Honduran or Costa Rican buyers for dollars, the Sandinistas offered sweetened deals to their erstwhile class enemies.

By the spring of 1984 the nine comandantes agreed that they would call for elections. Although they had not anticipated holding a vote for at least another year, the Sandinista leaders thought that this would meet one of the Americans' most pernicious charges – that they lacked popularity. At the very least, they would reassure their liberal and social democratic international supporters by submitting to the one criterion through which democracy was measured.

Their victorious election campaign in 1984 demonstrated that the Sandinistas could outorganize the opposition and rally the population to show support for the revolution. By winning over two-thirds of the vote they gained legitimacy in the eyes of much of the world, although the US government scoffed at the electoral process and much of the US media ran stories designed to undermine its credibility. Nevertheless, observers from scores of countries validated the election and, as one European commented, the procedure was at least as clean as the Salvadoran one, which Washington promoted and financed.

In 1985 the Sandinistas still held sway. Enough of the population still felt the vibrations of new possibilities that had flowed so dramatically through the society for the first three years of the revolution. International opinion also supported them, especially that of the regional powers in the form of Contadora, the regional grouping which quickly won European and Latin American backing.

Contadora is an island off the Columbian coast where members of the governments of Panama, Mexico, Venezuela and Columbia convened to present alternatives to US Central America policies. Frightened by the possibility that a US invasion of Central America would destabilize their own politics, the foreign ministers of the four countries set themselves up as an informal regional policy group to search for peaceful solutions to the conflicts in Nicaragua and El Salvador. Very quickly it became a serious player in the Central American drama.

The Contadora process, taken together with the humiliating decision against the United States at the World Court, caused the Reagan administration to lose prestige. The overwhelming majority of the judges at the International Court of Justice at The Hague ruled that the United States was guilty of terrorism against Nicaragua, and estimated that the Americans owed the Nicaraguans some $14 billion for damages caused by their illegal war. A third and final element that the administration had not built into its low-intensity conflict equation was the level of resistance inside the United States.

The campaign also took a toll on the popular Ronald Reagan. Because of the obsession with Nicaragua, and the Congress's vacillation on continued funding for the Contras, the president's top officials panicked that their beloved surrogate fighting force would perish from lack of nourishment. Reagan's advisers began to seek extra-Congressional means of continuing the flow of arms and money to the Contras, resulting in the machinations of National Security Adviser John Poindexter, Assistant Secretary of State for Interamerican Affairs Elliot Abrams, CIA Chief William Casey and his man on the National Security Council, Lt. Col. Oliver North. A major feature of their activities was the secret negotiations with the government of Iran to release hostages for US weapons, with the money from the arms sales going to the Contras. The American hostages were held by pro-Iranian sects in Lebanon.

## THE REAGAN OBSESSION

Had Washington's strategy worked, by the end of 1985 the Sandinistas would have been negotiating with UNO for a different political system. Yet in 1986 the Sandinistas continued to command popular loyalty. If the elements of low-intensity war were all added up, the overwhelming weight against the Sandinistas should have produced, if not a total collapse, at least some signs of submission.

In Nicaragua the war was all-consuming. Because of the tactics employed by the United States, the Sandinistas were forced to allot more than 50 per cent of the budget to defense. It was not just the Contras attacking on two fronts, but the ever-present fear of a US invasion, or at least an incursion by the Honduran armed forces, backed by US units. The psychological war, the threat of invasion, and the growing body count affected Nicaragua like constant body punching in a prize fight. Morale began to drop as the economic situation deteriorated alongside of the daily tragedies of the deaths and burials of young soldiers and civilians. The war also contributed to diminishing productivity, as young men were forced to leave work and go into the military, and because spare parts and raw materials were often in short supply. The economic troubles became a predictable and enervating part of daily life.

By 1985 the Contras should have accomplished substantial objectives: destroying the economy; winning the hearts and minds of the peasantry; and using the Miskito rebellion to detach the Atlantic coast region from the rest of Nicaragua. The pressures were also calculated to split the Sandinista leadership, which had come together late in the insurrection after bitter ideological divisions. However, various factors contributed to the failure of the CIA's strategy. One of the most important was the internal power of the revolution itself, which provided moral support for the hard-won unity in the leadership. Whatever grievances or differences existed among them were never allowed to disturb the vital outward appearance of harmony.

## THE US MOVEMENT

Inside the United States, opposition grew to President Reagan's intervention in Nicaragua. There were anti-Vietnam War protesters, now twenty years older, who belonged to Nicaragua solidarity groups, or liberation theology churches – or simply maintained their distaste for US interventionism. There was also a new generation, who saw in the Sandinista revolution a higher meaning than the commercial culture of their own country.

On the other side, the right wing mobilized through both the fundamentalist churches and its non-religious networks. For the anti-communist fanatics Nicaragua became the core of the struggle, the encounter that would determine America's will to resist communism. The right wing was led by President Ronald Reagan, whose speech writers produced extraordinary levels of hyperbole.

The majority of Americans never grasped the issue, according to polls taken throughout the 1980s. President Reagan made televised speeches and used his weekly radio program on scores of occasions to explain his version of the Nicaragua situation. The White House publicists released countless stories and 'leaked' documents to the media. According to newspaper polls, after eight years of inundation with White House information, the majority of the American public was still unsure as to which side the United States was supporting and confused Marxist guerrillas in El Salvador with the right-wing Contras in Nicaragua. The anti-interventionists, ranging from solidarity movement members to those who believed for religious reasons that US support for the Contra was wrong, to conservatives who simply did not see any compelling logic to the Nicaragua 'obsession', fared little better in reaching the public with a coherent explanation.

'Americans', quipped *New York Times* columnist James Reston, 'will do anything for Latin America except read about it.' This seemed an apt description of the public's obtuseness on the issue. What the activist left did accomplish, however, was to carry the Vietnam Syndrome into the 1980s. By staging sit–ins and other peaceful protests and demonstrations, the activists captured headlines in local newspapers and image space on the nightly local news. Whatever the public's confusion over US policy goals, there was none about the willingness of the anti-interventionists to disrupt daily life and business affairs. No matter how much the right wing carped about the threat of communism in Central America, it was not sufficient to arouse the public to support aid for the Contras.

Liberation theology played a role in the anti-interventionist movement and in tempering the warlike proclivities of Lt. Colonel North and William Casey. Religious groups from several churches organized Witness for Peace. Volunteers traveled to Nicaragua and witnessed the Contra violence against civilians. They sent their reports not only to their own congregations, but to the media and Congress as well. Because of their efforts, and those of thousands of students, professionals and idealists, the Sandinistas had a vocal if not terribly large support system in the United States. Campuses revived the teach-in technique, originated during the Vietnam War to educate students about the critical issues. Central America became the subject of countless sermons. Meanwhile, the Sandinistas wisely encouraged groups to visit Nicaragua and organized tours to show them what the revolution had done and was doing in the midst of the US-sponsored war.

Mass demonstrations throughout the country continued during the 1980s. One of the most dramatic occurred in the central California city of Concord, outside a military installation. One of the protestors, Bryan Wilson, lay down on the railroad tracks to prevent a train carrying weapons from leaving the installation. Whether the train driver saw Wilson and tried to stop or deliberately ran over him, the movement gained its martyr. Wilson's legs were severed by the locomotive.

After July 1979 people flocked to Nicaragua from scores of countries to offer their services, skills and talents to the revolution. Communists, religious liberals and ordinary people of good will tended the Nicaraguan sick, designed ecologically sound agriculture and industrial plants and manned some of the complex machinery that European governments donated to the revolutionary government. Among these 'internationalists' working in Nicaragua were hundreds of Americans. Some of the Contras warned that they would target the internationalists in their raids on villages and agricultural settlements in the remote areas.

One of the American volunteers, Benjamin Linder, was a twenty-six-year-old electrical engineer from Oregon, known by his colleagues as a good natured, modest and hard-working young man. One American working in Managua remembers Linder stopping by his home to chat on his way to the northern settlement where he worked. Linder joked about the Contra threats, his friend recalled, but also indicated that he knew how serious they were. On 29 April 1987, a Contra unit attacked the settlement at La Camaleona, killing several Sandinista militia members and Ben Linder. An investigation revealed that Linder had been unarmed and the powder burns on the wound in his head indicated that he had been shot at very close range – assassinated.

### THE SEEDY SIDE OF COVERT OPS: CONTRA DRUG DEALING

Just as the martyred internationalists achieved legendary and heroic status, the CIA actors earned the opposite reputation. CIA Station Chief Joe Fernandez had resources. Not only did the big boss, Bill Casey, give him the full-speed-ahead sign, but the messengers from Oliver North gave him further encouragement. The Costa Rican side of the war emphasized democracy; the Honduran-based front stressed hard-headed realism. This good–bad cop approach offered flexibility to the ideologues and speech writers in Washington.

The availability of resources played to the criminal proclivities of those involved. One of the leading CIA figures in Costa Rica was John Hull, an aging ex-marine (wanted by Costa Rican authorities for suspected murder), who had bought land in the north and raised cattle. An air strip on Hull's spread, not far from the Nicaraguan border, was a perfect supply link for weapons and narcotics.

The drug trafficking started from a simple entrepreneurial formula. Give a man money for which he does not have to account and the possibility of airplanes that can avoid US customs. For $50,000 a shipment of cocaine could be (and was) bought from a Colombian dealer, shipped to Hull's air strip, transferred to a CIA plane that is on Contra business and sent to the United States where the cargo was off-loaded without the inspection of a customs officer. This formula turned into a routine in flagrant violation of the law. In San Francisco, in 1983, several Nicaraguans were arrested by Drug Enforcement Agency officials, having been caught red-handed with a considerable amount of cocaine. One of the suspects pleaded that he was dealing drugs for the Contra on the authorization of the CIA. The case was mysteriously hushed up, much to the chagrin of the DEA.

As in all modern covert operations, the possibilities for shenanigans arose from the moment Congress authorizes funds to break its own laws. Once in motion as an illegal and thus covert action, it is difficult to control other crimes that are inevitably involved with, though not directed at the target itself. So drug dealing, and all that follows from it – bribery, corruption and murder – became part and parcel of the attempt to overthrow the revolutionary government in Nicaragua. The precedents for this were set in Southeast Asia, in the 1960s and 1970s, where CIA planes carried heroin in the name of supporting anti-communist guerrillas. In Afghanistan in the 1980s, CIA funds intended for the war against the communist government in Kabul also wound up in the heroin business.

## At the Battlefront

The Contra military strategy of 1982, to move through a corridor from Honduras, take and hold strategic positions, set up a 'Government of Free Nicaragua', be recognized by Washington and call for direct military aid never got past the first step. The Contra did infiltrate easily from the Honduran border into the mountainous areas of Jinotega and Nueva Segovia. And they often overwhelmed lightly armed border patrol units and village militia. Once inside the village, the Contra, no matter how much preaching and screeching they heard from their CIA handlers about avoiding human rights violations, seemed unable to act with restraint against the local populace. Murder, torture, rape and robbery were their ghastly trademarks.

In Matagalpa in the spring of 1986, a Contra platoon swooped down on a group of volunteer coffee pickers. After killing the militia members, one Contra recognized two of the volunteers and identified them to his commander as active Sandinistas. The middle-aged couple, Felipe and Mary Barrera, were then dragged off by the Contras and made to carry weapons back across the border into Honduras. Once outside Nicaragua, the Contra commander proceded to interrogate the husband and wife together, using the torture of one to persuade the other to talk. The difficulty that the Barreras faced was that they had no secret information and refused to give the Contras the names and addresses of their Sandinista comrades in Managua. One of the Contra raiding party, aptly named 'El Muerto', when subsequently captured by the Sandinistas, confessed to killing the couple. He also revealed that members of the platoon had taken turns raping the woman and beating her husband before they died.

The Contra may not have won major military battles, but they did discover ingenious methods of escape. After raiding cooperatives and small towns, they found back-country trails, with the help of local peasants who either sympathized with their cause or were sufficiently intimidated not only to guide them to safety, but also to feed and house them.

The Sandinistas, after suffering heavy losses owing to their poorly armed and ineptly trained troops, devised counter-guerrilla tactics with the help of their Cuban advisers, led by General Arnoldo Ochoa. Lightly armed and highly mobile units of well-trained troops would ambush Contra units located by Sandinista intelligence. The Contras would then retreat, whereupon they would be attacked by armed Soviet-built helicopters and surrounded by regular army units, cutting off their access to Honduran sanctuaries.

This method worked during 1985–86, but the CIA and US military advisers countered with other strategies, one of which almost brought the capture of Esteli, a key northern city. In the summer of 1986 a Contra company of some seventy-five men, armed with rifles, machine guns, mortars and a variety of grenade and hand-held rocket launchers entered the outskirts of Esteli. Undetected by Sandinista intelligence, the group penetrated well within the city limits before larger units of government troops, backed by armored vehicles and air support, were able to drive them out. In all the years of war, this marked the closest the Contras came to capturing a major military objective. It showed the Sandinistas that Contra collaborators were more numerous and bolder than they had estimated, since before reaching Esteli a Contra force that size should have been detected and its movement reported. It also showed that the Sandinistas, once activated, could outmaneuver and outfight the Contra. In part, this was due to superiority of weaponry and the availability of helicopter gunships and troop transporters. The Esteli victory could also be credited to the fact that the Sandinistas maintained a generally high morale and good combat training for their troops.

For most of the late 1980s, the Contras tried to elude Sandinista regulars and the mobile light infantry battalions (BLIs), and instead concentrate their attacks on lightly defended or undefended cooperatives and farms in remote areas. By 1987 the United States provided the Contras with Stinger anti-aircraft missiles that could be fired from the shoulder. This effectively neutralized some of the Sandinistas' fire power. The helicopter gunships had to be used carefully to avoid being hit.

The Contras' lack of military success was compounded by major cohesion problems. Calero, always obedient to his bosses, said whatever the agency told him to say. But the good parrot also wanted to retain control over his fellow Nicaraguan counterrevolutionaries, so that he and his cohorts could command the lion's share of the CIA support funds – which was the essence of the internal political fight.

As Colonel Bermudez sent his units over the border to snipe and pick at undefended targets, he argued that he and his men were risking their lives while the civilian elements of the Contra ate up the money. Similar arguments took place among the Miskito Contra leaders. Steadman Faggoth fought with Armstrong Wiggins and Brooklyn Rivera over CIA support funds in struggles that had less and less to do with ideology.

On the battlefield, the Sandinistas beat the Contras in place after place, from the northern and southern borders to remote eastern villages. But the Contras would run away, then return, kill a local official or a technician, steal material, destroy an agricultural substation, a school, or a clinic and retreat anew to the safe haven of their Honduran base camps.

Sandinista commanders sometimes ignored the border markings and pursued their enemy into Honduran territory. On several occasions in 1987 and 1988, Honduran forces engaged the Nicaraguan regulars in fierce exchanges of fire. The danger of having Honduras enter the Contra war was enough to intimidate the Sandinista leaders, who ordered their units to withdraw. The fear in Managua was that the Hondurans could call for US military aid, thereby justifying a formal US military presence in the war. Even in the brief border skirmishes, US military advisers ferried Honduran troops to the area. One US helicopter was shot down, but Nicaraguan officials apologized and defused the explosive situation.

The hot pursuit of the Contra into Honduras reflected the growing frustration not only of the soldiers and officers, but of much of the population. What the war meant by the late 1980s was a steady drain of resources and human life. Since the Contras could not defeat the Sandinistas, the US managers concluded, they would pursue a war of attrition.

The essence of low-intensity conflict is that a powerful and wealthy country expends a small amount of resources and energy to engage the government of a small and poor country, which has to expend enormous resources and spill much blood to counter the aggression. The CIA recruiters among the rural peasantry offered what appeared to be enormous amounts of money to teenagers. A US $50 bill looked like a million. Plus, CIA recruiters offered a brand new uniform, a powerful automatic weapon – the tricks that have seduced young men to fight for causes over the ages.

From tiny villages like San Francisco del Norte and San Pedro del Norte, to cities like Esteli and Jinotega, the low-intensity US effort became the major fact of life. Brother fought brother, cousin against cousin, neighbor versus neighbor. The dead and crippled teenage soldiers, the maimed civilian children, the refugees, the burned homes and schools and clinics – this was the low-intensity war. To Nicaraguans the intensity could not have been higher.

For the government the war was all-absorbing and their concentration on it meant neglect for the main programs of the revolution. The health and education systems, like other targets for social reform, became war victims. Key organizers were drafted, or murdered by the Contra. Funds were cut off from important projects so that they could be channeled to the war effort. The continuing and interminable war also meant that Nicaragua's leadership would perforce be of a military nature, not a situation propitious for the growth of popular democracy. So, Sandinista leaders, commanding a nation at war, began to lose the links that in the early days had bound them to the population of the urban *barrios* and rural villages.

The war not only drained resources; it spread corruption and cynicism. To the mothers of young boys the war appeared certain to consume their progeny. The Sandinistas suffered over five thousand military casualties; the civilian count was much higher. The draft became increasingly unpopular and the Sandinista ideology that in the early days of the war could inspire and bond young recruits began to lose its appeal in the face of the reality of grinding and relentless combat.

As the internal situation grew more difficult, with resources ever more scarce, some of the early and romantic nationalism turned ugly. The internationalists, once celebrated for their sacrifices in support of the revolution, became objects of resentment. Why should they hold positions of authority instead of Nicaraguans who were paying the supreme cost of defending the revolution? Although this feeling did not become public, the Sandinista leaders did quietly remove non-Nicaraguans from leadership positions or command posts throughout the economy and replaced them with Nicaraguans, who were often less qualified.

The glow of the early days was lost, both inside the country and among supporters around the world. Small solidarity groups remained, but by 1989 it was difficult to sell the Nicaragun Revolution as a success story.

## THE CONTINUATION OF THE REVOLUTION AND THE DEFENSE OF THE COUNTRY BECOME INCOMPATIBLE GOALS

In his reflection after the 1990 electoral defeat Tomas Borge, Minister of the Interior, characterized by the media as the 'hard liner' among the comandantes, said that two of the six major mistakes committed by the Sandinistas were failure to stop the draft and arrogance. Unwise economic policies, triumphalism, corruption and occasional fits of sectarian behavior also characterized the government.

But what really destroyed the first attempt by a Central American nation to build a genuine social revolution was the war waged against it by the United States. In December 1985 Secretary of State George Shultz summed up the US policy toward counterrevolution in Nicaragua. 'Our commitment', he said, 'is indefinite. It's just going to go on. I think the message is that ... we have staying power.' This proved correct. The Contras were discredited, militarily inept and unsuccessful in capturing territory. But the outcome was never in doubt. At a time in history when the Soviet Union was unwilling or unable to take on new clients, the fact that the Sandinistas endured for a decade was a minor miracle. The difference between 1959 and 1979 in world geopolitical and geoeconomic configurations counted heavily.

As Nicaragua grittily waged its defensive war against the United States and tried to maintain revolutionary impetus for its social reforms, it faced a world economy that was rapidly being integrated. Capital was ever more concentrated in fewer transnational operations and multilateral lending agencies. Nicaragua was not high on the receiving list of these entities. Indeed, the United States effectively prevented Nicaragua from receiving meaningful multilateral loans by vetoing them or threatening the World Bank with dire consequences should a loan be approved. In short, the time for Third World revolutions to flourish, even for two decades, had past. The contemporary world did not serve as a compatible back drop for the Sandinista experiment. The US government, when the ringing of the revolutionary bell sounded, seemed to be hopelessly stuck in its Pavlovian counterrevolutionary behavior pattern.

When the Sandinistas lost 60 per cent of the population to the opposition in the February 1990 elections, loyal supporters inside and out of Nicaragua felt deeply disappointed; some, however, breathed a sigh of relief. Indeed, thousands of those who had attended Sandinista rallies, as late as a day before the election, voted for UNO, not because they believed that Mrs Chamorro could deliver a meaningful program, but because war and suffering had tired them, their revolutionary fervor had been reduced to the mundane reality resulting from protracted low-intensity conflict.

It had become clear that the US government would not allow peace to prevail, or even the tiny political space that would allow for the trial of a reform experiment. The invasion of Panama in December 1989 illustrated that US interventionism would continue to be used as a policy instrument against revolutionary Nicaragua – or any other disobedient nation. The majority in Nicaragua voted accordingly: 'Basta!' – they had had enough.

## Postscript

The celebration in Washington over the victory of their candidate, Mrs Chamorro, was not matched by corresponding generosity. The cost to Nicaragua of ten years' warfare was estimated at over $20 billion of losses. President Bush, however, offered some $300 million in rebuilding aid, and imposed conditions on the money as well. The State Department appeared to be more concerned that Nicaragua drop its World Court suit against the United States than with rebuilding the country it had helped destroy. Most of the Contras were demobilized and disarmed under the supervision of a UN force. Some retained or hid weapons and supplies of ammunition. Few of the former CIA force reintegrated easily into Nicaraguan society. There were no jobs and no land for the returning men. Only months after her inauguration, Mrs Chamorro admitted that sporadic fighting had resumed in remote rural areas, mostly in land disputes between former Contras and Sandinistas.

Some Contras reformed under their old commanders and began once again to harass northern farmers and cooperatives. The Sandinistas fought back and the death toll rose to well over one hundred during the first year of UNO rule. In August 1991, the Contras planted a land mine in a puddle of water on a road east of the town of Wiwili. It exploded as a truck carrying sixteen people passed over it. All died. Sandinistas in the area vowed revenge. 'Wars', commented an OAS observer in Nicaragua, 'don't just end – especially in poor Third World countries.'

In 1993, three years after her election victory, Mrs Chamorro faced a divided nation, divided not between Sandinistas and Contras, but between the old elite and the affluent middle class on the one hand, and the vast majority of Nicaraguans on the other, who were not only dirt poor but deprived of the benefits that the revolution provided. There were sparse health or education funds available in the budget, and Washington even witheld some of the promised $325 million in aid until Mrs Chamorro complied with new demands. The State Department stipulated that she purge Sandinista members from the ranks of the officer corps of the armed forces and return the lands confiscated over the ten years of revolution to their former owners. Mrs Chamorro refused, explaining that such actions would cause civil war. She did, however, defuse a looming conflict with Washington by offering compensation to the former owners.

What she learned was that US intervention in Nicaragua had not ended. The US Ambassador behaved like her boss, not an understanding friend who would try to help rebuild a country destroyed by more than a decade of war. The covert war, she discovered, was more than a tactic for defeating the Sandinistas, weakening the Soviet Union, or containing the 'Cuban threat'. It was the tactic used by Washington to regain control of Nicaraguan politics. But what US national interests were served by continuing to demand supremacy over internal Nicaraguan affairs, a Nicaraguan businessman asked at a 1992 seminar in Washington? Indeed, what did the Contra war mean for US security? The point is, said a Bush Administration official in the corridor outside the seminar room, not that Nicaragua was strategically or economically important, but that everyone in Latin America should learn the lesson: the Monroe Doctrine still operates and, paraphrasing from Alice in Wonderland, it means exactly what we say it means.

# 3
# EL SALVADOR

"Let us unite the half-dead who are this country
That we may be worthy of calling ourselves your
children
In the name of the murdered
Let us unite against the murderers of all
All of us together
Have more death than they,
But all of us together
Have more life than they."
From *Todos* by Roque Dalton

El Salvador is the one Central American republic that remained free of US military intervention until the 1980s. Its neighbors had all suffered at the hands of various US governments, some for over a century. In El Salvador, the suffering was inflicted from within, principally by the ruling elite who dominated the country, in an alliance with the military, until the major social disruptions of the 1970s.

By 1979, the oligarchy's rule had produced a polarized, impoverished and unstable country: two-thirds of El Salvador's population received less than one third of the disposable income. More than 40 per cent of the rural population were now landless peasants. Tens of thousands of Salvadorans had been killed during periods of violent repression throughout the twentieth century. This situation was the starting point for a decade dominated by civil war, in which the army, the oligarchy, the political parties and the guerrillas fought for control over their country. This was also the decade in which the United States finally intervened, prompted by the threat of revolutionary political change in Central America. Those who supported revolution in El Salvador shared with their counterparts in Nicaragua and Guatemala a common set of grievances based on extreme polarization of wealth and power.

The name of El Salvador's modern revolutionary movement, the Farabundo Marti Front for National Liberation (FMLN), is well known, yet its origins are obscure. People throughout the world have now heard the name Farabundo Marti, but few know much about the revolutionary Salvadoran apostle. He was born at the turn of the century to a middle-class farming family with enough wealth and concern to send him to university. Throughout his childhood he had witnessed the naked exploitation of poor peasants. In the city he saw the working class living under similar conditions.

Once in the capital of San Salvador and surrounded by books, Marti immersed himself in Marxist and anarchist writings. Known as 'El Negro' because of his dark complexion, he fell in love with radical literature – and then with revolutionary politics. It was the age when, for young progressives, the Bolshevik revolution shone as the light of the future. By 1920 Marti had an arrest record stemming from his activities in student politics. Soon after, he was banished to Guatemala where he joined other Central American revolutionaries hoping to liberate their countries from oligarchies and Yankees. In 1927 Marti joined Augusto Sandino's rebellion in Nicaragua, and became a colonel in his guerrilla army. But Marti was first and foremost a communist intellectual and he found Sandino's nationalism too narrow and lacking in class consciousness. In 1929 he returned to an El Salvador corroded by the world depression.

By 1931, Marti had become the key organizer for the Salvadoran Communist Party. His task was to mobilize the peasantry – most of whom had become a landless proletariat – encouraging them to seize revolutionary control and establish a socialist system. What he saw on his return to his native country was a textbook example of what he had studied in Marxist literature. 'There appears to be nothing between these high-priced cars and the oxcart with its barefoot attendant,' commented a visiting US army officer in 1931. 'There is practically no middle class in El Salvador,' he continued. 'Thirty or forty families own nearly everything in the country. They live in regal style. The rest of the population has practically nothing.'

The American officer had observed accurately. When the world depression of the 1930s forced down coffee prices, along with those of other commodities, the handful of ruling Salvadoran families, who owned most of the coffee land, responded with capitalist economic logic. They cut back on production and halved the wages of the pickers, mostly Pipil Indians, thus setting the stage for violence. These pickers had already been robbed of their ancestral lands, traditionally held in communal estates, and converted into an agricultural proletariat. By early 1932, the conditions of the unemployed and even those who retained their jobs at reduced pay had become unbearable.

In the winter of 1932 Marti and other organizers promoted a massive peasant uprising. They convinced the angry pickers to challenge the control of the growers. This was revolution. Armed with their machetes, the Pipils congregated at the great estates. The most important instigator of the peasant uprising, Farabundo Marti, had planned the rural rebellion to coincide with an urban, working-class revolt.

But the revolutionaries' coordination was less than perfect, and the oligarchy, faced with a serious threat to their property, did not hesitate to communicate their sense of urgency to the commander of the armed forces, General Maximiliano Hernandez Martinez. Marti and other communist organizers were arrested and quickly executed. The army then moved into the countryside. The soldiers and bands of mercenary non-military squads tied together the thumbs of the peasants behind their backs (a trade mark renewed by the death squads of the 1980s), lined them up against the church wall and shot them, firing-squad style. When the days of bloodletting by troops and hired thugs were over, the death toll ran as high as 30,000 murdered peasants. Marti's name was deleted from official Salvadoran history texts. The members of the Communist Party, which he had formed and led, were virtually all eradicated.

The *matanza* (massacre) of the communists and the mostly Nahuatl-speaking Pipil Indians marked two important events in the beginning of the modern guerrilla war in El Salvador: the army officers, led by General Hernandez Martinez, set conditions for a marriage of the military to the oligarchy; and the name of Farabundo Marti, the organizer of the peasant rebellion, became associated in legend with social justice and independence. The *matanza* also marked the end of Indian culture in El Salvador, as the surviving Pipils thought better of retaining their traditional dress and language, for fear of reprisals.

The disorder of the early 1930s grew not only out of the greed and rapacity of the Fourteen Families, members of the super elite, and the military commanders, but also out of world economic conditions, which set the price of coffee. During the Great Depression the fall of commodity prices not only produced the conditions for radical social upheaval but also for reactionary rule.

General Hernandez Martinez fell into the latter category. Like Somoza in Nicaragua, Ubico in Guatemala and Carias Andino in Honduras, Hernandez Martinez ruled El Salvador as the *caudillo*, a strange mixture of feudal patriarch and contemporary fascist. The tiny *mestizo* (mixed race) officer surprised the sceptical oligarchy with his ability to govern. He protected their wealth, but would not be their servant. A reactionary autocrat, he demanded that the oligarchy live within the modest means of the country's agricultural export economy. The elite families who owned the majority of coffee-producing land agreed to temper their spending habits in return for a guarantee that the armed forces would maintain 'order' in the countryside. But Hernandez Martinez could not eradicate the legacy left by the massacre, nor the ideas generated by Marti, nor did he address the economic conditions under which those ideas flourished: the dire poverty of the majority and the opulence of the few. So the tyrant repressed. His soldiers and police arrested, tortured and shot the dissenters.

Under his despotic rule, however, some steps toward development were taken. Government operations, including banking, became centralized, a process that the ruling families saw as an erosion of their power and privilege. Until Hernandez Martinez' rule, the leading families had grown accustomed to establishing the social rules. In 1944 the upper-class resentment took political shape in the form of an attempted coup. The general dealt with the gentlemen plotters and suspected sympathizers just as he had with peasants and communists: blood flowed.

While Hernandez Martinez tried to extend his rule with a new wave of repression, the people of San Salvador responded with the equivalent of a national strike. Despite Hernandez Martinez's proven penchant for bloody retaliation against dissent, the populace dared to protest. In mid-April 1944, students from grade school to university went on strike. The laboring and professional classes responded – marching, carrying placards mocking the dictator, maintaining a vigil in front of Martinez's offices at the palace. He reacted predictably, by arresting and threatening to kill the strike's leaders. But the strike continued, shutting down economic life. A *Time* magazine correspondent on the scene described some of the opposition: 'It was a groundswell of popular indignation that dwarfed anything ever hatched by politicians. ... The people, who had served from time immemorial as a doormat for hob-nailed military boots, now reared, fierce, towering, and a bit more incredulous of their new might.'

Then, as Salvadorans waited for the showdown between immense popular anger and heroism pitted against the bloodiest of tyrants, the United States stepped in to influence their history. The police lashed out, killing even members of the Salvadoran elite. One of the victims of the National Police was Jose Wright, a student from a wealthy cotton-growing family, whose father had recently immigrated from the United States. The US ambassador indignantly demanded an explanation for Wright's death. The general, finally accepting the impossibility of ruling without Washington's blessing – and therefore without the Fourteen Families' approval – quickly vacated his office and went abroad. Hernandez Martinez thus followed an old tradition whereby *caudillos* went into exile when confronted with overwhelming evidence of hostility. Typically, one *caudillo* was replaced by an equally abhorrent military ruler – so little ever changed.

But the seeds of revolution sowed in 1932 by Farabundo Marti had begun to germinate, prompting the oligarchy and the new military leaders to arrest and exile the insurgency leaders. The very nature of class relations in El Salvador produced new revolutionaries. Sensitive people continued to respond to institutionalized injustice and poverty; the first step in the process of questioning the nature of the social and economic system. In addition, as Salvadoran society modernized and produced a middle class, democracy gradually became part and parcel of political discourse. The education system expanded to meet the needs of economic and social growth, and began to include arts and letters as well as technical subjects in its curriculum. Students were exposed to the anti-fascist ideology that inspired North, South and Central Americans to fight in World War II. Nevertheless, revolution remained, for some of the middle class, the only road to democracy.

One did not have to be a genius to note the correspondence between the descriptions in Marxist texts of the conditions necessary for revolutionary social change with the conditions of everyday life in El Salvador. Revolutionaries and reformers developed and, alongside them, right-wing ideologues arose intent on preserving the status quo. The left and liberal elements were buoyed by the democratic sentiment surrounding World War II, while the reactionaries took their inspiration from Hitler, Mussolini and Franco.

Political life inside the circle of the Fourteen Families was also fraught with conflict. Some oligarchs retained their semi-feudal ties to farming, though few ever got their hands dirty; others invested in urban business and technological enterprises. Some turned into playboys and jetsetters. Each courted aspirants inside the military to manage the state for their benefit. Families investing coffee profits in modern urban enterprises made new political allies by virtue of the investments themselves.

During the 1940s, US corporations became partners in certain enterprises and even began to use Central America to try out new communications technology. This development required the employment of skilled technicians. Most urban business also created a need for lawyers, accountants, advertising and public relations experts, and the consumer accoutrements that endow middle-class life. Class relations became more complex as the new middle class increasingly failed to identify their interests with those of the oligarchy, bringing new social tensions. The political stresses and strains arising from economic growth contributed to a growing independence on the part of the military establishment who, created as a necessary force to protect the wealth of the elite families, began to design means for the reproduction of their own class.

In the mid-1940s the passion for freedom produced countless demonstrations, strikes and political campaigns. It also induced deep fear inside the oligarchy that democracy would prevail if not stopped, bringing with it economic reforms that would diminish their fortunes. In late 1944, a senior policeman led a coup before the scheduled elections could take place. The progressive candidate fled the country, leaving a bland but conservative general as the only candidate.

The urban populace, however, continued to practise a lively politics. This produced unrest in the military, whose order-loving senior officers hated political expression, leading to several unsuccessful coups. Since the democratic groups had difficulty forming a common front around a strategy to govern, the right wing maintained the power of repression, albeit not with the same legitimacy as in the past. Gradually, social democrats and Christian democrats emerged alongside Marxists of various stripes when political openings allowed for the formation of political parties and associations. Begrudgingly, the aristocracy allowed some reforms, although nothing that touched on the distribution of wealth. As a result, the majority did not greatly benefit, but expectations rose that political protest could yield gains.

From the mid-1940s on, El Salvador's politics oscillated between the beginnings of formal republican government and military coups. Military men turned presidents continued to run the government for the benefit of the same Fourteen Families, making minimal concessions to other interests. While the oligarchy devoted its less than sophisticated intellects to work on how to maintain intact its wealth, power and privilege, major changes were occurring inside and out of the tiny Central American nation. At this time, many of the men and women who rose to leadership in the late 1970s had their formative political experiences.

The CIA maintained its agents inside the Salvadoran police and military high command and, during the 1950s, its analysts deemed El Salvador potentially unstable as a result of the absurdly lopsided division of wealth. In 1957, under the aegis of money from the US Agency for International Development, the United States began formal training of Salvadoran security forces. In the early 1960s, Alliance for Progress funds instituted by the Kennedy administration helped fuel a modernization of the infrastructure, after which foreign capital arrived to build factories. More peasants were forced off the land and became either rural proletarians or city laborers, making underwear for American women or chips for modern high-technology equipment. The new factory zones did not permit union activity – part of their attraction for foreign investors.

A Central American Common Market was formed in 1961. The idea behind it was to sustain industrial growth by amalgamating the separate markets of the region. It was not intended to rectify the uneven distribution of wealth that characterized most of the participating economies. US corporations liked the idea of the market as it would enable them to take advantage of the cheap labor costs in Central America and set up profitable subsidiaries. The local Central American business elite was also enthusiastic as the common market offered them the chance to form business partnerships with multinationals such as ESSO and Proctor and Gamble. El Salvador was best able to take advantage of the new economic arrangements because it was the most industrially developed of the Central American countries. In addition, unlike its neighbors Guatemala and Nicaragua, El Salvador was not engaged in a guerrilla war during the early 1960s.

But economic growth was accompanied at that time by greater political activity. Debate inside the Communist Party produced a split between the advocates of armed struggle, who pointed to the 'futility' of the electoral process, and the Moscow-oriented majority that eschewed the guerrilla model.

Salvador Cayetano Carpio studied Marxism-Leninism and the experience of the Cuban Revolution while he plied his trade as a baker. By 1969 he could no longer endure the 'moderation' of the Moscow-linked Communist Party. He founded the Popular Liberation Forces (FPL), whose purpose was to engage workers and peasants in guerrilla bands to fight for state power. The FPL combined grassroots political activity with the formation of a guerrilla army, aiming for a longterm struggle against the government.

The People's Revolutionary Army (ERP), another Marxist group, was formed in 1971. Led by an engineer, Joaquin Villalobos, their tactics differed from Carpio's, being more effective in the short term: they used guerrilla military actions to encourage political uprisings among the people. However, without a non-military wing, the ERP did not integrate so well with the populace.

## The Soccer War with Honduras

On 25 June 1969 El Salvador broke diplomatic relations with Honduras over what came to be known as 'the soccer war'. On the surface, the dispute was based on the disruption of the Honduran soccer team's sleep the night before their World Cup qualifying match against El Salvador. A large crowd of Salvadorans gathered outside the Honduran team's hotel in San Salvador on 22 June and created as great a disturbance as possible. Some manifestation of high spirits and rivalry might have been expected, but this action was far more serious. Not only was it led by General Jose Alberto Medrano, Chief of the Intelligence Services and Head of the National Guard, it also resulted in two deaths and seven people injured while the police attempted to break up the crowd. Honduras was held responsible by the local media and the Salvadoran government used the incident to whip up war fever. Behind this one bizarre event, the subsequent break in relations between Honduras and El Salvador and the resulting war lay years of border skirmishes, trade disputes and inter-governmental sniping.

The Central American Common Market was, by 1969, falling apart. Honduras had not fared well from the market, particularly in relation to El Salvador. El Salvador had taken over from the United States as the main supplier of manufactured goods to Honduras. But Honduras had little to offer El Salvador. A serious balance of payments deficit resulted. Salvadoran businessmen, the main benefactors of the market, had invested heavily in Honduran industries, leading to fears of foreign domination.

An older problem was that of the migration of Salvadoran peasants into Honduras in search of the vacant farmland that was so scarce in their home country. At the turn of the century, Honduras had encouraged this influx, pleased to have its remote lands developed. In the 1960s, however, Hondurans were facing similar problems to those of their Salvadoran neighbors: poverty, land shortages, unemployment. Successive Salvadoran governments still did nothing to stop the exodus – after all, it solved their overpopulation problem.

In 1969, there were 350,000 Salvadorans in Honduras. At a time when Honduras's own rural population faced underemployment on a massive scale, Salvadoran peasants in Honduras became easy targets for the military goverment of General Lopez Arellano. Invoking a 1962 law that required landholders to be 'Honduran by birth', and those not conforming to that description to leave the country in thirty days, Arellano caused tens of thousands of Salvadorans to flee the country, back into El Salvador. There the Sanchez Hernandez government was beset by problems, in particular labor strikes, and the growing popularity of the Christian Democrats. The evictions from Honduras were the last straw. Action had to be taken to respond to the Honduran insult and to prove the government's strength.

On 14 July 1969 the Salvadoran airforce bombed the airport at Tegucigalpa. In the resulting five-day war, 2,000 people died and more than four thousand were wounded. The Organization of American States (OAS) sent in a peacekeeping force to monitor the truce. Honduras closed its markets to all Salvadoran goods, thus delivering the fatal blow to the already ailing Central American Common Market. For Sanchez Hernandez, the war was a great success: the returning troops were greeted as heroes by the populace; the government's popularity soared and blocked the electoral hopes of the opposition for 1970. But for the military and the oligarchy this was to be a short respite. The 1970s saw the emergence and growth of the political forces that were to plunge the country into a protracted civil war.

By 1972 the majority of Salvadorans had voted in several consecutive elections, showing their preference for democracy and an end to military rule. The Fourteen Families and the military answered by nominating generals who stole the elections. This pattern continued in 1972.

Civilians of various stripes had put together a political coalition, The National Opposition Union, an electoral marriage of Christian and social democracy. Members of several parties agreed to nominate Jose Napoleon Duarte from the center and Guillermo Ungo for the democratic left. After the balloting the experts agreed that the National Opposition Union had won a clear majority. The armed forces and oligarchy's candidate, General Molina, controlled the vote counting. He also supervised the stuffing of the ballot boxes. After his self-proclaimed victory, he ordered Duarte's arrest and torture and initiated a nationwide campaign of repression against other members of the left and center. So much for democracy in 1972.

Duarte was to internalize this experience and re-emerge as a partner of the military in the 1980s; Ungo understood the 1972 election experience as a mandate for unity between social democracy and revolution in El Salvador. He became head of a coalition supporting the violent overthrow of the centuries'-old rule by the economic and military elite. During the mid-1970s, more revolutionary groups emerged as the struggle for 'the' correct approach to gain popular power consumed the factions.

In February 1977 another phony election was 'won', this time by General Carlos Humberto Romero. Demonstrations erupted in the streets of the capital, followed by brutal repression and the declaration of a state of siege. The pro-human rights administration of Jimmy Carter looked askance at these events and Congress held hearings about the allegations of fraud in the elections to determine future policy toward El Salvador.

## War on the Church

By March 1977, having failed to stop the continuing rebellions, the Fourteen Families and their military collaborators decided that the time was right to attack what they saw as the source of rebellion in El Salvador: the Church. The thought processes of the Salvadoran rich and their uniformed protectors fell short of sophisticated. To threaten the Church they decided to use force to intimidate the progressive wing of the clergy. In the mid-1970s, members of the repressive forces began to engage in the systematic torturing and murdering of priests.

Liberation theology was one response to the misery that resulted from the antiquated economic and social structures of Latin America. Some priests began to shift their allegiance in line with a new Catholicism that saw the meek, not the elite, as the inheritors of the earth. Like other members of his seminary class, Padre Rutilio Grande believed both in the rituals of the Church and a commitment to the poor. Born and raised in El Salvador, Padre Rutilio could relate his own life experience to the teachings of liberation theology. He and his fellow Jesuits throughout Latin America went to live and work in the *barrios* and poor villages, where the dramatic differences between rich and poor could no longer simply be explained by the cliché that 'this was God's intention'. Padre Rutilio thus identified with the dirt-poor peasants and agricultural day-laborers, who comprised his flock. The terrestrial enemy became the absentee landlords who occasionally dropped by to look at their sugar plantations and inspect the mills. They paid less than $2 a day in the 1970s to the young men whom they had only recently dispossessed from the land.

Rutilio and his team of priests set out to organize the poor of the Aguilares Valley into what they called 'Base Communities'. Using passages from the Bible the priests encouraged the peasants and workers to discuss the misery and injustice of their lives. 'Listen carefully, you rich people ...', the passage from scripture would begin.

Such readings were designed to show the similarities between God's Word and the conditions of daily life, and to bring forth the natural leaders to act as organizers in each community. Armed with Biblical justification, the priests would then encourage the villagers or *barrio* residents to discuss class struggle in very non-religious terms, and think about appropriate forms of organization with which to resist their oppressors and seize power over the state and the means of production. The Jesuit order that once supported oligarchical rule in Latin America was now producing priests who were revolutionaries. The propertied class was absolutely right to fear them.

Fear of revolution, in the minds of Salvador's ruling clique, meant violence. Priests in various parishes were arrested, some tortured, others killed. On 12 March 1977, Padre Rutilio drove his jeep toward the village of El Paisnal, where he was to say Mass. He was accompanied by a young boy and an old man, who acted as a kind of improvised bodyguard for the priest. En route, Rutilio's vehicle was overtaken by a truckload of non-uniformed soldiers, working in consort with a local police officer. The soldiers opened fire, killing Rutilio. His two companions escaped death and thus witnessed the crime.

Even those priests who were not part of the new spiritual movement felt the vibrations of the more revolutionary clerics. One of those thus affected was Oscar Arnulfo Romero, who administered a middle-class parish in San Salvador. He was one of the less threatening members of the clergy, although he admitted that he had 'always felt a preference for the poor, the humble'. Had it not been for the extreme character of the agents of repression, the quiet cleric might have remained a moderate, occasionally wringing his hands at the hopelessness of life on earth, while urging his flock toward greater piety and belief in the afterlife.

Romero was named archbishop only a month before the murder of Rutilio. He had been disinclined to pursue the activist path of his Jesuit colleagues, but the murder of his close friend transformed him. Conservative Vatican officials had hoped Romero would rein in the wilder priests; instead he became their outspoken leader. He demanded that the president investigate the assassination and called for demonstrations and the closing of Catholic schools to protest the act of barbarism.

In Washington, Congress held hearings at which witnesses denounced the government, the police and the military of El Salvador. President Molina took umbrage at this 'interference' from abroad, and declared that El Salvador would no longer accept military assistance from the United States on grounds of 'national dignity'. The total aid 'lost' by El Salvador due its president's righteous declaration came to $2.5 million, given as a low-interest credit toward the purchase of US military and police equipment.

Such farcical protestations drew laughter from Salvadoran revolutionaries and from US national security officials. Even under the Carter presidency, the human rights activists in the administration understood the requirement to accept national security dogma, which took as axiomatic an anti-revolutionary position. As long as El Salvador remained outside the revolutionary danger zone there could be gestures of disapproval made from Washington toward the beasts who ran the armed forces and police. But if serious insurrection developed, the beasts would again become necessary allies in the 'fight against communism'.

But the late 1970s were not like other periods. The march of revolution through the Third World was the dynamic of the age. The historical trajectory of liberation movements would also include El Salvador. The elite had become so desperate that they were attacking the clergy, their centuries'-old partners in hoarding the wealth of much of Latin America. The oligarchy's not always perfect marriage of convenience to the military proved more important than their ties to the Church.

It was in 1977 that the military declared that its opponents across the board were 'subversives', the nomenclature borrowed from the brutal repressors of Argentina and Chile. The war had begun, although the formal fighting had yet to commence. By April more than three hundred government opponents had been arrested, more than a third of whom eventually 'disappeared'.

In retaliation the FPL kidnapped Mauricio Borgonovo, the wealthy

Foreign Minister, whom they offered in exchange for thirty-seven political prisoners. The kidnapped minister's family agreed to pay a ransom, but President Molina claimed that only three of the thirty-seven prisoners named were held by the government. The Union of White Warriors, made up of military and police, declared that if Borgonovo died Catholic priests would pay the price, since they were behind the subversion. Borgonovo's bullet-riddled body was found three weeks later. As the archbishop became more vocal, the government moved more forcefully, deporting a dozen priests and threatening to silence the Church's press and its radio station. The day following the discovery of Borgonovo's corpse, men armed with sub-machine guns burst into a parish hall in San Salvador and opened fire, killing a priest and a teenage boy. The White Warriors claimed credit and delivered an ultimatum to all fifty Jesuit priests in El Salvador: leave before 20 July or die.

On 1 July another general, Carlos Humberto Romero (no relation to the archbishop), assumed the presidency. Archbishop Romero boycotted the inauguration because the president and his advisers had been involved in torturing priests. US Secretary of State Cyrus Vance leaned on the new president, telling him flatly that threatening, torturing and murdering priests did not sit well with Washington. The pressure worked. Just before the White Warrior execution date, President Romero attempted to draw an acceptable veil over the government and its connection with the right-wing murderers: he publicly denounced terrorists of all political stripes but supervised all right-wing terrorism.

In September 1977, the rector of the National University, a member of a wealthy right-wing family, was shot and killed along with his bodyguard. He had been in the process of 'purging' leftists from the university. By mid autumn, labor and peasant actions began. The government warned that it would deal harshly with such confrontations. It revoked constitutional guarantees and declared a state of emergency. The new US Ambassador, Frank Devine, although targeted by the ultra right for assassination, supported the government in its battle against 'terrorism', the euphemism that has come to mean the revolutionary left.

For Archbishop Romero the situation became clearer with each day. In El Salvador those who held great wealth supported oppression. Daily he grew less timid and closer to the people. But what the bespectacled cleric perceived as concern for the wretched of his country, the right wing viewed as communist infiltration of the Catholic Church. The

Vatican ordered him to decrease his criticism of the government and its handling of human rights. Romero's sermons reflected no lessening of his concern for social justice and peace; the revolutionaries stressed direct action. Their members kidnapped local and foreign businessmen, forcing the government to release some prisoners. Families paid ransoms, with which the rebels bought arms. The number of abductions induced foreign companies in El Salvador to recall employees on 'extended' vacations.

For members of the extreme right and their para-military executioners, and for the armed revolutionaries, the war had begun, even though it had no official recognition. The actions of each side became more dramatic and, on the part of the government's death squads, more violent. Following the models of other Latin American military dictators, the Salvadoran generals utilized members of the armed forces and police, in civilian clothes, to assassinate their political enemies and intimidate all their opponents. Death squads proved efficient. No records of arrests existed. Therefore, the families of people who 'disappeared' had no formal means of redressing their grievances. In the year ending in January 1979, more than one hundred people had 'disappeared'.

On 16 January armed members of FAPU (United Popular Action Front) seized the OAS building, the Red Cross offices and Mexican Embassy in San Salvador. More than one hundred and fifty people were held hostage, forcing the Romero government to release seventy-two prisoners, all of whom fled to Mexico. Three days later, the death squads answered the daring deeds by machine gunning five priests in their parish hall, just outside the capital city. Archbishop Romero excommunicated 'the authors' of the assassination and declared three days of mourning. The archbishop's office listed 715 people who had been arrested. The government acknowledged holding only forty-eight.

In May the guerrillas seized other embassies, demanding the release of prisoners. On 10 May their forces occupied the Metropolitan Cathedral in San Salvador. This gave the government and the right wing an opportunity for unified action. Police surrounded the cathedral and without warning opened fire on revolutionary supporters demonstrating on its steps; twenty-three died, more than seventy were wounded. Two days later a mass demonstration took place, as a funeral march. The message was clear: the majority would no longer be intimidated.

Confrontations continued throughout the late spring and into the summer. On 19 June the revolutionaries assassinated an army officer known to be a prominent member of ORDEN (Democratic Nationalist

Organization). On 20 June the death squads retaliated, killing Padre Rafael Palacios. Throughout June and July assassinations of teachers and political leaders were carried out.

## DEATH OF A POET

When revolution triumphed in neighboring Nicaragua in July 1979, the winds of that social change began to affect thinking in El Salvador as well. Revolutionary ideas grow best in a culture of oppression and there could be no better breeding ground than the social relations that existed in El Salvador. But there are no formulas to make successful revolutions, and those who have tried simply to transpose a model from one country to another have always failed. There was no repetition of the Cuban process, and even though Nicaragua was geographically and culturally close to El Salvador, there were enough dissimilarities to thwart attempts to emulate the Sandinistas. The struggle for the correct line is often bloody, as is well illustrated by the premature death of Roque Dalton.

Dalton, who became known throughout the world as El Salvador's revolutionary poet, was the illegitimate son of Frank Dalton, a member of the infamous gang that robbed trains and banks in the fading days of the Wild West. His father had fled to El Salvador and married into one of the elite families. Roque's mother was an Indian servant on the estate. But Frank liked Roque's independent spirit and his courage. He gave him the family name and bought the boy an education.

Roque, always the rebel, became a revolutionary after his first contact with radical ideas. He wrote short stories, poems and essays denouncing the system of exploitation. Once at the university, he also denounced his own family as capitalist exploiters. Roque was jailed, tortured and luckily escaped into exile. Thanks to comrades abroad he made his way to Czechoslovakia in the early 1960s and then to Cuba, where he remained until the early 1970s.

Roque lost no time rejoining the revolution, but he was not prepared for the ferocity of the ideological struggle rife among his former comrades. He was killed in 1975 by militants of the ERP, who accused him of being a CIA agent – the price he paid for ideological differences. The left was attempting to offer a revolutionary ideology that would establish its framework for debate, its cultural authority. Questions that appeared remote to casual observers were transformed into life and death issues. Revolution by its very nature produces a sense of crisis, a feeling that rapid change is in the offing. The fierce sectarian struggles that characterized the left reflected this sense of urgency until the FMLN took the struggle to the battlefield in 1980.

The right wing felt the pressure as well. As the Somozas dominated all of Nicaraguan political and economic life, so the Fourteen Families set the tone for life in El Salvador. The Fourteen Families, whose ideology and cultural tastes were imposed by force, feared for their own future. They observed in detail the overthrow of Somoza in nearby Nicaragua and his replacement by Sandinistas. This revolutionary virus was infectious. Thus, as had been the case since 1932, when revolution threatened, the armed forces stepped to the fore.

## WASHINGTON ENTERS THE WAR AND ENCOURAGES A COUP

Traditionally, Washington policy makers respond to revolution as if it was the sound of dominoes falling and ultimately landing on the US border. Viron Vaky, Assistant Secretary of State for Inter American Affairs, told a Congressional committee that El Salvador was 'the most volatile' nation in the region and that insurrection was brewing in this 'classic setting for social and political unrest'.

As if to prove Vaky right, in December 1979 National Guard, police and plain-clothes thugs opened fire on a large crowd of demonstrators in San Salvador, killing two and wounding eleven, including a US newsman. Politicians from the left to the Christian Democrats denounced the government; some political activists returned from exile and began discussing the formation of a broad democratic coalition to oppose the continuation of military rule.

The Nicaraguan events also had an impact inside the Salvadoran military. An important grouping of officers agreed that General Romero and his ilk had outlived their political usefulness. A reform-minded colonel, Adolfo Majano, emerged as the leader of the group that would stage a coup to depose Romero. At the same time, Archbishop Romero in his weekly homily warned the military not to substitute itself 'for the political institutions which should democratically decide the political course of the country'. US intelligence sources agreed also that General Romero's rule and his style of governing had become things of the past. The stage for the coup was set.

With a bright green light from Washington, the coup took place as planned on 15 October 1979, led by a group of junior army officers. General Romero packed his numerous suitcases filled with ill-gotten wealth, and went abroad into retirement. There was no formal resistance to the seizure of power by the junior officers. They named a civilian–military junta, which declared an end to 'the state of anarchy' that had warranted the coup itself. The young officers blamed 'extremists' for not complying with the constitution. They then called on extremists of the left and the right to join the 'democratic process', which would begin with free elections. A State Department spokesman, calling Colonel Majano and Colonel Jaime Abdul Gutierrez 'moderate and centrist', declared that Washington felt encouraged and would consider renewing military aid to El Salvador if the new government followed the course it espoused.

To demonstrate its Catholic nature, the new coup makers invited left, center and right to join the new governing junta. It authorized the release of political prisoners, and vowed to make the Romero government officials take responsibility for their bloody deeds, and to reorganize the security forces. Newly appointed Defense Minister Colonel Jose Guillermo Garcia and his Vice Minister Nicolas Carranza proposed a meeting which the new civilian members of the junta would meet the new young military officers, the progressives.

The optimism lasted for two weeks. For those who believed that real change was in the offing, this encounter proved devastating. Instead of meeting the young military who inspired the coup, the assembled politicians stared into the faces of thirty senior officers, all of whom had engaged in or actually commanded the repression over the last decade or more. It was clear to all but the very naive that Colonel Garcia, not the new junta, would be the ultimate authority. In the months that followed, the US government declared that it was satisfied with the new regime. The United States' main concern was to stop the revolutionary left.

Neither the revolutionaries nor the ultra right wing believed that formal political democracy could accommodate their interests. Thus violence re-emerged as the political weapon of both sides. On 24 October one of the revolutionary factions seized the Ministry of Labor, holding the employees and the minister hostage. Their demands: release 500 political prisoners and lower food prices. At this stage, US intelligence sources identified their key policy priority to be 'isolating and weakening the extremist left.' Washington began to gear up an aid program to ensure the new junta's survival.

Some of the revolutionary organizations agreed to suspend their activities in return for a pledge to release political prisoners and dissolve ORDEN. Even the US Embassy was skeptical, however, about the willingness of the members of ORDEN to dissolve, since some of them were the military officers proclaiming the dissolution.

In December the junta announced plans for an 'agrarian reform'. The very words enraged the right wing and simultaneously brought skeptical comments from the left, who doubted that the junta possessed the will to redistribute land. Archbishop Romero, however, pleaded for support for the Ministry of Agriculture. On 10 December street demonstrations recurred, this time with the left and right in violent confrontation. Some of the revolutionaries called for an offensive, urging peasants to seize land. The army reacted predictably, with overwhelming force, retaking two haciendas, a small slaughterhouse and a TV station, where strikes and takeovers had occurred. The armed forces employed armored vehicles and helicopters. Thirty-five strikers died; scores were wounded.

At demonstrations, which grew in number during this period of unrest, the police often opened fire. The number of dead and wounded mounted. National Guard leader Colonel Vides Casanova, clarified whatever confusion may have existed about who was in control: 'Colonel Garcia is the man from whom we take orders, not the junta. We have been running the country for fifty years, and we are quite prepared to keep on running it.' More than one thousand Salvadorans died in 1979 as a result of political violence. This would be the equivalent of 44,000 people dying in the United States as a result of domestic unrest. In El Salvador, this was just the beginning of the carnage.

## The 1980s

The military control of the government doomed the junta. By early January 1980 the majority of its civilian members had resigned from their posts due to the right-wing military command, refusing to serve as a façade for oppression. Guillermo Ungo stated that he could not serve as long as Colonel Garcia ran the government. The unofficial slogan in Washington remained: 'keep the center' alive. In reality, there was no center. So the national security experts in Washington helped to build one. Robert White replaced Frank Devine as ambassador, taking bold positions on human rights violations, which annoyed the right wing, and labeling the revolutionaries 'the Pol Pot left', a reference to the murderous regime in Cambodia in the mid-1970s.

As the first junta disintegrated and the violence escalated, Jose Napoleon Duarte announced that his party, the PDC (Christian Democratic Party) would, with conditions, join the government. The military, formally led by Colonels Majano and Gutierrez, agreed to reorganize the security forces, promote agrarian reform and disallow the representatives of the Fourteen Families into the new government. Washington had promised the colonels substantial help if they would cut the deal with the PDC. In mid-January, a second junta was formed, including Colonels Majano and Gutierrez and members of the Christian Democratic Party – but not Duarte, who cautiously remained on the sidelines waiting to see what developed. Christian Democratic leaders assured reporters that they, the civilians, would have power; that the military had made irreversible concessions. The colonels smiled for the TV cameras, appearing to support the statements of the civilians.

The right-wing press attacked the centrist junta as subversive and communist. Agrarian reform was equated with Bolshevism, theft and atheism by the Fourteen Families, whom God had endowed. The embassy and CIA heaved a sigh of relief: a center government existed – but it had no power.

While the junta was proclaiming itself, the revolutionaries announced their own equivalent of the left. As reporters gathered in a clandestine meeting spot and gaped at the masked faces of the men and women who had designed and carried out the revolutionary violence of the last years, Cayetano Carpio, Shafik Handal, Comandante Ana Maria and other near-legendary figures on the left assured the press that a coordinated political–military command had been set up, an equivalent to the unification of Nicaragua's three factions before their triumph.

The fact that Handal and Carpio appeared together shocked some of the journalists, who still believed that the left was made up of irreparably divided factions. What brought the revolutionaries together was the smell of victory. Like the Sandinista experience in Nicaragua, the Salvadorans listened to the grand master of revolution, Fidel Castro, who lectured to them about the need for unity above all if they were to prevail. The year 1980 appeared to be that of their success. At last, the Central American revolutionaries believed the fabled American domino theory would actually begin to realize itself.

The revolutionaries stepped up their street actions, seizing the Panamanian embassy and several ambassadors. The US national security apparatus elevated El Salvador to high priority and planned to increase military aid and send advisers to help stabilize the non-existent center. By mid-February the government had yielded to the revolutionaries' demands, releasing prisoners. The revolutionaries released their hostages and left the occupied Spanish Embassy. But as right-wing death squads and the official repressive agencies continued to slaughter, Archbishop Romero pleaded with President Carter to withdraw the $50 million military aid package because it 'will sharpen the repression'.

The archbishop was correct. The aid process began and the repression grew worse. The reformist religious sector was epitomized by Archbishop Romero. The center was developing slowly – too slowly for the State Department – but nevertheless had at its core the attractive figure of Jose Napoleon Duarte.

## THE ASSASSINATION OF AN ATTORNEY-GENERAL AND AN ARCHBISHOP

At this point each sector of Salvadoran politics was represented by powerful individuals. The revolutionaries had people like Carpio, Villalobos and Guillermo Ungo. The Christian Democrats had Ruben Zamora, who discovered most painfully the nature of the junta. His brother, Mario, served as Attorney General in both juntas and advocated forming links with reformist elements on the left. On 23 February he was hosting a dinner party at his home when a loud knocking was heard at the door. His servants were pushed aside by pistol-packing men who demanded to speak with Mario Zamora. The Attorney General stepped forward. He accompanied them into the bathroom. Shots rang out. The pistoleers raced off. Zamora's corpse lay draped over the bathtub, blood leaking from holes in his head.

On the right, the most imposing and sinister character came to prominence: Major Roberto D'Aubuisson. The handsome and charismatic young man from a wealthy family had chosen a military career. Inspired by fascist ideologies and a burning hatred of revolution, D'Aubuisson found his way into the intelligence unit of the National Guard, an ideal place to collect information on the 'subversives', as well as the perfect spot from which to attack them.

In 1980, as Ronald Reagan's political appointees replaced the more human rights-minded Carter diplomats, D'Aubuisson's appeal grew. After all, Reagan and his Secretary of State Alexander Haig vowed a war on terrorism, not protection of human rights. This was a no-nonsense administration and D'Aubuisson was certainly a serious character. He solicited, and found, some support in the US Embassy for stopping the nonsensical talk about reform and democracy, and using power to regain control of the country. He advocated a military government with right-wing civilian cooperation, one that would make all-out war on the subversives. The initially positive response to him, however, quickly dimmed as Members of Congress warned the administration that aid to El Salvador depended on distancing the United States from characters like D'Aubuisson. According to the file compiled by US intelligence sources, D'Aubuisson felt no compunction of torturing or killing. After reading the material, Ambassador White called him 'a psychopathic killer'. D'Aubuisson emerged as the presidential candidate of ARENA, the right-wing party.

Mario Zamora's assassination by right-wing thugs linked to D'Aubuisson and the resignation of Hector Dada, a leading Christian Democrat who had remained committed to the second junta, forced the Christian Democratic Party to reconsider its position in the junta. Could it continue to cooperate with a military wing that was clearly allied to right-wing death squads that had murdered one of their own ministers? They decided to split.

Duarte stacked the party convention in March 1980 with delegates loyal to him. He won the majority, and then impassively watched as all the government ministers in his party along with the entire progressive wing walked out in disgust. Duarte and his cronies then constituted themselves as the Popular Social Christian Movement (MPSC). Duarte would win the presidency, but not the power.

The strategies of the right, with close connections to the armed forces, and the left, in armed struggle, dictated the polarization of politics. The revolutionaries and Major D'Aubuisson and his less visible cohorts believed that only through violence could one side prevail.

On 23 March, Archbishop Romero preached to a packed cathedral, filled not only with his own parishioners but with visitors from the United States. Radio transmitted his words throughout Central America. Never had he delivered such a ringing message. In his 'stemwinder', as one visiting clergyman described it, Romero laid out his version of appropriate politics for his country. From the Bible he turned to comment on recent events, to talk of rapes and tortures, of murder by government forces, of support from US religious circles for withdrawing US military aid. He then endorsed the movement that had initiated the national strike, while recognizing 'its faults'.

What brought the churchgoers to their feet in a wave of emotion were his closing remarks. He called upon 'the peasants in uniform' (members of the repressive forces) to disobey orders, to 'remember the words of God', when men order other men to kill. 'Thou shalt not kill. ... No soldier is obliged to obey an order contrary to the law of God.'

He declared those who gave orders to kill to be sinners. 'The Church cannot remain silent in the presence of such abominations.' His voice rose to fever pitch as he addressed the government. 'I beg you,' he began, but then changed from a plea to a command. 'I order you, in the name of God, to stop the repression.'

The departing crowd agreed that the sermon marked a historic change in the role of the Church. Enthusiasm filled the air. The linking of religious power with revolution had been broadcast to the entire region and presumably to the rest of the Catholic world. The news did not escape the ears of the right wing in El Salvador and their allies.

The atmosphere in the cathedral returned to normal the next day. Romero began to lead the flock in the age-old rituals of the Mass. Then, from the back of the church, a man moved quickly down the aisle and, using a weapon with a silencer so that the parishioners would not hear, fired directly into the body of the archbishop as he raised his arms in mid-prayer. The killer then left the church.

The shots were heard around the world, but the message received from them was not uniform. The horror produced in religious and liberal sectors did not extend to the national security professionals, nor to the majority in Congress, which authorized more military aid to the Salvadoran government. The issue transcended human concerns: the Cold War had reached El Salvador.

Ironically, inside the Politburo in Moscow, little attention was paid to events in Central America. As late as 1982 the Kremlin's Central America experts worried more about a leading Guatemalan communist's conversion to 'the pro-Chinese line' than they did about events in Nicaragua and El Salvador. Contrary to what Reagan administration officials were reporting about Soviet beachheads in Central America, the Soviet leadership were completely uninterested in the struggle in El Salvador. Except for the special case of Cuba, the men in the Politburo believed that the Western Hemisphere was a US sphere and therefore beyond the scope of Soviet power. In public, however, they proclaimed their commitment to 'proletarian internationalism', portraying the Soviet Union as a potential insurance company for all liberation movements and Marxist revolutions.

In Washington the assassination of Romero went down badly in Congress, but the Democrats were so intimidated by Reagan's electoral victory and the aggressive arrogance of his new team that the various House and Senate committees authorized military aid to the new government on the grounds of 'national security'.

The US commitment began a process that would endure beyond the 1980s, one that did not involve economic interests and had little to do with strategic concerns or Soviet threats. From the moment that the situation in El Salvador was defined as one bearing upon US national security, the United States' president's credibility was deemed to be on the line – thus guaranteeing unwavering US support for the Salvadoran government no matter what atrocities it might commit. The interminable war in El Salvador became one more bloody chapter in the century-old campaign against revolution in the Western Hemisphere.

So confident were Major D'Aubuisson and his group of securing United States' backing, that they designed one provocation after another, continuously escalating the level and audacity of right-wing violence. On 30 March 1980, Salvadorans and visitors from around the world attended Romero's funeral. The mourners gathered at the entrance of the old cathedral, near the government headquarters. The coffin was placed next to the cathedral stairs. In the plaza, tens of thousands of Salvadorans pushed into an ever tighter mass. Then the contingent from La Coordinadora, the coalition of popular organizations, entered the square to a tremendous ovation to lay flowers by the coffin.

As Cardinal Corripio Ahumada of Mexico closed his eulogy, speaking in the name of the pope himself, a bomb exploded near the National Palace. Shots rang out and the crowd, thicker than ever, rushed toward the cathedral away from the noise. Panic spread and mourners became victims, trampled by their comrades trying to escape the shooting and bombing.

Inside the cathedral thousands pushed together, still able to hear the echoes of explosions and gunshots. The weaker died of asphyxiation, pressed against their loved ones or strangers who happened to be part of the human vice that crushed the terrified crowd. Some of the organized left shouted slogans; other people sought to secure Romero's coffin.

About an hour after the explosions began, the crowd slowly leaked out of the plaza and the cathedral. Blood, still wet, stained the stones; the wounded and dead lay in the hot sun, while teams of medical personnel and Good Samaritans began to tend to those who could still be helped. The death toll came to twenty-six; the wounded exceeded two hundred. The question on the minds of much of the policy establishment: who was responsible?

The US Embassy and Duarte assured the world that the government forces were innocent. Ambassador White, so outspoken in his denunciation of the right wing for Romero's murder, balanced his presentation on the cathedral massacre, attributing the blame to the left. Several priests swore that they saw snipers in the government palace. All witnesses agreed that members of the left fought back, either to cover the escape of people fleeing or as an act of resistance.

The assassination of Romero and its aftermath created the desired chilling climate for the new archbishop, Rivera y Damas. At the Vatican's behest, the previously outspoken cleric took a subdued position, retreating from Romero's commitment. The protest against the repression that had taken place in the streets with Romero's support no longer had a champion in the Church. D'Aubuisson had won the round. Although some of the left did not abandon the tactic of protest and civil disobedience, the toll in lives had begun to persuade many that the next stage called for a different level of resistance.

## Forming the FDR and FMLN

At a packed mass meeting in the auditorium of the National University on 18 April 1980, reformers and revolutionaries joined those centrist politicians who had 'seen enough', and forged a political alliance: the Democratic Revolutionary Front (FDR). The Front included the chiefs of popular organizations, union leaders and some religious figures. Enrique Alvarez Cordoba, a slightly left-of-center politician, was named as head man; Guillermo Ungo, who had run as vice presidential candidate with Duarte in 1972, emerged as its back-up leader. Ruben Zamora, recently resigned from the Christian Democratic Party, was chosen to complete the triumvirate. The emerging partners in the FDR agreed that El Salvador desperately needed basic political and economic change and that, unless overturned, the oligarchy–military alliance would eternally prevent the advent of democracy in their country. In addition, the FDR was outspoken on a platform of human rights and independence – especially from US intervention.

To meet the challenge from the right and the United States, the combined leadership agreed on tactics of public repudiation of the ruling elite. The majority would show its political thinking by demonstrating, protesting and organizing. FDR leaders would also appeal to the court of international public opinion, by making the Salvadoran case known abroad. On one issue the FDR leadership lacked consensus. In the late spring, they were still debating the correct position relating to armed struggle, although many of the politicians had friends who had recently picked up the revolutionary rifle. Inside the FDR a consensus began to form that endorsed political action and simultaneously recognized the need of some comrades to resort to revolutionary violence.

In Washington, those reasonable politicians who stood for the same values as President Carter found themselves talking to deaf ears both in Congress and the White House. The policy makers on Capitol Hill and in the Executive Office Building accepted the bizarre definition of US interests as maintaining a 'center' in El Salvador. The FDR representatives tried to convince the legislators and State Department officials that they were the real center.

It was not a communications problem, however. President Carter, having placed his 'credibility' on the line in El Salvador, began to circumvent truth through language. Administration officials labeled US aid 'non-lethal', and quickly approved a variety of military toys with which the 'center' could combat the extreme right and left. In fact, the real center had been forced to join the left. Duarte was no more than a fig leaf for the extreme right wing who, though they pledged loyalty to a lawful state, could barely control their contempt for laws that advocated democracy and justice.

Nevertheless, the US Embassy was told to accept the fabrication that finally a legitimate center party had emerged, personified by the appointed president, Duarte. Upon that nonsensical formulation the US government staked its prestige, backed by its formidable power. For Major D'Aubuisson, the spiritual and actual leader of the ultra right, the Americans' tortured postures signified a continued opening that allowed him to conspire with his legions to seize full control of state power, while keeping up the pressure through violence on the left. It was not an ambience in which even a fragile democracy could develop.

Uniformed military and police carried out raids and massacres, while at night the death squads caused 'subversives' to disappear, or simply murdered them. Scores of left and center leaders and middle-level personnel were wiped out. The reformist or moderate military wing, led by Colonel Majano, felt pushed and isolated from the other members of their corps.


## HEARTS, MINDS AND LAND REFORM

Inside the US Embassy some CIA and military sectors privately favored the ultra right, and some in memos and cables called for a full scale war against 'terrorism', the label given to the revolutionaries.

Others stuck to the somewhat confusing Carter line, faithful to the letter of the human rights dictum and the spirit of national security doctrine, which held that defeating communist insurgencies must be accomplished at all costs. The resolution of this contradiction in policy guidelines led to the return of the Vietnam War 'hearts and minds' formula, a plan to win over the noble peasants, while fighting a counterinsurgency war against the evil communists.

The key to the loyalty of the peasantry, claimed the experts and consultants who advised the national security elite, was land reform. The left, claimed the professors, had made gains over the years because of the unjust land tenure system and because of the greedy and selfish behavior of the oligarchy. Hey presto! Land reform became the cause célèbre of the Carter administration, which dredged up one of the Vietnam War land reform planners and sent him to El Salvador.

Agrarian reform plans were announced and actually began to develop. To the right wing, the notion of taking someone else's property and distributing it to those who do not have any, or who once had it, was tantamount to communism. D'Aubuisson and his supporters plotted assassinations and other violence precisely to force a showdown, which the right felt certain they would win. The plots included one on the life of the US ambassador. Col. Majano was tipped off and a sizable unit seized D'Aubuisson and several dozen followers at a ranch outside the capital. D'Aubisson was literally in the midst of eating a document when his arms were grabbed and the paper pulled out of his mouth. The evidence of his link to the death squads and other violence was overwhelming. In addition, several of the papers seized linked him directly to the assassination of Archbishop Romero. The reformists in the army had the evidence, the human rights advocates in the embassy had their prime violator.

When the Salvadoran officers met in assembly, Col. Majano soon discovered that the officer corps remained loyal to the oligarchy and ultimately to D'Aubuisson. Instead of supporting reform, the corps nominated officers linked to the right-wing violence. The bureaucratic Col. Jaime Abdul Gutierrez, who posed for the Americans as a reformer, was actually the lackey of Col. Guillermo Garcia, the Minister of Defense, known for his right-wing views. Majano fell precipitously from leadership to obscurity. Within a few days D'Aubuisson and the other plotters were freed.

The right wing had triumphed. Those Christian Democrats who had not resigned stayed silent. Duarte remained as the figurehead president, claiming with each act of violence that he could not control the military, but refusing to resign. The die was cast. The oligarchy celebrated a victory against the 'communists'.

## MORE VIOLENCE

Losing no time, the military, working unofficially with D'Aubuisson and his gang, began to eliminate the supporters or potential supporters of reform and revolution. As the non right-wing newspapers and radio heralded the anticipated changes in land policy, the military began its extermination campaign. In May 1980 alone the Catholic Church counted 1,400 dead, most of them peasants. Some died in a massacre on the Honduran border, where troops and ORDEN members destroyed an entire village of suspected revolutionary sympathizers. Such incidents were also used to intimidate other country folk from sympathy for the 'subversives'.

The military elite, a group singularly lacking in sentimentality or humanity, decided to retaliate against another intellectual center of the opposition. Having already launched a war against the Church, the military added the university to their official list of enemies. Like the sacred Catholic cathedral, the university had centuries of autonomous tradition behind it. The university was also, as the government believed, a hotbed of radicalism. It certainly performed useful functions for the left opposition. It served not only as a forum for necessary discussion and debate over tactics and strategy, but also as a talent pool from which the opposition leadership could draw.

Students played a variety of roles in the mass movement. Indeed, student leaders had been crucial in calling and organizing several of the protests and demonstrations. They could write, have material duplicated, and serve as links between the guerrillas and the political front. It was, like many universities, an information center. The elite families generally sent their children abroad to university, where they shocked even conservative American students with their expressions of contempt for their own peasant and working classes. A few upper-class youths attended the national university and some even became revolutionaries.

When, in late June, the opposition called for and achieved a successful strike, it showed that its members could not be intimidated. The US intelligence officers had written cables denying that the left opposition could respond. In fact they managed to shut down the capital.

On 27 June, while many students celebrated the victory of the general strike the previous day, armored vehicles and hundreds of uniformed troops crashed through the university gates, firing at the classroom buildings. Sixteen young people died. The university was shut down.

Throughout the summer two forms of struggle took place: the urban organizing and protests intended to weaken the legitimacy of the government and persuade the populace of the left's virtues; and armed clashes, mostly in the countryside, between the military and the various guerrilla factions.

As repression grew more ferocious and political space narrowed, members of various leftist parties and groupings began to engage in armed struggle – forms of guerrilla warfare. Their efforts, however, were uncoordinated. Theoretical and ideological differences led to organizational antagonisms that at first prevented a unified military command. But within months the leaders of each faction realized that their differences were less important than unity on the battlefront.

On 10 October 1980 the Farabundo Marti Front for National Liberation (FMLN) announced its existence. The leaders of most of the revolutionary groupings resurrected Farabundo Marti's name to promote a unified command to launch armed struggle. Ideological differences, the leaders agreed, should remain secondary to unified war strategy. The groups that composed the FMLN were the FPL, ERP, RN, the Moscow-linked Communist Party and the PRTC.

El Salvador had been at war without formal acknowledgement. The formation of the FMLN left no doubt in anyone's mind that an armed conflict to resolve who held state power was underway, full force. The façade of a government, held together exclusively by US aid and the authority of that empire's prestige, had little to do with the conflict – except as a front for the military and oligarchy whose instruments were the armed forces and para-military death squads.

The left, in the urban and rural areas, maintained a political and a military organization; its tactics, until the end of 1980, were primarily based on the various guerrilla models. During September 1980, before the merger of the varying factions, guerrillas bombed four government buildings; they also shot their way into and captured OAS headquarters in San Salvador. They took hostages, whom they tried to use as a lever against the armed forces and the oligarchy. However, D'Aubuisson and his team were not burdened with concern over a kidnapped ambassador, or the possibility of a poor public image.

On 21 November 1980 Jose Napoleon Duarte was inaugurated, the first civilian president in more than fifty years. As the non-elected president he would supposedly stand as a symbol of decency against a military machine and an oligarchy whom a critic had likened to vampires in their need for blood. Even though members of the ultra right and the oligarchy despised this short, stocky man of humble origins, the Americans had made it clear that there would be no possibility of large-scale aid without him. Duarte had good connections in the United States and his backers included the prestigious Father Theodore Hessberg, President of Notre Dame University, where Duarte had graduated. The human rights community revered him. He had survived torture – including the severing of fingers – by some of the very officers who stood before him at rigid attention. It remained a mystery how the enthusiasts in Washington could transform one well-intentioned man working against institutionalized barbarism into a credible hope of democracy in Central America.

At the time of his attaining the presidency in the autumn of 1980, over five thousand people had already died, most of them from military and para-military violence. The Salvadoran economy was in deep trouble; the government junta represented at best a thin patina of legitimacy. But, as one of Duarte's supporters pointed out, they 'love the little guy in Washington'. And that is where the ultimate source of Salvadoran authority remained.

The hopes vested in Duarte by people of good will around the world were first dashed when 200 armed police and military personnel stormed a Catholic school, murdered four prominent leaders of the political opposition and kidnapped twenty-five others. Although the Maximiliano Hernandez Martinez Brigade – one of the supposedly 'independent' death squads – claimed credit and the government denied responsibility for the raid, there was little doubt in anyone's mind where true responsibility lay.

## THE SLAYING OF THE SISTERS

American nuns and lay missionaries played a variety of supporting roles in the broad movement for social change in El Salvador, Guatemala and Nicaragua. As part of the new theology women who joined the Church to do service for God were no longer confined to convents or to teaching in parochial schools.

Jean Donovan, a lay missionary, and three nuns, Dorothy Kazel, Ita Ford and Maura Clarke, all met at the San Salvador airport in the early evening of 2 December 1980. Donovan and Kazel brought the van to pick up the other two, who were returning from Nicaragua. But they never arrived at the parish house. A security force van stopped their vehicle about thirty minutes from the airport. The men raped and beat the four young women, and then shot them in the head. The next morning the authorities declared the corpses to be 'unknowns' and dumped their bodies into a hastily dug grave.

But word of the missing missionaries reached the US Embassy, as did news of the burial of four 'unknown women'. The pressure brought by Ambassador Robert White and members of the clergy forced the government to exhume the bodies on 4 December. At the site White saw the bullet holes in the nuns' heads, their torn and twisted clothing. The blows to the heads and bodies of the women were obvious. 'This time', White declared, 'they won't get away with it.'

Ironically, over the course of the next few months and indeed years the perpetrators did get away with murdering the nuns as well as thousands of others. An investigation of sorts was mounted, bringing the arrests of some security officials and low-ranking Guardsmen, but witnesses contradicted themselves, evidence vanished and gradually the case simply eroded.

Ambassador White, however, who tried to promote support for the center as legitimate precisely because he believed in Duarte's commitment to human rights, soon grew disillusioned – if not with Duarte, then with his own bosses in Washington. Some Reagan administration officials suggested that the women might have been responsible for their own death. Secretary of State Haig commented that they 'may have run a roadblock'. Jeanne Kirkpatrick, about to be named as ambassador to the UN, was more direct, implying that the nuns might well have merited death. 'The nuns were not just nuns. The nuns were also political activists ... for the opposition', whom Ms Kirkpatrick labeled as violent totalitarians.

Following Duarte's inauguration, two and a half weeks after Ronald Reagan defeated Jimmy Carter in the US election, the right wing felt confident. The figurehead president had no support in the military. Majano and his small 'moderate' group were fast vanishing. D'Aubuisson, on the other hand, loomed as the man of decision: cold blooded and not intimidated by the bleeding-hearts gang in the US Embassy led by Ambassador White. If words were an indication of impending Reagan policy, White was on the 'to be replaced' list. Reaganites openly derided Carter's human rights policy and vowed to replace it with 'a war on terrorism'. And high up on the terrorism priority list were the Salvadoran guerrillas and their supporters.

Like other career diplomats during the Carter presidency, White believed that human rights abroad could be affected by US policy, and that the creation of a strong center was the only conceivable route to building democratic foundations. His tenure as ambassador to Paraguay in the mid-1970s had given him a strong dislike for authoritarian military governments. So, he found Duarte appealing and accepted the myth that there was real or even possible space for a political center in El Salvador. From experience, he thought that the replacement would take some months at least – the amount of time required for any new government to coalesce.

As if to underline the futility of White's quest for peace and stability, two *pistoleros* walked into the Sheraton Hotel dining room and assassinated two Americans and a Salvadoran, all associated with the land reform process. Ambassador White was disgusted and he informed friends unofficially that this had to be the work of D'Aubuisson's men.

## The First Final Offensive

The military, buoyed by its growing hold on state power, launched an offensive to wipe out the 'bandits', as they began calling the guerrillas. In Morazan Province, an FMLN stronghold, the army did not eradicate the *combatientes* of the left; instead, they marched into ambushes. Their boasts to the press simply did not match their performance in the field. And why should they? The officers who graduated each year had little or no real military experience. The rank and file, poor people who had little choice, possessed no sense of fighting for a just cause. The guerrillas, on the other hand, were highly motivated and better trained, albeit not as well equipped as the regular army.

After Duarte's inauguration, FMLN units undermined the government's legitimacy. They occupied scores of towns and villages throughout several provinces, attacked military posts and ambushed army columns. They appeared to have the upper hand. But the initiative they had seized could not be maintained.

FMLN leaders and soldiers suffered not from lack of will or ability to fight; indeed, they fought heroically and skilfully, overcoming great odds and superior weaponry. Some units fought with pistols, .22 caliber rifles and homemade hand grenades. Others used machetes. Twelve-year-olds and men of sixty engaged forces with superior armaments, including the air force, which bombed villages harboring the guerrillas. The Salvadoran brass cared little who suffered the impact of the bombs – poor peasant farmers or peasants turned guerrillas. Nor did they value the lives of the poor who were thrust into the battle wearing Salvadoran uniforms. Few officers died, but below the rank of lieutenant casualties were heavy. The blood from what was supposed to be the final offensive was spread thickly through the Salvadoran countryside and in the city and town streets.

One of the FMLN leadership's problems was triumphalism. They not only convinced members of the media, the diplomatic corps, the military advisers and even members of the Reagan team that they were a truly formidable force, but they also persuaded themselves. Their political and military vision omitted two decisive factors: their own inexperience in war, and the determination of the national security bureaucracy in Washington to prevent another 'communist victory' in the Western Hemisphere – no matter the cost to the people and land of El Salvador.

FMLN comandantes had confidently declared that the final offensive would occur before the Reagan inauguration, on 20 January 1981. They ordered the *militantes* to go to their stations in the cities and to their units for battle in the countryside; FDR and FMLN leaders coordinated political–military strategy. They called a strike for the city at the start of the uprising. But the revolutionary leaders had not gauged the extent to which the repression had decimated middle- and lower-level cadres. Neighborhood and local union leaders upon whom the success of the strike depended had already been murdered, arrested, or forced to go underground or abroad. Without leadership the strike was doomed to be less than the FMLN had envisioned.

The lame-duck Carter presidency did not have sufficient willpower to vote large sums of money – much less US military units – to back the nun-killers in power. Neither were they inclined to cut off the phony centrist government they had created. Three days before he left office, Jimmy Carter released the frozen aid money to the Salvadoran government. National security had ultimately prevailed over the human rights agenda proclaimed as the American mission by the religious Baptist president.

The decision to aid the killers committed the United States, once and for all, to the process of war in El Salvador. In January battles raged through much of El Salvador. The guerrillas, with their assorted and often primitive weapons, laid ambushes and assaulted military outposts.

Their initial successes in capturing towns and villages and routing ill-trained and demoralized troops were not sustained, however. Among the guerrillas, neither the top leadership nor the intermediate-level officers really knew how to follow up those victories. They could not successfully fight the army in conventional warfare. By mid-January their effort began to stall.

FMLN units were forced to retreat from some of the territories they had 'liberated', as they lacked the people to defend them, even though the villagers sympathized to one degree or another with the goals of the FMLN. The organization itself lacked the wherewithal to maintain the necessary administrative–military structures. When the revolutionaries abandoned villages the peasants fled and became refugees or faced the wrath of the military. On the other side, the Salvadoran military also learned painful lessons, and retreated to its barracks to lick wounds.

Despite the public relations campaign with which the US Embassy managed the major media, it became clear that the FMLN continued to control significant pieces of territory in the rural zones. Those reporters who ventured into the countryside discovered that the revolutionaries had set up their own systems of government in villages throughout several provinces, and that the Salvadoran military was reluctant to seek them out. Although claims of the 'final offensive' proved boastful, the guerrillas showed their mettle and won the respect, if not fear, of their foes. The FMLN military achievements, however, only strengthened the resolve of the Reaganites, who used the offensive to dramatize their plea to Congress for more aid to deal with the threat of communism in El Salvador.

Those in the officer corps, who thought about more than accumulating wealth and living an easy life, understood from the first month of battle that there probably would be a protracted war, in which the United States would cast itself in the role of the permanent insurance company. Time and certainly money were on the army's side. They would wait for more aid and advisers before taking the war to the FMLN's strongholds. Confidence came with word from Washington that help was on its way.

President Reagan brought no bleeding-heart liberals into his inner circle. Quite the opposite. His Secretary of State, General Alexander Haig, told reporters that the guiding theme for his foreign policy toward El Salvador would be anti-terrorism, and he left no doubt that the FMLN were the terrorists. Worse, they were terrorists tied to Moscow and Havana, and would be treated as serious enemies. Haig assured the skeptical reporters that they would soon see the evidence in black and white.

## The White Paper

Secretary Haig met reporters several times in barely off-the-record sessions and assured them that the Reagan administration 'meant business' with respect to terrorism. 'It's not rebels in El Salvador who are causing these problems,' he said in early February 'but people in Havana and Moscow.' And, Haig told the skeptics in the crowd, 'we'll show you plenty of proof'. When asked how aiding the dubious government in El Salvador would hurt Havana or Moscow, Haig shook his head and proclaimed: 'We're going to the source.' He meant Havana, he informed the press corps. Fidel Castro took him seriously and began to shore up Cuban defenses.

In fact, Cuba was hardly the source. Unlike the Americans who stationed military advisers in El Salvador, Castro offered to provide Cuban military experts in Cuba to train new Salvadoran cadres for the FMLN. He also opened Cuban hospitals for wounded Salvadoran guerrillas who could find their way to the island. These forms of aid were hardly decisive to the FMLN's efforts.

'Evidence' for the Haig thesis came in a much heralded White Paper released by the State Department in late February 1981. The US government, the document claimed, had 'definitive evidence' that the Soviet Union, Cuba and other communist countries were sending weapons 'to the Marxist–Leninist guerrillas'. It went on to say that the Soviet Union, using Cuba as its surrogate, was conducting 'indirect armed aggression against a small Third World country'. Tons of weapons, the report continued, were to be delivered by the Soviets to the guerrillas.

Among the other key documents that Salvadoran security forces allegedly captured to show the international links to the Marxist–Leninist terrorist uprising were the diaries of FMLN leader, Shafik Handal. Handal went to Moscow and other communist capitals, the report detailed, in order to secure a flow of weapons. This made the insurgency 'a textbook case of aggression'.

State Department emissaries carried the report and supposedly cor-roborating proof of this 'textbook aggression' to Latin America and Western Europe to convince allies and win endorsement for the US position, which was to offer increased support to the Salvadoran forces of repression. Simultaneously, Reagan administration staff hit the mass media, in off- and on-the-record briefings. El Salvador, announced spokesmen from the State and Defense Departments and the White House, would be the place where Washington would draw the line against communism.

Another administration heavy weight UN Ambassador Jeanne Kirkpatrick, announced that 'Central America is the most important place in the world'. By that she meant that it was *the* test of American will to resist the 'totalitarian empire'. If 'authoritarian' regimes had to be backed in order to thwart the goals of the 'red empire', then so be it. Authoritarian regimes were subject to change; not so the totalitarian ones.

The new administration spared no expense to legitimate its view of the world, one that Reagan would later articulate as the war between the forces of good and those of the 'evil empire'. But, for the less gullible parts of the population, healthy skepticism met the dramatic pronouncements and claims of the Reagan ideologues.

If energy and militancy could have been converted into truth the Reagan administration would have carried the day. The problem they faced was the dubious accuracy of the White Paper. The Europeans did not accept the premise that the Salvadoran insurrection was Soviet–Cuban inspired – regardless of the 'facts' of the White Paper – and Congress was not about to be bamboozled into simply doling out cash to murderers of American nuns. The Speaker of the House, Thomas 'Tip' O'Neill, had been raised by Maryknoll sisters and was appalled at the idea that those who killed women of God should be the beneficiaries of US taxpayers' largesse. Both Houses placed human rights conditions on future US aid. The Reagan officials dealt with this obstacle by simply fabricating reports that the Salvadoran government was complying with the human rights standards required by Congress. The State Department's human rights progress report to Congress grossly underestimated the gravity of the situation. A more accurate and harsher monitoring effort came from inside the Catholic Church of El Salvador, but the Reagan administration downplayed the clergy's assessment and presented a wholly unrealistic version to Congress.

Regardless of the skepticism surrounding the charged ideological pronouncements from the White House, the mass media reported the publication of the State Department's White Paper on El Salvador as if it actually contained irrefutable evidence of Soviet–Cuban subversion. It was not until months later that the first critical reports emerged and, when they did, they destroyed the document's credibility.

## WHITE PAPER REFUTED: BUT TOO LATE

By the spring several journalists had studied the February White Paper and reported serious shortcomings in its evidence and methods. John Dinges in the *Los Angeles Times* and Jonathan Kwitney in the *Wall Street Journal* both concluded that the White Paper did not prove that the Soviets were supplying the FMLN. Indeed, Handal's diaries, when read carefully, proved exactly the opposite. When Shafik Handal arrived in Moscow, representing not only the Salvadoran Communist Party but the entire FMLN, not one high-level official agreed to meet him. His request for aid was not even answered. The total reward for his trip and the ensuing wait in his Moscow hotel room was a free Aeroflot ticket out of the country. Handal, disappointed at the lack of Soviet interest in El Salvador's revolution, traveled to other communist capitals without receiving any significant promises of aid. Only in Havana and Managua was there open support for the FMLN, but hardly of the quantity or quality alleged by the State Department. In addition Jon Glassman, the principal author of the paper, admitted to Kwitney that much of the document was based on speculation, not evidence.

Those who opposed US aid to El Salvador did not have the public relations operators of the White House, nor did they command the attention of the major media. So the news of the international conspiracy to subvert Central America dominated the headlines and the TV news, but the refutation of the story attracted minimal attention.

In any case, truth meant little to those in the National Security Council who managed the affair. First, they circumvented Congress' stipulations when in February 1981 they 'found' $25 million in the pipeline that could be funneled to El Salvador. Next, more than fifty military advisers and instructors went to El Salvador under the guise of training their Central American counterparts in communications and other 'skills' required 'to respond to terrorist attacks'.

In Washington, the intellectuals of the military, CIA and State Department concluded that there was little need to worry about these dubious activities because 'the war should be over within ninety days'. Within a month of Reagan's inauguration, Bob White was replaced as Chief of Mission by Deane Hinton, a man with orders to 'get the job done', a euphemism for 'don't be a bleeding-heart liberal'. The Reaganites decided to stay behind Duarte, but to reinforce the military and police apparatus as the effective means to deal with revolution. After the war, they thought, elections would be called. With US help, and Duarte as a candidate liked by Congress, the planners in national security circles foresaw full victory in El Salvador – a healthy step on the road to defeating Havana and Moscow.

To show their cooperation with the Washington sixty- to ninety-day war plan, Salvadoran commanders ordered their units, with US advisers guiding the battle plan, to bring the war to the guerrillas in the rural provinces where the FMLN controlled territory. Once again, the guerrillas, with accurate information provided by sympathetic peasants and informers inside the military, set traps and ambushes into which the poorly trained soldiers walked. The Salvadoran officers invariably fled, leaving their troops leaderless and helpless before a smaller but smarter guerrilla unit.

In the cities, death squads resurfaced, murdering those targeted as leaders of the opposition. With Ambassador White gone, and the new Reagan team operating from the embassy, there was no eagerness to hear reports of assassinations or slaughters in the rural area. In March, White was dismissed from the foreign service for attacking the Reagan aid policy in testimony before Congress.

The FMLN, led by Joaquin Villalobos and Ferman Cienfuegos, divided their units into discrete military fronts, ranging across the northern frontier. These areas, they believed, could be controlled against army encroachment by creating an infrastructure that included civilian government, health and education facilities and supply and training operations. A rear guard defense perimeter was established, and an offensive capability created so that guerrilla units could attack vulnerable army posts or stage ambushes of units that went out on patrol.

In the spring, the Salvadoran army employed conventional war techniques taught in military school with the result that officers continued to lead their units into ambushes. Washington's advisory team, employing methods learned from more than a decade in Vietnam, began to train the army in some counter-guerrilla techniques. They concentrated their pedagogy on a new unit called the Atlacatl Battalion.

## THE REFUGEES

By July, having failed to knock out the enemy in the allotted time, and having watched their highly trained Atlacatl Battalion suffer devastating losses as a result of superior guerrilla strategy, the US advisers reverted to other tactics. A decision was made to cut off the guerrillas' source of sustenance: the villages from which they gleaned new recruits, food and supplies. This tactic led to the same result as it had in Southeast Asia – the destruction of villages and the removal of the population by death or by forcing them out of their homes with threats and intimidation.

Soon reports filtered in from the countryside that the inhabitants of small villages supposedly sympathetic to the FMLN had been massacred. News spread fast and helped spark the inevitable refugee explosion. The exodus of Salvadorans from their war-torn county produced effects that no one in Washington or San Salvador had anticipated.

The logic of war often escapes the policy makers. A mass migration to the United States began that endured throughout the 1980s. To escape the war, the draft, the poverty and the uncertainty that revolution and counterrevolution bring with them, Salvadorans poured into the United States. This migration in turn caused unanticipated consequences in the Salvadoran economy and, to a much lesser extent, in the US workforce as well. By the end of the 1980s, some one million Salvadorans, 20 per cent of the population, had moved to the United States; about a half of these earned income, a portion of which they sent home to El Salvador to help support their families.

By 1989, those remittances totalled approximately $2 billion annually. This money not only allowed for family survival in the villages of San Miguel, Chalatenango and the *barrios* of San Salvador, but it also kept the Salvadoran economy afloat. Remittances were second to coffee as the country's biggest foreign exchange producer, outstripping even the various forms of US aid.

The money flowing in from the United States was welcomed by the Salvadoran oligarchy as well. It allowed them to continue to pay low wages, even as prices rose. In the United States, employers found similar satisfactions: Salvadoran workers were excellent house servants, dish washers and construction laborers. They did not complain about low wages for fear that the immigration authorities would arrest and deport them.

So important had the export of labor become that in 1985 President Duarte pleaded secretly with President Reagan to instruct the US immigration police to relax their efforts to find and deport Salvadorans. In the early years of the war, Salvadoran men were routinely rounded up, deported often without due process, and sent back home to serve in the army. Reagan acquiesced, and the immigration agents often looked the other way when they discovered Salvadorans working illegally in the United States. By the end of the 1980s the Immigration and Naturalization Service (INS) estimated that one million or more Salvadorans had entered the United States.

Between the autumn of 1979 and July 1981, an estimated 200,000 Salvadorans out of a population of just over five million had been displaced or had fled their homes in fear. Over thirty thousand had crossed the border into Honduras and were then herded into refugee camps. The Salvadoran army, having failed to win their three-month war, and having suffered great losses in one battle after another, attacked a refugee camp inside El Salvador, killing and wounding hundreds and causing the displacement of over two thousand people.

Following further defeats, the army attacked and burned villages, raping, torturing and often murdering the inhabitants. The FMLN's control of territory was a military asset, but the cost on civilian life was far too heavy for the revolutionaries. Through 1981 and 1982, FMLN commanders debated new strategic plans. Meanwhile hundreds of thousands of Salvadorans continued to leave their villages, their barrios and their country.

The US advisers, few of them schooled in unconventional warfare, taught the conservative Salvadoran commanders what they had learned in military school. The government forces had superior fire power, controlled the air, had armored vehicles and trucks to transport troops, possessed more sophisticated radio communication equipment and outnumbered the guerrillas. In addition, thanks to the US commitment, there would be no money or equipment shortages.

Even though the FMLN's first offensive petered out, its forces nevertheless controlled significant sections of the countryside. And, reasoned US military advisers, they would learn from their mistakes and launch other attacks. So, by mid-1981 the American advisers devised a strategy for the Salvadoran armed forces: cut the FMLN off from their supplies and interrupt or disconnect their communication lines; then move those villagers supporting the FMLN to other locations, or create depopulated zones in the areas controlled by the guerrillas. In this way FMLN units would have to confront the Salvadoran army, who would then overpower them with superior numbers, firepower and air force and refined detection technology. After these plans succeeded, a Special Forces-type unit would deliver the decimating blow to the teetering revolutionaries.

In the meantime, the US military team looked the other way or even smiled tacit approval for the death squads that assassinated individuals with leadership potential whom D'Aubuisson's henchmen had labeled 'subversive'. Intelligence tactics, learned from a myriad of counter-revolutionary exercises, were employed against the urban infrastructure of the FMLN. Informers and sophisticated monitoring devices helped the government's hit squads pinpoint which houses to target. And, even when they hit the wrong house, few tears were shed by the brass. Nothing succeeds like sheer violence when the targets can be located. So, the police and death squads carried out effective search and destroy operations in San Salvador, wrecking the FMLN's cadre structure in the trade unions, civic organizations and inside the universities.

In the countryside the story was different. The plan that looked so good on paper proved less viable in practice. In August 1981 the army trumpeted an operation to wipe out the guerrilla presence in Morazan Province. Heavy ground artillery backed the government force, as A-37 Dragonfly bombers dropped their deadly loads on 'the proper coordinates', in the words of a US colonel, and Salvadoran army units, ferried in on Huey helicopters, circled the guerrilla positions, allowing only one escape valve for the FMLN troops, which would lead them into ambush and annihilation. The only problem with the operation was that the guerrillas slipped away before the Salvadoran armed forces had completed their positioning. When the troops arrived in the villages after intensive bombing and shelling they found no trace of guerrillas. Then, as frustrated Salvadoran army units returned to their bases some of the guerrillas reappeared, as ambushers lying in wait. Not all the villagers returned to their Morazan homes, or what was left of them after the bombing, but enough did for the FMLN to reactivate its infrastructure.

The failure of the army and its US advisers to administer battlefield defeats emboldened the FMLN to take the offensive. As 1981 drew to a close, the guerrillas attacked and won victories in Usulutan, San Miguel, Cabanas, Morazan and Chalatenango. A typical attack would begin before dawn as FMLN units surrounded an army base and poured mortar rounds into the compound along with rocket-propelled grenades. In some cases the guerrillas captured the compound, and made off with the weapons. In other instances, the Salvadoran army fought sufficiently well and bravely to prevent the capture of their bases.

From the offices of those national security officials whose job it was to convince Congress to fund the counterrevolution, the situation in El Salvador looked messy. The US-backed ruling civilian–military junta had won for itself a world-wide reputation for human rights abuse. This meant that each year the administration had to present Congress with a series of promises it could not or did not intend to keep about improving the behavior of the military and police officers whose salaries and pensions were being financed by American taxpayers. 'Don't worry,' one Reagan official assured members of a House Committee on Foreign Affairs, 'we will be training the Salvadoran military in our way of conducting war, with emphasis on protecting human rights.' He was referring to a contingent of sixty officers and sergeants who had arrived in early January at Fort Bragg, North Carolina, to begin infantry training with American Green Berets. This contingent would form the basis of a Salvadoran military that would be modern in its war making and in understanding the need to win the hearts and minds of its own people. Others were receiving instruction at Fort Benning, Georgia. The administration argued that the Salvadoran military command understood the need to improve its image and was already well on the road to good behavior.

This public relations gimmick did not correspond with the facts, however. A former Salvadoran soldier told a *New York Times* reporter that two US advisers were present when Salvadoran officers tortured guerrilla leaders. The Pentagon denied the story, but members of Congress were skeptical. In addition, two human rights monitoring organizations, America's Watch and the American Civil Liberties Union, provided Congress with details of consistent abuse, including the shocking claim that the Salvadoran repressive forces had killed more than twelve and a half thousand people in 1981, the vast majority of whom were civilians.

## Elections 1982: Made in Washington

To deal with the criticisms from liberals and centrists in Congress and the growing body of revelations in the media about the abusive character of the military and the right in El Salvador, the State Department set out to build a counteroffensive, to show that good intentions, agrarian reforms and democratic procedures as understood by Americans were on the ascendancy. And the *sine qua non* for this offensive was the one institution understood by the US public to be 'our way of doing things': elections.

The architect of the elections plan was Thomas Enders, Assistant Secretary of State for Inter American Affairs. He saw the promise of a ballot as a way to slide funds out of Congress into El Salvador. Like most State Department strategists, Enders did not question the goals of the policy: his job was to make it work. The fact that for Salvadorans the word elections had been synonymous with the word fraud made little difference. Enders did not care about Salvadorans or their feelings. Nor did he project any notions of long-term US interests in El Salvador or in the rest of Central America. Like other Ivy Leaguers in policy posts, he simply assumed a permanent imperial presence without concern about details. And, like the gentlemen aristocrats in his social circle, he cared about success – or, as the less cultivated Reaganites put it, winning!

The military was sent in to assess the situation and recommend a plan. Enders knew that this would guarantee at least a blueprint for five years of 'aid' and 'advice'. Ironically, the strongest opposition to Enders came from the right wing of the administration, the gang that wanted to win the war and then think about democracy. Senator Jesse Helms, National Security Adviser Richard Allen, and his successor, William Clark, wanted to confront Congress on the 'soft on communism' issue. The confrontationalists wanted to face the enemy in both places: in El Salvador to smash the FMLN-FDR; in Washington to put Congress in its properly subservient place.

Enders prevailed. Using the promise of reform and free elections, while keeping secret his knowledge that the Salvadoran military and oligarchy were unreformable, he twisted enough Congressional arms to win a substantial aid package. Duarte's presence in Washington helped sway the doubting members. If he and his Christian Democrats won the election and controlled the politics of the country, they would initiate agrarian reforms to answer the left and simultaneously offer some semblance of decency to rein in the brutes who ran the armed forces. If...

Many Salvadorans who spoke honestly, which often meant anonymously, with journalists and visitors, did not understand why the FDR and FMLN considered the 1982 elections so important as to try to stop them. Salvador's history of elections was ample evidence of their futility. In the rare instances where relatively free and fair balloting took place, the military and oligarchy invariably overthrew the elected government.

In Washington there was no sense of history. Life and politics revolved around television and if elections could be staged for TV then they would *ipso facto* become real, and thus legitimizing. The national security advisers knew they could lure the US media to a voting spectacular, and that they could hire appropriate people to make the election look at least plausible from the government's standpoint.

The FMLN leadership, not on the same public relations wavelength as their enemy in the old Executive Office Building, set out to stop the electoral process, assuming that any intelligent person abroad could cut through the farcical façade of balloting in a nation at war, where at least a third or more of the electorate would not be able to vote for its parties. The last time the left had tried to compete in civilized politics they had been slaughtered by the death squads and military units. To hold an election under these circumstances, they felt certain, would not withstand the scrutiny of foreign public opinion.

They were wrong, but so was the White House. The elections, although a far cry from free or fair, went down well in key public sectors, especially Congress. The Reagan administration erred because they were certain that Duarte and the center would emerge from the process. Instead, D'Aubuisson and his gangsters from ARENA polled the largest amount of votes.

Peasants historically have tended to vote for candidates or parties who were known intimidators, rather than unknowns. The rural people understood from their past that elected officials traditionally steal their land and underpay them for crops and labor. ARENA was at least a known if exploitative entity, familiar and predictable. Voting for a reform candidate was inherently risky. Peasant history was replete with reformers who did not deliver. Reformist candidates might be assassinated or removed from office. In such circumstances, the consequences of voting against ARENA or its historical equivalent could be severe. In addition, voting was also mandatory. Without an official identity card, issued when the voter cast his or her ballot, any Salvadoran was subject to arrest – and to whatever might subsequently befall him.

## With the Guerrillas

Like most wars that endure beyond the initial offensives and counteroffensives, the conflict in El Salvador is the story of numerous individual battles, most of which were not reported on the TV news or in the morning papers. And, unlike the myth that grows around each side, the battles themselves were the product not just of superior or inferior weapons, good or bad strategies, but of decisions made by commanders of platoons and companies about whether or not to attack, where and when.

Several days before the scheduled March 1982 elections, a column of men and women, all young, some barely in their teens, left its base in

Guazapa to launch an attack. Their mission: to prevent people from voting in the town of San Antonio Abad. They trooped over small mountains, cutting away foliage as they went. They carried an assortment of weapons manufactured in various countries for various wars. Carrying light packs, with just enough nourishment to make it through a three-day hike, the former peasants and city youth, who had witnessed the repression at the cathedral or in the *barrios*, had grown accustomed to living in discomfort and even pain. Few had understood the adversity of guerrilla life, the bodily rigors of being dirty and unable to wash, change clothes, or eat when hungry. They followed strict orders to buy, not to take, food from peasants and villagers.

Often drinking water was in short supply, and, aside from wounds inflicted on them in battle, the guerrillas had to fight all the pestilence that nature had to offer, from poisonous snakes and insects to sharp thorns and thistles that tore the flesh. And of course there were mosquitoes, mites and lice.

In the seemingly endless marching in a tropical climate, guerrillas frequently collapsed from heat exhaustion, suffered from an assortment of bone, muscle and ligament damage, and some from psychotic episodes caused by the stress of guerrilla life. None of these conditions had anything to do with actual fighting, which brought forth traumas of a different order – and death.

With the FMLN was an American doctor, Charles Clements, a Vietnam veteran who volunteered to treat the wounded in the guerrilla zone. Like other religious people he was profoundly moved by the idealism of the Salvadoran cause and totally unprepared for the conditions of guerrilla life. Before attacking their target, the town of San Antonio Abad, Clements recalls, two guerrilla officers exchanged bitter words over whether or not to attack the city. 'Luis', a guerrilla *nom de guerre*, argued that the column was obliged to fulfill its mission of disrupting the election. 'Pico', also an alias, felt an attack would be frivolous and that flexibility, not rigidity, should guide guerrilla field commanders. After hours of arguing the decision was made to go ahead.

Clements remembers one young city woman called La Chinita because of her Oriental eyes. She had joined the FMLN after Romero's murder. On the way from the guerrilla-controlled zone to the area above San Antonio, Clements observed her drinking too much at one time from her jar of honey, the only break in her discipline that he had seen on a three-day hike, during which he could barely walk. Now in the early

March evening she lifted her AK-47 and her pack on to her shoulders and back and marched off.

Later, Clements learned, her *companeros* saw a Huey helicopter gunner open his machine guns on her and literally cut her in half. The column was ambushed on the outskirts of the small city. The guerrilla losses were seven dead. It was one of those rare instances in which the army used a guerrilla tactic against the FMLN.

Secretary of State Haig told the Senate Foreign Relations Committee that he had 'overwhelming and irrefutable' evidence to prove that 'foreigners' were controlling the Salvadoran guerrillas. Haig, speaking through a bare slit in his mouth, with a serious scowl on his face, told the senators about massive arms shipments coming from Cuba and Nicaragua. Along with Enders, the secretary went from House to House, committee to committee, telling lies about human rights improvement, the dire state of the military situation and the Soviet backing for Central American revolution.

A key component of the State Department's 'Show and Tell' package was a Nicaraguan revolutionary, Orlando Tardencillas, who was captured in a battle between the Salvadoran army and an FMLN platoon. This man, announced the Reagan administration, was living proof that the Sandinista government was directly involved with the Salvadoran insurrection. His testimony would leave no doubt about foreign control of the operation.

On 11 March Tardencillas was unveiled to the press. Instead of affirming the statements he gave privately, he retracted his 'confession' that he had been sent from Managua to command FMLN forces. 'I was tortured,' he told the press, demonstrating his fresh scars. 'I said whatever they wanted me to say so they would stop torturing me.' The youthful Tardencillas proudly admitted to his Nicaraguan citizenship, but when asked if he was sent by Daniel Ortega's men he denied any official connection. He also recanted earlier statements about being trained in Cuba and Africa. 'I volunteered,' he told the astonished media and the embarrassed State Department officials, 'because I am a revolutionary and the Salvadoran cause is just.' Tardencillas hinted that the Nicaraguan government ought to be, but was not doing, what it was accused of by the State Department.

The media responded to expressions of Tardencillas's revolutionary enthusiasm with a yawn, but found credible, if not damning, his refutation of the State Department's claims of proof that the Sandinista government was controlling the Salvadoran rebellion. The US officials stared helplessly at the man who was to have been their star witness. The media victory in Washington, however, was short-lived.

In El Salvador, the FMLN announced intentions to disrupt the upcoming 28 March elections, by cutting off electricity in several areas and blocking public transportation. Salvadoran army chief Gutierrez told the press that he feared that his army could not stop the guerrillas from carrying out their plans. More military aid from the United States was necessary for a free election to take place, he gravely informed the media.

Using his declaration, the Reagan lobbyists made their Congressional rounds and fabricated stories about improvements in human rights. In the midst of this effort to wring money from Congress, a Salvadoran army unit assassinated four Dutch journalists in Chalatenango Province. The Salvadoran government denied responsibility for their deaths, claiming the four were caught in a cross fire. However, the denial was weakened by the fact that on the same day that the four men died, a group calling itself the Martinez Anti Communist Alliance left a list with a San Salvador radio station, stating that if the thirty-five journalists cited did not mend their subversive ways, they too would join the dead from the Netherlands.

During the month of March, preceding the elections, fierce battles took place. The army sent out units to trap guerrillas. Most of the plots failed to kill or catch the mobile rebels; some succeeded in routing the FMLN from their camps and forcing them to move to others. The guerrillas meanwhile proved they could disrupt life, by cutting power and blocking inter–urban transport. But the elections took place, with the TV cameras showing people lining up and the interviewers conducting quick conversations with befuddled Salvadoran voters.

The guerrillas had miscalculated how the public at large would respond when they announced plans to interfere with the elections. They thought that they could organize a popular uprising to coincide with their actions on the military front to demonstrate the lack of support for the balloting. They believed that because the urban poor sympathized with their cause, they could coordinate a dramatic revolt. But by March 1982 death squads and arrests had wiped out or caused the relocation of a substantial number of the trained and disciplined urban cadres upon whose shoulders any successful uprising had to rest. In their strategic planning, the guerrilla leaders failed to acknowledge that the FMLN no longer controlled the urban *barrios*; the repressive forces had broken their network.

The FMLN also miscalculated their ability to shape public opinion. The White House 'spin men' staged the election so expertly that the media reported on a blatantly fraudulent process as if it were legitimate. Rarely did a TV reporter mention the fact that left or even center candidates could not compete for office without risking assassination, the reason the FDR and the FMLN gave for not participating in the elections. Instead, TV viewers watched government troops 'protecting' the right of citizens to vote, while the 'terrorists' burned buses and attempted to stop people from casting ballots.

The results of the election, however, disappointed Washington's Salvador managers. The wrong people won. Of almost one and a half million votes cast, the extreme right polled some 60 per cent. Thus, D'Aubuisson controlled the assembly, which made the prospect of future Congressional assistance appear dim. The US Embassy brought pressure to bear, holding the aid package in front of the noses of Salvadoran military and political figures as if it was a honey-dipped carrot. The American dollar muscle worked wonders. A compromise was reached. Those elected to the Constituent Assembly were only to write a new constitution and select an interim government until the constitution was approved.

The extreme right agreed, under US threat, that Duarte could serve as president of a temporary coalition government until the next election, at which point El Salvador would be functioning under the new constitution. Garcia, seen as reliable by the right-wing military officers, remained as chief of the armed forces. Duarte accepted the fact that the fledgling reforms initiated under the junta would be stopped – especially changes in land policy, which the right wing equated with communism. The fact that Duarte would be president, even though he had no power or control over the military and police, left State Department officials enough space to squeeze Congress for more aid – and Reagan signed the necessary papers acknowledging improvement in human rights, a lie that Congress nevertheless accepted.

Centerists in both Houses feared being labeled 'soft on communists' more than they did 'weak on human rights violators'. Thus as spring settled in on El Salvador in 1982, so did the beginnings of a long-term US presence. The fact that Members of Congress accepted the prevarications of Reagan officials, even though they knew better, meant that the military advisers and the support systems that emanated from Washington had taken on the character of bureaucratic intractability.

This process did not escape the attention of the FDR–FMLN

leaders. The war against the Salvadoran armed forces, they realized, had become a war against the United States as well. The Americans called it low-intensity war; for the combatants and the residents of the areas in which fighting took place it was just plain war.

From the perspective of the ruling oligarchy and their military allies the war had to be fought to the death – of the guerrillas and the rest of the non-military left as well. For the Washington team assembled to direct the war and the aid package that was married to it, the future was not important. They had a task and they would prolong it. For the policy elite in April 1982 the issue was somewhat different. The Salvadoran army was suffering defeat on the battlefield, and seemed incapable of improving its behavior toward civilians, causing its already horrible reputation to sink further in the court of international public opinion. To dispatch US troops was not really an option. The president did not want to discuss the possibility of sending US troops to Central America. His wife, Nancy, was firm on that subject. Nor did he want to hear the word 'negotiate', since that was not how one dealt with communist terrorists. He smiled at the policy staff and assured them they would come up with a solution.

## ON THE BATTLEFIELD

General Wallace H. Nutting, head of the US Southern Command, who oversaw the US military operation, told Congress that the Salvadoran army 'faced deficiencies in command and control, tactical intelligence, tactical mobility and logistics'. The US military establishment did not share President Reagan's interest in Central America, because they did not see strategic value or economic importance in the area. The West Point graduates tended toward skepticism or disinterest in low-intensity varieties of conflict.

Except for the Special Forces and Green Berets, the old counter-insurgency gang from the 1960s and 1970s, the US military was ill prepared to advise and guide a war in the rural areas of a country the size of Massachusetts. Salvadoran military attending training at Fort Gulick, Panama, and other US academies designed to train foreign military officials, learned the doctrines of conventional, not irregular warfare. That was what those Salvadoran officers brave or energetic enough to leave their comfortable and safe barrack quarters practised upon their return home. And, as long as they did engage in more or less conventional warfare, the guerrillas maintained an edge.

A good example was the offensive that began in June 1982 when some three thousand troops and a squadron of newly acquired US fighter bombers, called Dragonflies, prepared for a major offensive to oust the guerrillas from their stronghold in Morazan Province. According to the US military advisers, who had taken under their wings the Salvadoran officers, this offensive would answer the doubters in Washington.

The planes bombed, fired rockets, and strafed the FMLN positions. Ground artillery pounded away at the same sites. Then the troops moved in, not green teenagers, but US-trained battalions, the best the Salvadoran army had to offer. The assault was aimed at two towns, the capture of which would give the army a major strategic advantage. But, unknown to the army commanders, the FMLN had reinforced their units and, when the troops tried to penetrate the perimeter of Perquin and San Fernando, they were met with withering crossfire. When the confused lieutenants and captains called for a rapid retreat they led their companies straight into an ambush.

For more than five days the government forces probed the defenses and found no entrance along the various approaches to the two Morazan cities. The losses sustained by the crack battalions were devastating. More bombing and shelling followed the unsuccessful attacks. Reinforcements were sent up from other areas and Honduran soldiers also entered the fray at the behest of the American advisers.

They captured both cities, but found no FMLN units left. The guerrillas had pulled out just before the massive onslaught began. The Salvadoran army controlled two virtually empty towns, whose buildings had been turned into smoking shells by the amount of bombardment they sustained. The guerrillas took casualties as well, though far fewer than the army.

## RADIO VENCEREMOS

The FMLN leaders, understanding the need to maintain a source of information and even analysis about the events of the war, established a radio station, called Radio Venceremos. With movable transmitters the FMLN could give its version of the battles and the political intrigues and maneuvers in San Salvador as well as in Washington and other important capitals. And even in the most remote village there was always someone with a transistor radio.

The rebels tried to keep their reports accurate so that they would earn a reputation for honesty. In October 1982 the government reported a successful sweep through Chalatenango, claiming that their forces had killed 137 guerrillas. In fact, they had massacred more than five hundred non-combatants, as Radio Venceremos reported, a fact that was later confirmed by members of the mainstream media. The success of Radio Venceremos was measured by the attempts of US officials to jam it. From the Gulf of Fonseca military experts used sophisticated equipment to interfere with the wavelength used by rebel radio. In turn, the guerrilla *tecnicos* changed the frequency on which they broadcast, usually by going up just a notch or two on the dial, so that listeners would not have to search the entire band to find them.

### AIR WAR AND ANTI-AIRCRAFT MEASURES

The arrival of A-37 Dragonflies and the increased use of helicopter gunships made the guerrilla war more difficult and muted some of the sting the guerrillas had previously caused in the flesh of the army. Although the Salvadoran pilots were hardly top guns, willing to risk their lives to make a successful dive and hit a target, they nevertheless launched plenty of destructive poundage and deadly gasoline bombs on villages in the guerrilla-controlled area. This made not only for immense civilian casualties, but for an ever increasing supply of refugees. While FMLN comandantes debated what kind of countermeasures to adopt against the aircraft, they continued to apply the guerrilla formulas, attacking at vulnerable positions, feinting at one place to draw army units, then attacking at unguarded spots.

By the end of 1982 the guerrillas had proven that they were better fighters, smarter tacticians and more committed than their enemy, but the US supply line, the infinite source of money and weapons had changed the war. Some called it a stalemate, but that did not describe what was happening and would continue to happen throughout the rest of the decade: a dynamic equilibrium was established. Each time one side would begin to demonstrate clear superiority the other would counter, with a change in weapons, tactics, or even overall strategy.

The FMLN attacked, ambushed, sabotaged and harassed government forces. Almost at will, guerrilla units shut down power installations, blockaded roads and took over villages, towns and even provincial cities – sometimes executing the local officials to show the powerlessness of the Duarte regime. These victories played well in the Cuban press, which was eager to show the power of armed struggle in nearby countries, but in the hands of the US and European media reports tended to portray the revolutionaries as ruthless and bloodthirsty rather than to demonstrate Duarte's impotence. Images aside, the FMLN was not winning the war.

By October 1983 the guerrilla leaders had shifted their objective. Offensives were no longer aimed at taking power, but at proving the government could not destroy them. They showed during the summer of 1982 that they could fight on two separate fronts, in Morazan and Chalatenango, deal with air attacks and even recapture areas that the government claimed were impregnable.

The FMLN proved that it was a formidable force. In early 1982 guerrillas attacked and destroyed US-supplied war planes at the heavily guarded Illopongo base. Then at the end of the year they sabotaged a major bridge spanning the Pan American highway. Guerrillas interfered with business at every level, cutting off electrical power, telephone and transportation – including blowing up commercial trucks, and making highways impassable for vehicles engaged in conveying goods – areas necessary for the functioning of all modern economies.

By the end of 1983 US government sources estimated that the bill for FMLN-caused sabotage of private and public sectors of the economy ran as high as $1 billion. Not only did the guerrillas destroy installations and interfere with coffee picking at the estates of some members of the oligarchy, but they made all property owners fearful of sabotage, thus increasing security and insurance costs throughout the country.

However, the FMLN did not destroy basic pieces of the Salvadoran infrastructure, such as dams or major power generators. The FMLN still hoped one day to govern the nation, and did not wish to inherit a pile of rubble. The Salvadoran government responded to the sabotage campaign by dispatching an ever larger percentage of the growing army to guard the technological foundations of the economy.

While proving their might, and certainly their value as a major nuisance, the FMLN's economic sabotage plan also turned some Salvadorans against them. Not all poor people shared the revolutionary commitment to 'sacrifice' for the cause, which meant yielding some of their livelihood. As much as they may have despised the government, they did not smile on the destruction of the bus that took them to work, or the crippling of the power substation that generated the electricty running their television and refrigerator. In addition, the sabotage tactics generated unintended benefits to American companies, who built new airplanes to replace those destroyed by the FMLN at

Illopongo, or who repaired the damaged bridges, highways and power substations.

As war became a way of life for peasants who remained in Morazan, Usulitan, Chalatenango and parts of other provinces, so the US military and civilian bureaucracy attached to the Salvadoran government acquired an attitude of semi-permanence about their task. While repeating that Salvador would not be the Central American translation of Vietnam, there were frightening parallels. On the battlefield itself the US advisers could not enforce 'civilized' war conduct, nor induce Salvadoran officers to behave like ideal US unit commanders. By late 1982 and early 1983 the A-37 Dragonfly crews were deploying phosphorous bombs and rockets not as target markers, but as anti-personnel weapons. Doctors treated children whose skin had come into contact with such bombs. Their wounds were horrific: the volatile metal burns at high tempartures, penetrates deep into the tissue and continues burning.

The guerrillas also participated in the war-related cruelty. They 'executed' government appointed village officials, shot notorious officers associated with the most violent repression and in the capital planted car bombs, which killed not only those targeted, but innocent civilians as well. But there was no comparison in the levels of bestiality. For their part, Salvadoran patrols would almost automatically kill peasants encountered near suspected guerrilla strongholds and leave their corpses as 'lessons' for others who might possibly think of aiding the FMLN. And there were massacres; the tragedy of My Lai was repeated several times in El Salvador.

Defying government orders and strong US recommendations not to try to travel to 'guerrilla controlled' areas, reporters arrived at the site of a mass grave in Usulatan. Residents told them how on 4 November 1983, the soldiers of the Atlacatl Battalion, under orders from their senior officers, systematically slaughtered more than one hundred peasants. One of the commanders, Colonel Monterroso, confirmed to US and Mexican journalists that his men had indeed done the killing. He trivialized the massacre, attributing it to his men confusing 'the civilian population with the guerrillas that operate in the area'.

The Mexican press reported additional massacres two weeks later in a nearby area. Salvadoran commanders did not deny the report. Military massacres of civilians had long been both a way of war – and peace. In their education as cadets they were taught that Maximiliano Martinez's 1932 massacre of peasants was not a horrible crime, but rather a master stroke in defeating 'subversion'.

These attitudes frustrated the Americans who, whether they acknowledged it or not, were involved in nation building. Once members of the Reagan elite admitted that revolution stemmed from the conditions of life, not from Soviet and Cuban manipulators or weapons shipments, they had to defend their Central America policy on the grounds that they were interfering to make El Salvador a better, more democratic place. Even before the 1984 Kissinger Commission formally acknowledged the social roots of the war, US advisers were trying to explain to their pupils in the Salvadoran armed forces that they had to try and win the 'hearts and minds' of the people, not just exterminate them. So the Salvadoran army nodded gravely when US advisers spoke about halting human rights violations. Then they took their companies on search and destroy missions. Invariably, they did not find the guerrillas. Instead, they were often ambushed or tricked into making moves that left them vulnerable. And they lashed out at unarmed peasants – men, women and children.

With the right wing controlling the assembly and blocking land reform and other measures promised by Duarte – to his own people and to the US Congress – the government had little to offer in a hearts-and-minds-winning contest. In late December 1983 news leaked out that the FMLN had killed 800 Salvadoran soldiers in a week. Other statistics amassed by the Americans by the end of 1983 showed that US military training and advice had failed to turn the tide of war. Even the occasional entry of the Honduran forces – always officially denied – into battles had done little to oust the FMLN from its controlled areas.

In the United States the Committee in Solidarity with the People of El Salvador (CISPES) and a variety of religious and anti-imperialist organizations used information on massacres and death squads to educate the public and lobby Congress to withhold aid and condemn the murderous regime in El Salvador. The Reagan administration countered with a more intense campaign to label the guerrillas as terrorists and, more ominously, tools of Moscow, Havana and Managua; to make them intrinisicly part of the greater Cold War.

By the end of 1983 the US public was perplexed. The majority, according to polls, did not know whom the United States was supporting in either Nicaragua or El Salvador. People confused the right-wing Contras with the left-wing Salvadoran rebels and some thought that the United States was aiding the guerrillas in El Salvador and opposing those in Nicaragua. Those who did follow the lines of the unfolding story were unconvinced by the Reagan arguments. Congress grew more and more obstinate when funding time came near. The result of this confusion and dissent was the naming of a commission to study the issue and recommend policy guidelines.

## The Kissinger Commission

The people who comprised the National Bipartisan Commission on Central America ranged from right wing to liberal, the majority being establishment figures. Besides its chairman, former Secretary of State Henry Kissinger, the commission included Lane Kirkland, head of the AFL-CIO; John Silber, President of Boston University; Henry Cisneros, Mayor of San Antonio; William F. Clements, Jr, former Governor of Texas; and Nicholas Brady, the future Treasury Secretary in the Bush administration.

The report first ackowledged that the violent upheavals in Central America had their roots in a history of repression and the continuing unequal distribution of wealth: 'Discontents are real, and for much of the population conditions of life are miserable; just as Nicaragua was ripe for revolution, so the conditions that invite revolution are present elsewhere in the region as well.' It also repeated the old Reagan administration adage that the Soviet Union and Cuba were acting as both *agents provocateurs* and financiers of revolution in the region, although as usual this was more an ideological statement than a proven fact.

The Kissinger Commission recommended a $400 million 'emergency stabilization program' and large increases in military aid to El Salvador, Guatemala and Honduras, and it tacitly approved the continuing covert war against Nicaragua. The Commission's report also recommended an $8 billion five-year aid program that would escalate US involvement in and responsibility for the economies of Central America to an unprecedented level.

With a nod to the concerns of the US Congress, and the American public, the report tied further military aid to El Salvador to a requirement of proof that the government was no longer violating the human rights of its people. Both the US and the Salvadoran governments knew that this requirement was not worth the paper it was written on. The Salvadoran military had no interest or motivation to change their ways. Killing and torturing the opposition and terrorizing the people kept them in power. Furthermore, despite their dependence on the US government for continued aid to pay their salaries and provide arms, they knew that the United States was also dependent on them: having made prevention of revolution in El Salvador a key national security objective, there was no way the US government would abandon their Salvadoran clients.

The most significant part of the report concerned the Commission's economic proposals for the region. It was here that the report's nation-building character could clearly be seen. The Commission called for the establishment of two new economic institutions: a Central American Development Organization (CADO) to oversee the allocation of approximately 25 per cent of US bilateral economic assistance to Central America; and a Central American Development Corporation (CADC) to promote and help finance private enterprise. The report also proposed that the United States join the Central American Bank for Economic Integration (CABEI) which already existed to finance both public and private economic projects in the region.

What these economic proposals meant in effect was that the United States would take responsibility for managing the societies and economies of Central America. Nothing would be left to chance – or open to the possibility of local ineptitude. North American 'experts' would train the professional classes of Central America, and they would plan and oversee the region's urban and rural development programs. Guidance would also be provided for the political development of the region.

## An Euphoric Moment in a Bloody War

As experts on both sides attacked and defended Reagan policy, the numbers of dead and wounded mounted alarmingly in El Salvador – as did the refugee population. Amidst the brutality of this war fought by poor young men against other poor young men there were moments of extraordinary pathos. One story involved the attempt of an FMLN commander to turn over prisoners to the government.

The gesture, which Charles Clements witnessed and described in his memoir, *Witness to War*, had both magnanimous and practical motives. It showed the FMLN in a powerful light and it allowed them to get rid of several POWs including one badly wounded man. The nature of his bullet wounds required him to be fed intravenously, and the delicate operation required was beyond the scope of guerrilla hospital facilities.

So Pedro, the *nom de guerre* of the FMLN commander, sent another POW to Suchitoto to call upon the authorities to receive the men. The guerrilla commander wanted to make a gesture, so that the government would have to admit that the FMLN was releasing prisoners. The prisoner announced his mission over a bull horn. But no one came into the streets, which showed how frightened the village officials were of the FMLN. The lone prisoner despaired as no one acknowledged his presence. Then, hours later, to the surprise of the FMLN, the commander of the local garrison radioed his enemies that he would receive the POWs.

The guerrillas carried the wounded man, accompanied by the other prisoners. Some of the captured men refused to return, either because they feared reprisals or because they could no longer in good conscience serve in the Salvadoran military. The guerrillas not only cared for the wounded troops, but gave them an indoctrination as well.

The Salvadoran major appeared, received the wounded man and the other POWs and then proceeded to embrace each of the accompanying guerrillas. He conversed by radio with the guerrilla commander, congratulating him on his noble behavior and declaring his desire for a peaceful solution. Pedro responded in similar terms, stressing his respect for the major and hopes for an end to the conflict.

After this rare and euphoric moment amidst a bloody war, each officer returned to his mission – the annihilation of the enemy. Most of the Salvadoran officers, the American advisers noticed, were less than eager to engage the guerrillas in a fire fight. Salvadorans tended to step aside and let the *gringos* do their jobs for them, while they collected their salaries and had extra time to relax. Among the eerie military parallels to the Vietnam experience, the US officers assigned to Salvadoran units noted that commanders rarely accompanied their troops on patrols or search and destroy missions. Those officers who did try to press the war were not popular with the ruling military clique, and the Garcia-run army saw such officers as troublemakers who did not understand the real meaning of US aid. If the war was won quickly the Salvadoran officer elite would lose out on millions of dollars which came in the form of aid, but was easily diverted into personal gain for those with entrepreneurial sense.

Lt Col. Sigifrido Ochoa Perez was an exception, an outspoken critic of the Garcia-run military and the lip service paid to human rights. Ochoa won the approval of the US advisers because he wanted to win the war quickly, and brutally if necessary. In early January 1983, Garcia removed Ochoa from his command of Cabanas Province and posted him to Uruguay as a military attaché. Ochoa defied the order and openly labeled Garcia as a traitor for turning the military into a political institution. Ochoa called upon his fellow officers for support; some came forward, the majority formally backed Garcia. (Garcia resigned a year later, as was customary for commanding officers in El Salvador.)

Routinely, the guerrillas would pull off dramatic military acts that reinforced the poor image of the Salvadoran military. On 27 January 1983, rebel units hit the San Carlos army barracks, one mile from the US Embassy, killing eleven and taking quantities of arms. Two days later, as army patrols fanned out to roust the FMLN in Morazan, the guerrillas struck in San Vicente, taking the town of Berlin, decimating the police and National Guard stations. The army retook the town when the FMLN retreated and unleashed violence on the townspeople.

The guerrillas had their own internal disputes as well, not all of which were resolved with words. Melida Anaya Montes, known as Comandante Ana Maria, was the number two person in the FPL. Aged fifty-four the former teacher was a dedicated Marxist–Leninist whose life was the revolution. Based in Managua, where she helped to coordinate FPL activities, she began to doubt the impractical militancy preached by Cayetano Carpio, her *jefe*, and she took issue with his sectarianism, challenging his leadership.

On 6 April 1983, Nicaraguan police announced that Comandante Ana Maria had been murdered. The killers had stabbed her repeatedly with knives and ice picks. On 9 April, Carpio read the eulogy at Ana Maria's funeral in Managua. Carpio's distress was evident. He looked pale and tired and he had trouble concentrating on his speech. Ana Maria had been with him for more than a decade not only as a comrade, but as a friend as well.

Inside revolutionary circles Carpio had acquired the reputation of an inflexible dogmatist, someone increasingly removed from the kind of practical grasp of reality needed to make decisions in a guerrilla campaign. The Sandinistas and the Cubans had both pressured him to resign. While speculation abounded that the CIA had assassinated Ana Maria, the Sandinista police traced the slaying to Carpio's closest followers, laying the responsibility for her gruesome death ultimately at his feet. Three days later the founder of the FPL, the deacon of Salvadoran revolutionaries, shot himself.

## ASSASSINATION OF SCHAUFELBERGER

The leaders of the groups that comprised the FMLN had shown in two years an amazing ability to work together and suppress their ideological differences. The growing role of US military advisers, however, tested the revolutionaries' ardor. Not only were the *gringos* participating on the battlefield – against the orders of the White House – but they paraded openly in San Salvador, often with native women on their arms.

So, the FPL leaders took action, testing the resolve of the other FMLN commanders and provoking the Americans. On 25 May, an American military adviser, Lieutenant Commander Albert Schaufelberger, sat for a moment in his car at the Central American University campus in San Salvador, waiting for his girlfriend. Neglecting to take proper security measures – he had removed the bullet proof glass on the windows a few days before and was sitting with the window open – Schaufelberger was shot in the head by a FPL gunman and died almost immediately.

The effect of the killing was to make the military advisers angrier, more determined and careful. Within days, hundreds more US troops were flown into Honduras to train Salvadoran soldiers. For the FPL the act dramatized their growing frustration at the inability of the revolutionaries to prevail.


## 1984

Two days before the end of 1983, units of the FMLN confounded the optimistic predictions of US and Salvadoran officials by capturing the El Paraiso army base in Chalatenango, about forty miles north of the Capital. They killed more than one hundred soldiers, wounded scores more and took over one hundred and sixty prisoners. Two days later their sappers blew up the Cuscatlan Bridge that spans the Lempa River, cutting the main link between the east and west of the country.

Congressional voices raised notes of despair. 'It seems to me the situation is deteriorating,' said Senator Bennett Johnston, a conservative Democrat from Louisiana; 'that we are losing the war ... because we are losing the war for the hearts and minds of the people ... because of the death squads and the lack of human rights.' Other members filed a law suit to try to force President Reagan to adhere to his agreement to make human rights a priority before more aid requests were granted.

In response to Congressional threats to cut aid, the Salvadoran high command announced the transfer of two of its most notorious death squad officers to diplomatic posts abroad. But others, arrested for death squad related murders, were set free.

The Kissinger report offered justification for continued US aid to El

Salvador on defensive grounds, but did not convince Congress that the American taxpayers should fund the building of a mini model of the United States 1500 miles south of the border. In addition, the consensus had formed that the human rights record had to be a basic element in measuring the merits of any aid request, and the Salvadoran performance continued to be mediocre.

Congress, however, did not have clear alternatives to the policies of the administration, though they did place conditions on and cut the size of aid. The administration countered with warnings and threats about communism, subversion and more of the tired rhetoric of late Cold War colonial policies. Stale as it was, it scared the spineless Congress into continuing appropriations and, more importantly, into keeping the debate restricted to technical questions of how and where aid would go, the monitoring procedures, certification and disbursement.

The solution to the administration's Salvador problem came with the ability of US government, private public relations promoters and the mass media to convince the public of the notion that a free election was the supreme and indeed only test for the functioning of democracy. On 25 March, the staging for TV of the first round of presidential elections could not have been better. The guerrillas, unable to cope with the professional media warriors on the enemy side, made the same old mistakes. Some FMLN units tried to intimidate voters; others cut transportation links to polling places. Their argument – that fair elections could not be held when the left was effectively prevented from participating – was not heard in the US media. The fact that FDR and FMLN representatives would be certain targets of death squads did not seem to register.

Viewers saw people lining up to vote, heard quick sound bites from 'average' Salvadorans and then listened to commentators rattle off numbers and percentages of voters from strange sounding places. While the off-camera voice prated on, campaigning montages filled the screen, including the familiar handshaking and baby-kissing with which the American public could identify. The election, despite the cogent arguments of the FMLN that it was inherently fraudulent, looked good on television. The guerrillas were put into an uncomfortable position: 'What are you going to believe,' they symbolically asked the TV public, 'us or your own eyes?'

As expected, the Christian Democrats' Duarte and the right wing's D'Aubuisson emerged as winners, neither with a majority. To the State Department's relief Duarte won the run-off election in May, receiving

53 per cent to D'Aubuisson's 46 per cent, a difference of 100,000 votes. Almost one and a half million voters had turned out in another display of TV elections at their best. The media played up the triumph of the popular democratic personality and virtually ignored the fact that the right-wing vote was not only very large, but sufficient to block any significant reforms in the National Assembly.

The voting booth and public relations wars and the action on the battlefield turned against the guerrillas by mid-1984. The see-saw began to tilt toward the US side as more air power – in the form of bombers, gunships and reconnaissance craft – began to force the guerrillas into constant movement, depleted their population base and killed and traumatized growing numbers of combatants.

In addition, more Salvadoran junior officers, having graduated from US military schools, possessed both the training and will to confront the FMLN, which up till then had proven itself superior to the government's forces in courage and logistics. The work of the death squads had also taken a tremendous toll. The State Department declared that they had substantiated reports of 104 corpses per month in the later part of 1983, compared to 177 monthly victims during the first half of 1983. This, to the State Department men in pinstriped suits, was progress.

One reason for the decline in bodies was that the death squads had already killed a substantial number of Salvador's best and brightest – students, doctors, lawyers, labor leaders. They had depleted the urban cadres of the revolutionaries and the reformers, forcing people into exile or into the ranks of the guerrillas in the countryside. The target list had therefore diminished. There was no evidence to show that US government threats or warnings had convinced anyone involved in these killings to behave differently.

The government knew that D'Aubuisson was behind the assassinations. Former Ambassador White even made public information concerning Salvadoran exiles in Miami who had funded and conspired with D'Aubuisson. White offered evidence of the cashiered major's direct involvement in the slaying of Archbishop Romero. The Reagan administration's spokesperson mumbled that its information was 'limited and incomplete'.

Duarte assumed the presidency in June and proceeded to make the formal moves that won him the continued backing of the Congressional consensus in Washington. The land reform program that was effectively dead he promised to revive. He ordered commissions to investigate charges of massacres and declared that the Salvadoran air force would no longer bomb civilian populations. The fact that he had no power to enforce this new decree, and that his commissions had no teeth, mattered little to a Congress eager for proof that their funding was leading to real democracy. Indeed, leading Christian Democrats offered to debate publicly with FDR leaders – in the United States.

On the battlefield and in the *barrios* of the cities things had changed little. Troops continued to slay civilians and murder guerrilla prisoners; the air force bombed at will, including in its arsenal an occasional canister of napalm. Death squads still used their own criteria to decide which citizens should die. And the army continued to massacre, oblivious to US embarrassment and the Geneva Conventions. In July, the Atlacatl Battalion wiped out much of Los Llanitos in Cabanas. The US trained officers and soldiers systematically slew sixty civilians. A month later troops machine-gunned fleeing men, women and children caught in a river in Chalatenango. 'In the conflict zones, there simply aren't any civilians,' explained Colonel Carlos Aviles, who spoke for the army. 'The people who move in zones of rebel persistence are identified as guerrillas. Good people are not there.'

## An Olive Branch

Few who knew Jose Napoleon Duarte doubted the sincerity of his pledges to control the army, and to bring to trial the murderers of the nuns, Archbishop Romero and others. The facts of power, however, did not permit him to keep his commitments. The civilian authorities could not control the military or its paramilitary offshoots. The FDR-FMLN was forced to adapt to the changing reality. Their launching of the 'final offensive' in 1981, and their belief that they could win a military victory, no longer prevailed. The extremists like Carpio were gone. By 1984 the majority in the rebel leadership accepted the goal of power-sharing as a reasonable response to the facts of political and military life. The US government's commitment to an indefinite role in preventing a left victory forced the decision. The period between the Duarte election and late 1988 proved the most difficult for the insurrectionary forces. The reasons were not only the increases in US military assistance and the growing roles of US advisers in intelligence and actual combat, but the political campaign waged by Napoleon Duarte and his US allies.

Duarte, ever the astute political manipulator, offered the FMLN an olive branch. During an address in early October 1984 to the UN General Assembly, he vowed to meet his enemies within one week at the village of La Palma to explore means of ending the war. Duarte laid out a forceful, albeit less than genuine, position. Democracy, he declared, existed in El Salvador in the form of a constitution and free elections; human rights violations had been sharply reduced and would soon be controlled. 'The democratic process' could now incorporate groups that were driven to armed struggle so as to end 'the scheme of violence'. There would be a general amnesty so that the guerrillas could move freely in the country, travel abroad at will and form their own political party or parties. Even the wounded would receive special rehabilitation. Thus, on 15 October, the meeting took place and, after five hours of face-to-face encounters, the two sides agreed to meet again and establish a body of delegates on each side to eliminate some of the savagery from the war.

Even though his language and logic were sophistic, in that he was calling for the FMLN to surrender without any guarantees for their safety and that he was calling the US-staged elections 'democracy', Duarte genuinely wanted peace. But those who controlled the scenario of battle had little interest in anything but either the continuance of the war or total victory. Even though a second meeting was planned for late November, the best of Duarte's intentions remained unrealizable.

As the FMLN commanders shook hands with Duarte, the Salvadoran army launched an attack on a guerrilla zone in Morazan to try to capture the transmitter for Radio Venceremos. The follow–up meeting was postponed indefinitely as it became clear that the right wing and the oligarchy would not permit a settlement with the 'subversives'. President Reagan had staked his own ideological reputation on continuing the war. He insisted that the Salvadoran insurrection was part of an overall Moscow-based plot, albeit the Soviets remained decidedly disinterested in the Central American conflict. Reagan's November landslide re-election victory was the single biggest blow to the peace process. It guaranteed the bureaucrats who managed the Salvador war four more years of a policy whose only aim was to ensure that the left would not win, or even become a partner in a government coalition. It meant four years of negative and aggressive policies based not on a vision of a new El Salvador, nor of a developing region, but of bureaucratic commitment to a bizarre process of seeking appropriations because the extraction of funds from a reluctant Congress amounted to victory itself. 'Our job', said a State Department official working in the Salvador policy group, 'is to assure the yearly appropriations by Congress to El Salvador for military and non-military uses.' When asked what the aim of the policy was, the official smiled and said: 'just what I told you.'

## MONEY AND BUREAUCRACY

The inability of the FDR–FMLN, or any other revolutionary group, to grasp fully the banalities of day-to-day US politics led them to continue to see events more in ideological than bureaucratic terms, a less useful measure of power politics in Washington. Elections, for example, no matter how obviously fraudulent they appeared to FMLN leaders, were sacred symbols in US politics. FMLN attempts to block them played into Reagan's hands. The US president used TV images of flaming buses on Salvadoran election day to portray the revolutionaries as terrorists; the revolutionaries fighting in the name of the victims became the anti-democratic villains.

It was money, however, and not public relations that told much of the war story in El Salvador over the next four years: US military aid to El Salvador jumped from $533 million in 1985 to $3.55 billion in 1989. The number of soldiers grew from 12,000 in 1980 to more than 70,000 during the decade of war, while the guerrilla forces remained relatively stable – fielding between 6,000 and 12,000 guerrillas. When the FMLN leaders decided to contract their forces some guerrillas quietly slipped back into civilian life; when they were needed for battle they returned to soldiering.

The military dynamics with which the war began continued to prevail. As soon as one side achieved a tactical advantage, the other learned how to counter it. In turn, that advantage would be diminished and a new theory of war devised to meet new conditions. The guerrillas usually reacted faster and with more imagination because they had to – they possessed less resources, firepower and reserve manpower than the US-financed government.

The army increased the size of its attack units and, although the guerrillas almost always avoided confrontation with larger and better equipped units, they began to suffer serious, corrosive damage. In July 1984, a guerrilla commander, Ana Guadalupe Martinez, confirmed press stories that the FMLN was drafting young men to fight for the guerrillas, a reversal of their previous policy of only accepting volunteers who could demonstrate their ideological commitment. The young woman explained that if the guerrillas did not actively recruit these young men, then the army would get them and turn them into 'enemies of the people'. Even Cuban sympathizers of the rebels shook their heads in disapproval over this policy, fearing that it demonstrated that the guerrillas were desperate.

Despite the enormous logistical advantage held by government forces, the FMLN clung tenaciously to certain territory, like Guazapa, the volcanic area near the capital which they had controlled since the onset of the war. Colonel John Waghelstein, who led the US military group in El Salvador, laid out the plan for a national counterinsurgency: take the war to the guerrillas. With this kind of encouragement from US advisers, the Salvadoran army set out to accomplish both a military and psychological objective: to prove they could rout the guerrillas from their strongholds. In late 1985 the army began preparing its troops to remove the guerrilla's traditional base of support: the population. On 10 January 1986, the army launched Operation Phoenix. Aircraft laid down a carpet of bombs in and around the extinct volcano which the guerrillas had made their home base. Then artillery was poured into the area. The 'softening up' phase was followed by the invasion of 5,000 troops swarming the area that was supposedly occupied by the FMLN's rear guard.

After two months of sweeps and search and destroy patrols amidst periodic bombing and shelling, the army killed over two hundred and fifty civilians, forced one thousand more to evacuate and left Guazapa a virtually depopulated area. The army had estimated that up to eight hundred guerrillas occupied the area, but could not locate them in the course of the prolonged operation. Unlike the uniformed soldier who operated under traditional army discipline, the guerrilla could slip back into the population – and re-emerge as a warrior when needed. But most of the rural people were not mobile guerrillas. They were members of families, with small farms and animals to care for.

A peasant from El Zapote described the experience from the non-combatant point of view. 'We had to leave everything,' said Mario, who survived the ordeal of the two-month army sweep. 'We fled into the mountains searching for hiding places. If they find us in our homes they kill us.' He saw bodies of neighbors killed by the bombing and shelling as he and his children scrambled through the rocks. 'After five days the children began to cry because of the hunger and thirst.' Mario watched from behind some boulders as an army patrol ambushed unarmed villagers and sprayed them with machine-gun fire. 'We felt desperate,' he told church officials later, 'because they were pursuing us tirelessly and they didn't give us a chance to eat or sleep.'

During the first half of 1986 the military carried out similar operations in Morazan, Chalatenango, San Miguel and other provinces. Each sweep, as Catholic monitoring groups later ascertained, was preceded by aerial bombing and artillery shelling. The pilots made little effort to pinpoint their bombs on military targets. Thus, the primary victims were the civilians living in areas allegedly controlled by the FMLN. *Soldier of Fortune* magazine printed a candid statement from a Salvadoran army colonel:

Take the population away from the guerrillas. That's the way to win. It's like malaria in this area. You can do two things: you can treat people with malaria for as long as you stay in the area, for the next three thousand years maybe, or you can drain the swamp and not have to worry about malaria any more.

With this kind of talk the army was hardly winning the hearts and minds of the peasantry. It did, however, reflect the actions taken by the military. 'The only good peasant living in the area controlled by the subversives', another colonel quipped, 'is a dead one.' This attitude, pervasive in the officer corps, effectively prevented Duarte from carrying out serious peace initiatives. Without the ability to replace the top brass, he could not establish civilian control over his military.

He did, more importantly, ensure the flow of aid from the United States, thanks to his popularity with Congress. Even though some of the high command claimed to despise him, by keeping Duarte as president the military death squads could continue to assassinate opponents. Duarte, whom some of the extreme right accused of being a communist, could always persuade the skeptical American legislators that El Salvador was en route to democracy.

In October 1986 a severe earthquake struck parts of the countryside, exacerbating the already miserable lives of the poor. The dead numbered some fifteen hundred. Thousands of peasants moved from the rubble of their farms and homes to the capital, setting up make-shift villages of scrap metal and cardboard. The shanty towns had no running water, electricity, or sanitation. The populace had no jobs. Military trucks roared into the new neighborhoods and armed men rounded up teenage boys, often tying the army 'recruit's' hands behind him.

Under Duarte, El Salvador became what a Jesuit priest called the perfect example of low-intensity democracy. The constitution, the elections, the judicial system all functioned on paper, or for occasional subjects of television news, but in fact the public had no say in the major decisions made on foreign, military, or economic policy. Duarte, whose political life had been spent fighting the abuses of the military and the oligarchy, became their servant. Although the mutual distaste never disappeared, Duarte made it possible for the high command and the idle rich to receive mounting sums of US government money and a guaranteed protection of property pledge from the US Congress.

Duarte promised peace, but delivered war – because the oligarchy, military and US Administration wanted total victory and saw no reason to permit a peace that did not serve their interests. As the army was routing people from the countryside in pursuit of the FMLN, Duarte continued to pretend that he was offering peace. For the majority of Congress this was sufficient, but in El Salvador the scene was grim. Following the army sweeps in 1986, the government formed military-led administration and development programs, called United to Reconstruct.

The purpose was to control the rural population by relocating them, terrifying them with threats and then turning them into informers. By rounding up those who had not fled to refugee camps or abroad, the army would then prevent the remainder of the rural populace from supporting the guerrilla. The Americans had invented 'strategic hamlets' for this reason in Vietnam, and convinced the Guatemalan military to employ 'development poles', a similar method, in their anti-guerrilla war.

## 1987: Peace Plan and Counterinsurgency

As in the Nicaraguan war so too in El Salvador unexpected external factors entered the power equation. Before the formation of Contadora in 1982 there had been no initiatives from Latin America. By 1987 the initiative had become a routine part of diplomatic life and it intruded on everyone's war plans. The peace initiative, although it was built gradually and openly, nevertheless came as something of a shock of recognition to the major protagonists: President Duarte in San Salvador, FMLN Comandante Villalobos in his mountain headquarters and President Reagan in Washington.

International attention was focused on the town of Esquipulas, Guatemala in February 1987. Media from all continents covered the meeting of Central American presidents. Most reporters agreed that the sessions marked a turning point for the region. The presidents of El Salvador, Nicaragua, Costa Rica, Honduras and Guatemala had met before. By 1987 President Reagan's apparent obsession with the Central American civil wars began to cause deep concern among Latin American,

West European and Soviet leaders. Their greatest fear was that of US troops once again invading the soil south of the Rio Grande. This concern was expressed as backing for the Esquipulas initiatives, concepts that flew in the face of the national security zealots in the Executive Office Building in Washington.

The assembled presidents agreed that compromises were needed to end the wars and prevent further damage to the already battered economies and societies of Nicaragua, El Salvador and Guatemala. The presidents also realized that Central America had indeed become an important place and that the entire world was pushing for peace in that region. The US presence there was seen as a decidedly mixed blessing.

Thanks to American manipulation the Contras operated mostly from Honduras, now a nation only in name, but actually a US basing port. The Pentagon was discussing sending more US military advisers to El Salvador, where the war scenario appeared doomed to take a turn for the worse. It was fear of direct US intervention that had prompted the Contadora presidents to call for compromises to end the wars. In Esquipulas the Central American heads of state concurred – concessions were demanded from the FMLN and the government. The real target of the message was the US government, which was in the full and unquestioning process of developing a Vietnam-style counterinsurgency war.

As the counterinsurgency plan developed, United to Reconstruct began to resemble ever more closely the strategic hamlet operations in Vietnam. The Salvadoran military disrupted almost all village life. The plantations, owned by the oligarchy, were exempt from the disruption; indeed, they were protected. Many rural villages were bombed and shelled, then invaded. The population fled or hid. Those who stayed could not harvest their crops nor transport them to local markets.

Military commanders became the distributors of meager survival goods and services to the people who remained, with conditions: as the price for receiving enough food to survive, the peasants had to join civil defense units to 'defend' their villages. Those villagers who remained were totally dependent on the army.

The army also fashioned roving propaganda teams that delivered lectures, military style, against communism, liberation theology and disobedience to authority in general. Peasants had to come to the village square to listen to these recitals. 'Democracy', chanted a lieutenant, staccato style, in a San Miguel village, 'means elections. You have elections. Therefore, you have democracy. The alternative is terrorism.

All those who cooperate with terrorists and reject the government program will be shot.'

Some army units assassinated villagers suspected of collaborating with the FMLN, or because they showed signs of disobedience. This process, labeled development, had as its objective the destruction of the guerrilla bases in the countryside. Once villagers had suffered the fear and pain of army occupation, and had listened to the terrifying threats of reprisals should the rules be defied, FMLN units would not find the conditions propitious for a return to the villages they had controlled for up to six years.

The army commander often placed a government stooge in the local town or city hall as mayor, and declared the captured area secure. The guerrillas, warned by scouts or spies of the imminent arrival of government units, quickly fled the targeted zones. But the Salvadoran army did not have sufficient forces to occupy each village indefinitely. As soon as the government troops left, the FMLN would either execute the newly appointed mayor – who had been assured of protection by the government – or force him to resign. By 1988, the majority of the more than two hundred and fifty government-appointed mayors had lost their posts or their lives. In many instances the guerrillas quickly resumed control of villages which the army had declared secure. But their size and vitality had diminished. The dynamic equilibrium between the two sides continued, but each year took its toll – especially on the civilian population. Those who fled to San Salvador found difficulty getting work, but not getting into trouble. The new *barrios* were rife with begging, prostitution, drugs and crime – along with unemployment.

## The FMLN Counteroffensive

The army's strategy disrupted the FMLN, whose units moved by necessity from their traditional strongholds into new areas. But in addition, the guerrillas developed new tactics. One was to attack the oligarchy by attacking their property. Moving into areas previously thought 'safe' by large land owners and the government, FMLN commanders hit coffee plantations, and sabotaged power supplies and small dams, thus making harvesting difficult or impossible.

In a dramatic and successful counteroffensive that required months of precision planning, in March 1986 FMLN units converged to attack the army barracks in San Miguel. Catching the sleeping soldiers by surprise in the early hours of the morning, the guerrillas fired small artillery and machine guns, then penetrated the base in a spectacular raid. The army suffered hundreds of casualties and the FMLN captured a new stock of weapons.

But the victory at San Miguel and their successful organizing efforts in the newly created slums could not stop the erosion of the FMLN's coherence. The government made it impossible for the guerrillas to hold territory; when they did try, it brought terrible consequences to the civilian population. Their forced recruitment policy of 1984 proved disastrous. Those who were not committed to guerrilla warfare with intense ideological belief behaved poorly in battle situations – like their drafted counterparts in the Salvadoran army.

The FMLN began to respond to the army's brutal tactics with their own cruelty. As the government had used death squads against FMLN cadres or sympathizers, so the FMLN began to target individuals. In 1987, according to the Catholic Church, the only organization able to keep such records, the FMLN slew over thirty civilians. In 1988 approximately forty-five victims died, mostly from car-bombings directed at military officers or right-wingers associated with repression. The mayor-killing episodes sullied the FMLN's image abroad and even some of the FDR leaders expressed open dismay at the executions. FMLN leaders were denounced by some of their own supporters for using such bloodthirsty tactics. Villalobos, seeing that one of the FMLN's great advantages was its ability to project a humane image, ordered the cessation of these activities.

In the rural areas the FMLN continued its policy of planting land mines in order to increase the number of casualties when the army entered guerrilla territory. Officers, however, rarely led their columns along the trails and dirt roads. Instead, fresh recruits stepped on the explosive devices and those that did not die were often left legless or footless. Worse for the FMLN's image, peasants and their wives and children frequently detonated the mines.

In late 1986, Villalobos and the other commanders held a series of meetings to assess their position and to plan ahead. They continued to speak in the revolutionary rhetoric that was fast becoming anachronistic. Their Marxism–Leninism, in its five varieties within the FMLN, became evermore cumbersome and failed to offer a vocabulary to describe the changing international order and its relationship to the struggle for self-determination and social justice. 'The masses', a term used frequently, offered little help in understanding the political psychology of El Salvador's poor. Expectations shared by Villalobos and the other commanders about popular uprisings had become unrealistic. The FMLN did not enjoy majority support, despite the claims of its leaders. Nearly a decade of living in the mountains and using a discourse emanating from another era made the FMLN leaders a species of revolutionaries fast disappearing.

Villalobos, the thin, handsome, bearded ex-engineer, could have been a great mathematician, scientist, or perhaps even a chess grand master. His ability to think and plan the logic of a defense or offense inspired his junior officers and confounded the US advisers and the Salvadoran high command. When he translated political theory to practical politics, however, Villalobos did not overcome the tendency to rely on dogma. This intellectual flaw, exhibited in 1975 when he ordered the execution of Roque Dalton for holding heretical views, carried over into his vision of a guerrilla victory on the battlefield, coinciding with a mass uprising in the cities to overwhelm the decadent order. In the late 1980s such thinking did not conform with geopolitical reality. Even before Mikhail Gorbachev announced his intention to withdraw from the superpower contest with the United States, it was clear that the Soviets would no longer serve as the *de facto* insurance company that offered policies to revolutionary movements throughout the world. The Sandinistas and Cubans continued to provide some moral and material support, but the possibilities of an FMLN victory had become improbable, given the commitment of the US national security apparatus to prevent it and Soviet disinterest in promoting the endeavor. While maintaining triumphalist rhetoric in their speeches and pamphlets, the guerrilla leaders began also to compromise, to talk about negotiations, power sharing.

The FMLN directorate had developed keen strategic minds for the battlefield and the political moment. Although their original goals had receded with events, they could not surrender without risking serious consequences for those who had followed them, and, more importantly, abandoning the ideals of sovereignty and social justice that served as the revolutionary impulse. Rumors about the corrosion of the FMLN had to be proven wrong, they agreed, by launching a coordinated offensive. Throughout 1987 the see-saw war continued, the army displacing the people, the guerrillas returning as soon as the army removed large-scale units from the area. Even as the army continued to grow in size, it lacked sufficient troops to occupy its own country, which would have been required to defeat the FMLN. The FMLN countered army strength by increasing the mobility of its units, and changing their size; alternately decreasing and increasing the number of combatants for certain kinds of confrontations – ambushes, or attacks on major installations or fortifications.

Throughout late 1986, 1987 and into 1988, the FMLN commanders began to move units toward targets with precision and remarkable secrecy for a coordinated series of surprise attacks designed to dramatize their strength and force the government into realistic negotiations. The FMLN also capitalized on the opening of political space, which allowed cadres to rebuild in the urban areas – where the death squads had assassinated key members of the organization.

In addition, the revolutionaries took advantage of the political aperture to revive popular movements that the death squads had disrupted or annihilated since 1981. In 1986, FMLN organizers began drifting quietly into the newly erected shanty towns where earthquake refugees lived, and into the *barrios* on the outskirts of the capital, where the working class and unemployed poor resided.

Taking advantage of the new climate inside the university and other arenas of political life, revolutionaries began to replace members of the disintegrating Christian Democratic structure that by 1987 had fallen into a state of chaos and bickering. Into the places vacated by Christian Democrats tainted by scandal moved a new left leadership. They organized anew street demonstrations and large public gatherings, unseen since the slaughters in the streets in 1980. In the second half of the 1980s, strikes broke out and political and cultural activities took place that would have been unthinkable two years before.

By November 1987 the members of the FDR felt the time was propitious to form an open political party. Led by Ruben Zamora and Guillermo Ungo, the Democratic Convergence would participate in the 1988 elections. The FMLN had tried to block past elections because, its leaders said, they were inherently illegitimate. How to reconcile that position with the emerging new politics, which stressed electoral democracy and compromise?

## The Failure of Christian Democracy

The new political climate created by the Esquipulas meeting and the broad support for a settlement in El Salvador did not correspond with the actual political configuration. Democracy and compromise required a strong and durable center. Yet, in 1988 El Salvador was in the throes of political polarization due to the disintegration of the very center that

US ideologues had assured Congress would become the core of the new 'fragile democracies' in the region. The right wing staged its comeback with a re-energized ARENA party, led by D'Aubuisson. Their rhetoric focused on attacking the Democratic Convergence as communists disguised as candidates and on the center politicians as corrupt failures. These charges were true.

The moderate middle, symbolized by Duarte, had both failed to deliver on any of their promises and had enriched themselves greatly. Their supporters in El Salvador and the United States received a devastating blow in May 1988 when doctors in Washington diagnosed Duarte as having inoperable stomach cancer and warned him that he could die within weeks.

As Duarte's disease progressed, scandal shook the fragile political coherence he had built up since the early 1980s. The Christian Democrats stank from corruption. Duarte's cohorts erected mansions with swimming pools and tennis courts using funds stolen from the US aid programs. The voters watched in dismay as Duarte's team grew greedier in office, and fought over how to carve up the US aid dollars.

The FMLN's ability to infiltrate units into the slums and into the working-class *barrios* was due not only to their own planning but to the horrendous failure of the Duarte regime to deliver on its promises. After four years Duarte's only solid support remained in the US Congress, where he exuded the charm, wit and democratic language that endeared him to the backslapping members of both parties, with few exceptions.

He promised peace. He presided over a grinding war in which more than five thousand people died each year. He promised land reform. Under his rule, land reform disappeared. He promised democracy. If elections were the sole measure of that word, then El Salvador should have been the most democratic country in the world since the country had been inundated with them. But there was little protection for dissent, since neither Duarte nor the pressure of the US Embassy could curtail the abuses of the death squads and the overachievers in the army. Duarte promised economic recovery. The economy was in a shambles, in part because of the direct effects of war; indirectly, because the Salvadoran capitalist class invested abroad rather than in their own precarious country. Over the 1980s, the poor grew poorer; the oligarchy – some absent, some in the country – remained in control of the lion's share of the national wealth. Duarte promised sovereignty. Under his rule, US advisers effectively administered the government, but could not reform the antiquated structures of the military.

One feature of Salvador's martial class was institutionalized spoils system. The means for perpetuating the unwritten perquisites of officerdom was the promotion system, a function of time served rather than merit. Officers of each class understand that twenty-five years after graduation, the members of the *tanda* (graduating class and brotherhood) are traditionally named to the commanding positions inside the armed forces.

## THE TANDONA

The 1966 class successfully lobbied for their 'rightful' command posts before they were due. They argued persuasively that the war was not going well. But the concerns of the new *tandona* were more banal than patriotic. Only top officials had a share in the spoils to which the officers had become accustomed, spoils that grew enormously as American military aid increased. There were complications, however, in carrying on the tradition. When Colonel Emilio Ponce, *el numero uno* of his 1966 class, became chief of staff, replacing General Adolfo Blandon in November 1988, the army was more than four times the size of the 1980 force. But the number of command positions had not expanded accordingly. In other words, there were plenty of officers, but not enough top spots whence the loot could be pocketed. Although the US advisers expressed disgust for the system, they could not change it. Ponce assured the Americans that under his guidance the Salvadoran military would rise to their task and rapidly defeat the FMLN. The 1966 class was tough, he postured.

The FMLN tested him on his first day on the job. Guerrilla units hit the headquarters of the Salvadoran National Guard with mortars and light artillery. The FMLN demonstrated their ability to penetrate not only working-class *barrios*, but upper-class residential areas as well. On 1 November in the capital they took the Estado Mayor (military high command headquarters) and occupied the neighborhood of Escalon. The army retook its headquarters and the FMLN retreated from Escalon. But their dramatic successes showed the new military commander and his *tandona* in a poor light. The populace witnessed the arrogant, strutting officers, who each year boasted of victory, prove unable to defeat the guerrillas in battle. Salvadorans grew accustomed to blackouts as the FMLN sabotaged electricity substations at will.

'Duarte', commented a Salvadoran banker, 'has presided over the destruction of the social fabric of our country. Not only have we lost all semblance of sovereignty, but we have lost confidence in the ability of a moderate and well-meaning group of Christians and democrats to govern.' The retired financier concluded that 'the right wing will win the 1988 elections'. And so they did. As a preview of the coming presidential contest, in March ARENA swept away the centrists and took over as the assembly majority. ARENA also captured the lion's share of mayoral elections. However, the disappointment over Duarte and the victory of ARENA at the polls did not tell the story of what had happened to El Salvador.

## The End of the Cold War: Glimmers of Peace in El Salvador

Even though the term negotiations became permissible in Washington, real bargaining remained difficult. On the side of some form of settlement were members of the FMLN leadership, the remainder of the Christian Democratic center and a handful from the political right – along with the vast majority of the Salvadoran people.

Villalobos still believed that a general insurrection could take place. Other FMLN commanders and some of the political representatives were unsure if the majority would respond to the call. There was one way to test the projections and at the same time demonstrate to the persistant optimists in the US Embassy that the FMLN still possessed the ability to launch major offensive drives.

On 11 November 1989, the guerrillas, who had moved unseen from the provinces, reconnoitered and hit the capital and other major cities. While mortars fell on the compound which housed both President Cristiani and the barracks of the brigade defending the city, squads and platoons entered and captured the entire northern arc of the city. With obvious popular support, they occupied the working-class *barrios* and controlled access to the major roads leading out of San Salvador.

The army counterattacked with heavy artillery, tanks and armored vehicles. The FMLN responded with anti-tank weapons, some of them homemade but nonetheless effective. The residents collaborated with the FMLN, serving as spies, couriers and makers of homemade bombs. After three days of fierce fighting, the army failed to dislodge the guerrillas. Joaquin Villalobos's voice, over Radio Venceremos, crackled throughout the country. He called upon Salvadorans to join the uprising. The revolutionary moment, he told them, was at hand. He was wrong.

The guerrillas dug in and held off the better equipped army. Faced with their inability to dislodge the guerrillas from their emplacements, the armed forces resorted to their tried and true methods. Shocking even some of their loyal acolytes in the US Embassy, the generals sent the bombers in with orders to drop their loads on the neighborhoods, with no regard for civilian lives.

Along with the massive, indiscriminate bombing of the poor *barrios* came repression of the groups that had moved into the political space opened in the late Duarte years. The leaders of the various civic, political and cultural organizations, anticipating violent repression, had already left their homes and abandoned their offices. Most were either in hiding or abroad when the police and army units raided their offices in mid-November.

Frustrated by their failure to move the guerrillas or find their leading political sympathizers, the general staff ordered an intensification of the bombing. Every ramshackle hut became a target, every moving human being an excuse to strafe a street or neighborhood. The excitement over the rebels' ability to take and hold territory in the capital faded quickly and panic overcame the people.

The bombing made it impossible to organize the poor into militia-style units. Instead of a full-scale uprising, the residents of the *barrio* took flight. Rebel commanders even advised the gritty *muchachos* to leave. To make a final statement, however, the retreating FMLN troops took one of the city's wealthiest sections. As the shabby, tired and often bloody guerrillas lounged by the swimming pools and experimented with the imported barbecue grills, the rich and powerful cowered and begged. The guerrillas and the oligarchy shared one certainty: the air force would not drop bombs on the property of the aristocracy.

The FMLN offensive taught lessons to almost everyone connected with the war. The guerrillas' audacity and skill and the inability of the army to drive them out of the capital without resorting to massive aerial bombardment convinced some of the wealthy Salvadorans and some of the US national security elite that a compromise had to be reached. The rebel commanders understood that their vision of a massive uprising to coincide with a daring military move was a pipe dream. For one thing, one third of the Salvadoran population had been displaced or made into refugees. It was not the same country as it had been when the war began.

On 23 January 1989, the FMLN offered a peace proposal. In it they accepted the legitimacy of elections and said they would support the moderate-left coalition, the Democratic Convergence, if the government would postpone the elections from March to September so that there could be 'guarantees against election fraud'. In essence, the FMLN announced that it now possessed the political will to make peace and overcome the numerous obstacles created by a decade of war.

Duarte, living on borrowed time, dismissed the offer as a 'propaganda ploy' and ARENA labeled it a 'tactical ploy'. Ironically, the change in attitude came from Washington. Vice President Dan Quayle flew to San Salvador and delivered the message from President Bush: reconsider the proposal.

In the United States, the November 1988 elections had brought George Bush into the White House with the assurance that Central America would no longer be 'the most important place in the world'. Indeed, the new Assistant Secretary of State for Inter American Affairs, Bernard Aronson, was told to keep that region's name off the front pages.

Bush changed priorities to coincide more closely with those of the older establishment, who never understood Reagan's fascination with an area that had little strategic or economic importance. By 1989 many Washington insiders accepted the fact of the end of the Cold War. And without the ideology of anti-communism, the concentration on stopping the Soviets in Central America appeared ludicrous.

Yet wars do not end simply because the reasons for their being no longer exist. The ten years of fighting had created not only over seventy thousand dead bodies, but also a sizable bureaucracy with its own vested interest in continuing the same outmoded US policies in El Salvador.

## THE SLAUGHTER OF THE JESUITS

Throughout the war, the Jesuit fathers in San Salvador did not leave their residence to run from the fury of the frustrated military. They knew that the high command identified them with the rebels, but the prestigious priests were beyond partisans; their vows, they believed, offered them some shield from the senseless violence unleashed in response to the FMLN's dramatic moves.

On 16 November 1989, one year after the FMLN offensive in the capital, a squad of men led by an officer entered the Jesuit residence grounds in El Salvador and systematically executed six priests and two servants who might have acted as witnesses to the slaughter. Among the dead was Father Ignacio Ellacuria, head of the Jesuits in El Salvador, a brilliant theologian, recognized universally as a scholar and a man of peace. He was 'sentenced' to death by a 'group' inside the officer corps because he had 'defended terrorism' and led a campaign to 'defame the armed forces'.

The right-wing military apparatus held the Jesuits, like the late archbishop, responsible for legitimizing – if not covertly directing – the insurrection and undermining the military. Their method of dealing with those who disagreed with them had not changed. D'Aubuisson was no longer the one bad apple that somehow corrupted the whole barrel of military life. The rot went deep and pervaded the entire system, beginning with the day the cadet entered the academy where an armed force was trained not to defend the country against external enemies, but against its own people. The high command of the Salvadoran army could make no distinction between dissenting opinion and treason. Those who disagreed with the military's policy were seen as enemy soldiers or agents who deserved to die. The church, the monastery, the home – all became simply the battlefield in the minds of those who commanded the means of official violence.

Like the other murders ordered by members of the high command, the slaughter of the Jesuits remained 'unsolved' until September 1991. For the first time, thanks in part to pressure from Washington and the Vatican, the government of El Salvador carried out an investigation and a trial. In the dock stood the head of the cadet school, Lt Col. Guillermo Benavides and Lt Rene Musshy Mendoza, who commanded the hit squad. Both were convicted, Benavides of having ordered the slaying of the Jesuits, Lt Mendoza of murdering the servants.

US Embassy officials leaked information to reporters that implicated the entire high command of the Salvadoran military as well as members of the US military mission, who tried to cover up for their clients. The same embassy leakers felt confident that Benavides and Mendoza would be pardoned by a general amnesty and that the murders of the priests and their servants would go unpunished as had the other crimes committed by the military and their agents.

The shock felt from the murder of the Jesuits was not of surprise but of recognition. They were an assault on the personal decency of President Alfredo Cristiani, most members of the US Embassy and those who handled their cables in Foggy Bottom. The politically astute community knew that in the changed world of 1990 the United States could not continue to support a crude gang of thugs in power.

However, those on trial were US-trained and educated thugs. Major

Eric Buckland, a US military adviser who gave information to the FBI about the murder of the Jesuits, expressed the moral sentiment that prevailed inside the military elites of both countries. He did not understand the uproar over the killings because by advocating such concepts as human rights in the midst of an anti-guerrilla war, 'you're going to get your butt kicked'.

## THE FINAL PHASE

The Salvadoran bloodshed continued throughout 1990 and into 1991. The guerrillas attacked, fought and retreated. The government forces retaliated against the civilian population suspected of supporting the subversives. More people fled the country. The FMLN's ability to enter the capital at will demonstrated that after a decade of war the Salvadoran military could not secure its home base. World and regional conditions, however, changed dramatically. By 1990 the revolutionaries could no longer hope for anything more than a peace plan that would allow for their reintegration into Salvadoran society.

The changes in the world and more than a decade of war turned most of the revolutionaries leaders, by necessity, into reformers. Those rebel leaders who survived had witnessed some of El Salvador's best and brightest gunned down in battle or fallen victims to assassination squads. In all, the war claimed more than eighty thousand lives. One and a half million Salvadorans had fled the country, some to refugee camps, others to become members of a cheap labor force in foreign lands.

# The Peace Process

Although the peace dialogue had moved forward seven leagues over the 1980s, the obstacles to ending the bloodshed remained formidable. The American dollar flow appeared as one of the impediments to peace. Everyone in the government depended on it and worried about their futures when it stopped – when the war ended.

In May 1991 President Cristiani asked for more US military aid, unfettered by human rights clauses. Indeed, said Cristiani, the peace process itself would be moved along by unrestricted US military aid. At the same time talks were taking place between the government and the FMLN. UN representatives sat in at the talks and quickly began playing an active role in the dialogue.

The FMLN insisted, logically, that El Salvador did not need a large armed force since it had no foreign enemies, and that before the rebels laid down their arms and accepted the possibility of integration into civil society, the army must disband. Law and order was the task of a police force, they said. Look at the record, the FMLN argued. From 1980 to 1991 the armed forces of El Salvador – financed, advised and supplied by the United States – murdered more than fifty thousand civilians and unleashed untold destruction upon villages and neighborhoods by practising indiscriminate bombing.

Despite these facts, some US officials insisted to House and Senate committees that unrestricted aid to the people responsible for all this violence would bring about a peace process. Rather than extricating the United States from that internal conflict, these US bureaucrats still saw their job as wresting a yearly Salvadoran aid package from Congress.

Like the Salvadoran high command who enlarged their wallets as a result of US assistance, the Americans argued that more military aid would bolster President Cristiani and help ensure democracy and peace. But the facts accumulated for more than a decade showed that aid had produced little more than continuous action by death squads and the overflowing of mass graves.

The leitmotif for El Salvador in the 1980s and into the 1990s was death. At the end of ten years of unmitigated struggle, two of the men who led the politics of the left and center died within a year. Duarte hung on to finish his term in June 1989. Hated by the right and the left, he managed by his personality and perseverance to make Salvadorans accept elections as the institutional means of change. But the peace, prosperity and economic development he sought never materialized. The cancer took Duarte's life on 23 February 1990.

One year later Guillermo Ungo, Duarte's running mate in 1972 and his political foe for the decade of the 1980s, died from complications relating to a brain tumor. Like Duarte, Ungo came from the generation of Central Americans who saw national sovereignty as more than a political goal; it was the poetry of their lives as well. Ungo, the best that Latin American social democracy produced, never wavered in his faith that through struggle the people would prevail. He did not foresee the amount of blood that would have to be spilled just to carry on the mission which Simon Bolivar had inspired almost two centuries before.

Roberto D'Aubuisson, who alone remained of the original key players, began to make regular trips to the United States in 1990 and 1991 to receive radiation therapy for his throat cancer. The man who had looked like a matinée idol, or at least the lead in an afternoon soap opera, now appeared in the assembly with burns on his face and neck, his mouth distorted by the massive dosages of radiation. When he surprised his rabid followers by accepting the left-wing legislators into the assembly, it meant that left candidates could run for election without risking assassination. The Salvadoran business class, the professionals, even some of the aristocracy grudgingly accepted the inevitability of a negiotiated end to the war.

President Bush was not tired of the war, but rather relegated it to one of those low-priority issues that needed to be solved. For the cosmopolitan Republicans who took over the reins from the Reaganites, Central America was low on the foreign policy priority list. The order from Washington was sent to the US Embassy in El Salvador: 'Settle it'.

In early September 1991, army Colonel Mark Hamilton, the head of the US military mission to El Salvador, along with US Ambassador William Walker and a small staff, including bodyguards who were totally outgunned, met commanders of the FMLN in Santa Marta, guerrilla-controlled territory in northern El Salvador. Raul Hercules, *nom de guerre* of one of the FMLN leaders, hosted a meal for his erstwhile enemy and the men drank from a bottle of Johnny Walker Black Label. They discussed what guarantees the guerrillas needed for a real cease-fire to take effect. Col. Hamilton did not disclose their response, but cabled the information to Washington.

He called the encounter 'fruitful', and then explained, 'I didn't go up there to break bread with the guerrillas. We've got to pass through this phase to get to peace.' The order had come to 'wind down' the US investment in El Salvador. The guerrillas previously shunned by the Reagan-Bush administration became parties with whom to negotiate.

The Salvadoran government denounced the mission as 'ludicrous'. The story received minimal cover in the US media. In government circles in Washington, few officials cared, or even noticed the incident. By 1991 Central America had become among the least important places in the world.

In late September 1991, at UN headquarters in New York, President Cristiani and the leaders of the FMLN announced an agreement to stop the war. Although a cease-fire was not put into place, the guerrillas accepted concessions by the government to reintegrate into the society and politics of the country, without reprisals. Many questions remained unsettled, such as what force would restrain the military or induce it to comply with the peace accords. But the rebels, under the accord, would join the police force and the good offices of the UN would be utilized to oversee the implementation of the peace entente.

In early October 1991, two weeks after the announcement of the agreement, the Salvadoran air force and ground artillery launched a massive bombing and shelling attack on the Guazapa volcano, a site that the guerrillas had held for twelve years. The army spokesman said that the attack was in retaliation for ambushes and other incidents initiated by the rebels since the peace accord. The high command, according to a US Embassy source, was angry at President Cristiani for failing to consult with the military on the peace agreement. The majority of the business community, however, was tired of the war, as was President Bush.

In May 1991, in Washington, DC, an incident occurred that dramatized the plight of the majority of the Salvadoran people, one million of whom lived in the United States. A policewoman encountered a Salvadoran man drinking in the street in the racially diverse neighborhood of Mount Pleasant, where a large proportion of the district's Salvadoran population live. She claimed he drew a knife before she shot him. The facts became unimportant, however. Within hours, thousands of Hispanics, accompanied by blacks from the neighborhood, and watched by their white middlle-class neighbours, poured into the streets to express their anger against the police. The riots lasted for two more days. The police responded with tear gas, not with automatic weapons or tanks. No one was killed.

'I'm not happy here,' a Salvadoran refugee commented. 'But who knows when I can go home, and what I'll find there when I do.'

Under the agile guidance of UN negotiator Iqbal Riza, the FMLN and the government survived a dozen nearly catastrophic impasses and by January 1993 both sides were close to compliance with the peace agreement. The FMLN disarmed and transformed itself from a guerrilla army into a political party. The government began to reduce the size of its various security forces and allow some of the former rebels to begin the process of joining the system. The peace was an uneasy one. Both sides mistrusted the other – with good reason. Key generals and colonels balked at being dismissed from the military, as the accords stipulated. They might lose some of their pensions. President Cristiani pleaded with the FMLN commanders to allow a little more time to get rid of these troublesome and dangerous men.

The US Ambassador sided with the UN. From Washington's perspective, the point had been made: the United States had prevented the FMLN from winning a military victory. If the former guerillas eventually won an election, the policy-makers would deal with that situation as it arose. Intervention, the Americans had demonstrated in Central America and elsewhere, was not just a one-time tactic, but a way of policy life.

# 4
# GUATEMALA

For decades tourists have enjoyed the pleasures of the quaint market plaza in Chichicastenango. There, foreigners can purchase Indian artifacts before touring the Mayan ruins to view the pre-Columbian pottery and architecture, clues to the complexity and profundity of the ancient civilization – whence descended the majority of Guatemalans. Most tourists do not see the homeless population, the wretched conditions of the majority, or signs of the guerrilla war that has been raging intermittently for three decades.

There were two roots for the unremitting guerrilla wars fought in Guatemala between revolutionaries and government troops from the 1960s into the 1990s. One was the skewed division of wealth and property in the country, which, for centuries, deprived the majority of access to land or social justice. The other was a 1954 decision by President Dwight D. Eisenhower to overthrow the elected government of President Jacobo Arbenz.

In the early 1950s a series of events converged to bring about a crisis whose consequences led to the bloodiest sequence of military governments in Latin America, a phenomenon that Guatemalans will continue to endure for years to come. To understand what provoked Eisenhower to intervene, thus altering the destiny of the Guatemalan people, one must return to leitmotifs that guided American policy since the early nineteenth century.

The Monroe Doctrine etched its imperial premises into the chairs occupied by successive generations of presidents and State Department officials. For more than a century the United States guided or coerced the politics of the Western Hemisphere for a variety of reasons; either American companies needed the resources and labor of the area; or US security 'required' decisive action from Washington; or the imperial elite perceived disobedience on the part of a Latin American upstart.

US troops had landed in Guatemala in 1920, in the words of the State Department, 'to protect the American Legate and other American interests, such as the cable station, during a period of fighting'. US troops stayed for eighteen days and helped the government defeat the insurgents. Washington's next 'problem' with Guatemala developed in 1944, when the majority of the people demonstrated in the streets to show their hatred for the continued rule of Jorge Ubico, the latest of a long line of dictators. The coalition that emerged from the street protests and political struggle announced that the next president of Guatemala would be chosen by free elections.

In March 1945, Guatemala was a country far removed from the center of Washington's focus. That changed when the newly elected government of Juan Jose Arevalo announced a series of reforms, including the seeds of an agrarian property redistribution program – which would affect the assets of the United Fruit Company (UFCO). Not only did the proposed land reforms conflict with the interests of powerful Americans with investments in that property, but the very idea of expropriating property for any reason was linked to communism in the minds of both the Cold War Democrats under Truman and the crusty Republicans who comprised Eisenhower's cabinet in 1953.

President Arevalo (1945–50), was a commited nationalist, who also believed in 'spiritual socialism', an abstract concept that no one could ever concretize. He said that Guatemala's destiny was to spread its reform program throughout Latin America. At least two dozen unsuccessful coup conspiracies were hatched during his presidential term, mostly by cliques inside the military or oligarchy.

By 1948 US Embassy officials were already sending cables to Washington about the 'red danger' in Guatemala. By 1951 these reports warned that communists were being appointed to minor posts in the Guatemalan government. This scenario ran foul of a primary tenet of Cold War rules and regulations as set by the United States: communists were not allowed to participate in governments. Those countries that permitted 'reds' into their governments would receive no aid from the

United States, and could count on strong US animosity.

After the election of Jacobo Arbenz in 1951, members of the Truman and then the Eisenhower national security bureaucracy sent their superiors a stream of alarmist memos and cables over Arbenz's apparent lack of interest in US complaints that Guatemalan communists held subcabinet posts and were reportedly friends of the president and his wife.

US Ambassador to Guatemala Richard Patterson demanded that the 'reds' be fired. The ambassador threatened serious repercussions if Arbenz remained 'soft on communism'. Instead, Arbenz requested that Patterson be removed. The State Department recalled Patterson for 'medical reasons', but once in Washington he continued his campaign to alert the public to the danger of communism in Guatemala. In the process, Patterson invented the notorious 'Duck test' to illustrate the difficulty of actually proving that an individual was 'a card-carrying communist'. Patterson offered a barnyard analogy: 'The bird looks like a duck ... he swims like a duck ... and quacks like a duck. By this time you have probably reached the conclusion that the bird is a duck whether or not he is wearing a label.'

For Patterson and a slew of less-than-brilliant bureaucrats the Guatemalan nationalist experiment quacked like communism. Worse, the State Department accepted the allegations of their legal officers and of ranters like Patterson who were seeking to establish a basis for intervention under the OAS Charter.

Indeed, in March 1954, Secretary of State Dulles was presenting these arguments before the OAS ministers in Caracas. The Arbenz government, declared Dulles, represented a communist threat to the hemisphere. Some laughed nervously; others recoiled in fright at the thought of yet another landing of US troops on Latin American soil. Only the boot-licking ministers from Nicaragua and the Dominican Republic willingly cooperated with the Dulles position.

John Foster Dulles was the quintessential Cold Warrior, whose conviction that the Moscow-based communist conspiracy was plotting day and night to capture the world spurred him to proselytizing zeal. For him, the United States had a mission: to prevent the spread of atheistic communism and support the American way of life – for those countries civilized enough to understand it.

Dulles harrangued and threatened the diplomatic officials of the weak and poor countries of Latin America, many of whom understood the Guatemalan reform process as both necessary and indigenous. Finally, under extreme US pressure, the OAS majority reluctantly backed a US resolution aimed at Guatemela that referred to 'dangers originating outside the hemsiphere'. Mexico and Argentina abstained. Guatemalan Foreign Minister Guillermo Torielo denounced 'the systematic campaign' against his government. Dulles needed little sensitivity to see that the majority in the OAS did not approve, albeit they voted for the US resolution. So, the Eisenhower administration decided to go it alone – in the spirit of the Monroe Doctrine, which State Department lawyers interpreted to empower Washington to move by itself when it perceived a foreign threat to the hemsiphere. Aid and arms shipments to the Guatemalan government were cut; in Europe the US ambassadors carried notes to the allies to ensure that the NATO nations did not make any deliveries.

In 1932, the Guatemalan communists had been virtually wiped out in bloody raids and executions ordered by dictator Ubico. But a few surviving members gradually rebuilt the party. By 1951 they had established themselves as a small but diligent group of intellectuals and organizers who proved themselves indefatigable allies of Arbenz. They had shone in the labor struggles of the late 1940s and, more importantly, they had adhered to agreements supporting Arbenz's general program. They were also efficient in carrying out their assigned tasks. Communism, however, was a non-issue in Guatemala, where the nationalist impetus that had propelled the Arevalo coalition through difficult coup attempts carried Arbenz into office. In Washington, where an institutionalized Cold War mentality reigned, 'reds' in government became a central issue.

State Department intelligence officials were wary from the beating Senator Joe McCarthy gave them over the 'coddling' of communists in Foggy Bottom. They joined FBI agents in a fervent attempt to scour every nook and cranny of the hemisphere for subversives. In Guatemala they found some juicy prospects. They ignored Arbenz's affirmation of capitalism, and concentrated on the dangerous germ of communism there, to which they applied their bureaucratic magnifying glasses. Thus, a benign situation in a poor Central American republic arrived on the crisis agenda in national security circles.

Whereas centuries of Guatemalan history had established a skewed distribution of wealth that cried out for reform, President Eisenhower was uninformed and uninterested in the Guatemalan past. Along with the urgent national security briefings from the CIA, Eisenhower's close associates owned parts of the targeted property. He was easily convinced that Arbenz was a communist, so he ordered the CIA to plan a covert operation to overthrow him.

The very notion of confiscating property, even with compensation, appeared to John Foster Dulles and his associates as a form of communism. The crotchety Ohio Republican went so far as to characterize the Arbenz regime as a 'communist-style dictatorship'. Coincidentally, Dulles had been a long-time partner in a Wall Street law firm that handled the United Fruit account. President Eisenhower's personal secretary was married to the public relations director of UFCO. Important members of Congress, high State Department officials and CIA officers either owned major stock in the company or had family ties to United Fruit executives. The quintessentially Republican cabinet accepted without skepticism the idea that the democratically elected Guatemalan government was on the road to communism. Their thinking was rooted in a narrow notion of property rights and on a tradition of Latin American obedience to Washington, established since the Monroe Doctrine in 1823.

Arbenz's land reform called for the expropriation of hundreds of thousands of acres belonging to the United Fruit Company. UFCO bought up Guatemalan land early in the century for a tiny percentage of what it was worth, and bribed a series of cooperative dictators to avoid paying proper taxes and obtain a series of monopolies. By mid-century UFCO owned not only some 40 per cent of the country's most fertile soil, thereby making it difficult for potential banana-growing competitors, but also the nation's railroad and communications systems as well as the port facilities.

United Fruit was not just a big banana company: its size, wealth and power made any Central American government appear a shade less than sovereign. The tiny Guatemalan oligarchy – who had welcomed the American giant because it offered the possibility of US government protection – possessed some 70 per cent of the remaining acreage, while the majority of the rural population held only 4 per cent of the total land. This absurd class division, which persisted from Spanish colonial times, was perpetuated by autocratic rule and repression.

## The History

Guatemala's 42,000 square mile area, about the size of the state of Kentucky, contained some four million inhabitants in the 1950s. More than half of the indigenous population were non-Spanish speaking people, descended from the Mayans. They had lived in rural areas before the Spanish conquest. For centuries the *latifundistas*, with the cooperation of the Catholic Church hierarchy, virtually enslaved the Indians. The young Indian men walked bent almost in half, their spines permanently curved from years of carrying heavy bags of coffee beans down the mountain trails to the markets. The bags were attached to a strap that went across their foreheads. It was cheaper to use people than mules. Life expectancy among the poor was thirty-eight years. Illiteracy among the rural, non-Spanish speaking Indians was close to 100 per cent.

These conditions pervaded Guatemala as they did other Central American countries. And Guatemalans, like their neighbors in the early 1940s, absorbed the heady democratic rhetoric that allied leaders expounded to win support for the war effort. President Franklin Roosevelt had informed the world that poverty and injustice should be challenged, not accepted as something natural.

By 1944 Guatemalans of different classes and political backgrounds forged a political coalition, under the broad themes of independence and social justice, and staged a revolt. It brought many thousands into the streets to oust Jorge Ubico – who had won an uncontested presidential election in 1931 – the latest in a string of self-styled dictators. The military, reading the pulse of the changing times, did not come to Ubico's defense; as a result the demonstrators prevailed. In their first free election Guatemalans chose as president a brilliant intellectual, writer, and college professor. Among the reforms Juan Jose Arevalo promised was land redistribution.

Slowly, under the new president, the wheels of reform moved to dismantle dictatorship and install systems of accountability and mechanisms to ensure some modicum of social justice. Arevalo's rule was hardly smooth, however. Several military-led coup attempts failed, and officers jockeyed for position to win the next election. Some of the top military were simply paid employees of political leaders or economic barons. The majority of the colonels and generals understood that the old semi-feudal order had come to an end and believed that the officer corps could provide solid national leadership.

The most intellectual and political man in the corps was an army colonel, Jacobo Arbenz. In 1951 he won the presidential election. He had garnered support from liberal and reform-minded fellow officers and, more crucially, from progressive sectors of civil society. Arbenz was labor's candidate; he was the man favored by the Communist Party and he had wide support among the middle class as well. Accompanied by his elegant and beautiful wife, Dona Maria, he also showed great poise at the cocktail parties and receptions attended by the aristocracy and the diplomatic corps.

'Red Jacobo', as he was affectionately named for his radical ideas and his closeness to certain communist intellectuals, picked up the threads of the agrarian reform promises and wove them into laws that called for the expropriation of more than a thousand estates, including some of United Fruit's uncultivated lands. During the two-year life of the land reform, the Arbenz government expropriated some 15 per cent of the farm land, compensating the owners at the rate declared on the tax assessment. More than fifty thousand peasants, which meant, with their families, over a quarter of a million people, received deeds to the land.

In addition, Arbenz challenged UFCO's electric power monopoly by ordering the construction of a rival power plant that would sell cheaper electricity. He also began to build a new port that would compete with the United Fruit controlled loading and unloading facility. Arbenz explained that he had no intention of attacking foreign capital that was 'subordinate to Guatemalan laws, cooperates with the economic development of the country and strictly abstains from intervening in the nation's social and political life'. This statement was no different from the US government's approach to foreign capital.

The objective of the agrarian reform was not to punish the UFCO, but to settle 100,000 people on the land – and assert sovereignty. This created a problem for United Fruit executives and major stockholders: the company had grossly undervalued the worth of its property in Guatemala on the tax declarations and thus would receive far less in compensation than the real value of the land. For decades UFCO had cheated the Guatemalan government in its tax payments. But regardless of UFCO's unscrupulous behavior, there was a basic principle of business that no government could expropriate US property and get away with it.

In decision-making circles the perfect conditions existed for the banal to wed the heroic, in an ideological marriage of convenience. Since Arbenz did not take the hard line against communists, it was relatively simple, in the era of rampant McCarthyism, to transform an issue of national sovereignty into a Cold War confrontation in which the Soviet Union was establishing, in Eisenhower's words, 'an outpost on this continent'. The Guatemala issue put a new twist on the old imperial formula, in which US military forces traditionally solved bank or corporate problems in Central America. In the Cold War atmosphere, Guatemala acquired a crisis label.

Once the decision was made to get rid of Arbenz, the facts of the case mattered little. By late 1953 the CIA had taken on the Guatemala project and UFCO officials immediately cooperated with the agency. From the late 1940s on they fought every reform tooth and nail, spread lies and rumors that Arbenz and other government figures were thieves or Kremlin agents, and created as many legal obstacles as possible to every measure proposed by the government. UFCO had been at war with the reformers since the first glimmer of agrarian reform appeared in the eye of President Arevalo in the mid-1940s. Company executives exercised influence on the powerful in Washington that Arbenz thought inconceivable in the post World War II era.

Even during Truman's two terms as president (1945–52), UFCO officials had convinced some of the CIA alarmists that Arbenz, then Minister of War, was a communist. Truman, however, dismissed agency initiatives to launch a clandestine operation against the Arevalo government. Eisenhower, however, gave the green light to the covert action squad, after less than a month in office. UFCO officials contributed money and access; the CIA bought and distributed arms to a group of right-wing Guatemalan officers for the express purpose of inspiring an uprising to overthrow the government.

As the clandestine operation was beginning, American foreign service personnel tried to persuade other skeptical Latin American governments to isolate Guatemala because of the 'communist influence' over Arbenz. Agency operatives, with the aid of New York's Cardinal Spellman, convinced the bishop of Guatemala to write a pastoral letter denouncing Arbenz and warning Guatemalans to beware of the communist takeover of their country. CIA pilots dropped copies of this document over villages throughout the country.

While US officials were testifying to Congress and making headlines about the Soviet presence in the Arbenz government, the men in the Politburo in Moscow wondered what the United States was up to. The Soviets had conceded that the Western Hemisphere was a US sphere and in the early 1950s had not even opened embassies in much of Latin America, much less fed weapons to unknown governments. The Politburo cared little about Latin America and assigned only one man on the Central Committee to act as liaison to Latin American communist parties. The Guatemalan communists sent delegates to major meetings and congresses in Moscow, but were never received there by officials with more than ceremonial powers.

Arbenz had accepted Guatemalan Communist Party support during his presidential campaign, without considering the impact this would have in Washington. The communists were a small party, which captured only four of more than fifty seats in the legislature. Their leaders, whom Arbenz knew socially, did not aspire to take over the country. Indeed, they were thrilled to be accepted as very junior partners in his government.

American pressure from 1952 on created serious economic problems for the government and hardship for the people. Washington punished Arbenz for his 'pro-communist' policies by making trade difficult and credit impossible. Other nations that offered loans or favorable trade to Guatemala were 'leaned on' by State Department officials.

Despite the adversity, the Arbenz reforms sparked excitement that spread throughout Latin America. Once again, Latin revolutionaries concluded, 'a brave leader is embarking on needed changes without asking permission from Washington.'

Radicals like Dr Ernesto 'Che' Guevara traveled to Guatemala and offered their services to the new government. Guatemala was not exactly awash with trained and educated people, so when Guevara, a young Argentine physician, arrived, he easily secured a position at the Ministry of Health. He observed a depressed, sick and illiterate population that desperately needed the nascent Arbenz reforms.

Most of the changes planned by the Arbenz government to deal with the misery of the Guatemalan majority never went beyond the planning stage. In March 1953, CIA and UFCO executives staged a collaborative dress rehearsal for a coup. UFCO paid some disenchanted army officers to instigate revolts. The agency supplied them with arms, and plans for fomenting insurrection, which erupted subsequently in several cities. But the coup makers lacked sufficient coherence and the army suppressed the revolt. The officers, however, were less than delighted at their situation. Under Arbenz they were experiencing not only a cut-off of US military aid, but a weapons embargo imposed by Washington.

More than a year later, in June 1954, CIA pilots took to the air again. This time their leaflets demanded that Arbenz step down; if not, bombing would begin. Radio messages broadcast from clandestine transmitters repeated the threats, saying they represented the 'Voice of Liberation'. World War II fighters strafed areas near some of the military barracks. Guatemala was flooded with disinformation.

A young CIA operative, David Atlee Phillips, began what turned into a long agency career by making up lies to spread confusion in Guatemala. In his autobiography, *Nightwatch*, Phillips called himself the 'world's greatest liar'. His superiors, E. Howard Hunt and Tracy Barnes, went on to work together with Phillips on the Bay of Pigs and other infamous clandestine jobs. Hunt's career ended dramatically when he was caught by the Washington, D.C. police in the 1972 Watergate break-in of Democratic Party headquarters. Most of those who did the dirty work, which permanently altered Guatemalan history, did not reflect – at least publicly – on their actions, except to rejoice in their 'success'. One CIA officer, Phil Roettenger, later apologized to the Guatemalan people for his role in the plot. He acknowledged that he had participated in an evil deed. 'You just don't think about consequences during the excitement of the action,' he cogently explained.

As the CIA destablization campaign proceeded, a prelude to invasion, Arbenz finally received a small shipment of relatively useless Czech weapons, which became, in the hands of the CIA prestidigitators, the final offering of 'proof' of Soviet intentions to subvert the hemisphere.

Meanwhile in Nicaragua a sleazy band of former Guatemalan officers and men, along with foreign mercenaries and criminals were 'training'. Somoza, ever cooperative with CIA requests, provided the facilities for housing what one of the CIA officers called 'the flotsam and jetsam' assembled by agency recruiters. Nicaragua also served as a take-off and landing base for CIA aircraft that strafed, bombed and leafleted Guatemala.

The agency found its replacement for Arbenz in the person of Colonel Carlos Castillo Armas. His main virtue as leader of the counterrevolution and then president, according to the CIA man, was his 'willingness to obey orders without question'.

The CIA's multifaceted destabilization effort sowed confusion and division inside Guatemala. The military leaders could not figure out the situation. Who was bombing? Who was broadcasting? Arbenz lacked both the personal will and the institutional forces to mobilize the population to defend the fledgling reforms. On 18 June 1954 the CIA army of some one hundred and fifty men attacked from the south. A voluble radio propaganda effort and much posturing from US Embassy officials followed. Ambassador John E. Peurifoy, who was even more zealous than Patterson in his anti-communism, ordered giant speakers installed on the embassy roof, which then played super-loud martial music or beamed propaganda messages. Peurifoy, a former elevator operator in the US Senate, rose in the foreign service to become ambassador to Greece at the time the left was being violently ousted and the right-wing monarchy reinstated.

To Peurifoy's frustration, Castillo Armas's airforce, which had caused much confusion and some damage, was reduced to one plane. His troops, meeting even light resistance, refused to take the offensive. On the few occasions in which the CIA troops engaged Guatemalan forces the outcomes were indecisive. Meanwhile, 'Che' Guevara and a few other revolutionaries attempted frantically to induce Arbenz to organize and arm a popular opposition to the few hundred men in the rag-tag CIA army. But Arbenz appeared reluctant, even confused about what to do.

Eisenhower, receiving hourly reports on the invasion from the fanatical Ambassador Peurifoy, sent more aircraft to Castillo Armas. The CIA pilots bombed and strafed targets at will. One of the CIA cowboys sank a British freighter. He explained later that he mistook the Union Jack for a Hammer and Sickle. Arbenz, seeing his own army paralyzed by the sound and light show, finally agreed to form and arm a militia of peasants and workers. Groups of union members and peasants from several areas did gather and declare their willingness to fight the invaders. But they had neither weapons nor men with military experience to train and lead them.

The majority of the officer corps reacted with intense hostility to this attempt to create what they considered a rival military machine, and refused to offer any resistance to the invading army. Hearing this, Arbenz resigned, just ten days after the invasion, further undercutting any legitimacy the government had. Guevara and other revolutionaries desperately tried to set up resistance at factories and other labor centers. But it was too late! The moment for resistance had passed.

As CIA officials had scripted, Colonel Castillo Armas was flown into the capital on a US government plane. But even though no organized resistance impeded the agency's plan, spontaneous outbreaks of rebellion occurred. One took place at the Cadet School in Guatemala City, where the mercenary unit that was sent to take it over was confronted by armed opposition from the young officer candidates. The cadets forced the invading soldiers to surrender and made them parade, arms raised high, through the city streets. Finally, a combined CIA and army force negotiated their disarmament, but the rebellion signalled problems that would arise again with members of the officer corps.

Castillo Armas named himself president, while the agency bribed other high-ranking military officials to accept the CIA candidate as president. Before taking a plane to Mexico, Arbenz named a progressive army colonel to succeed him, thinking that some reforms could be salvaged under military rule. But Ambassador Peurifoy was ready for the occasion. Armed with a pair of .45 caliber automatics, he appeared at the colonel's residence and, hands on holstered guns, he intimidated the less-than-eager officer.

Peurifoy's wife later published her fractured verse commentary on the subject:

> Sing a song of quetzals, pockets full of peace,
> The junta's in the palace, they've taken out a lease
> The commies are in hiding, just across the street;
> To the embassy of Mexico, they beat a quick retreat.
> And pistol-packing Peurifoy looks mighty optimistic
> for the land of Guatemala is no longer Communistic.

The US government then denied any involvement in the plot. Dulles denounced the Kremlin for interfering in the American system, attacked Arbenz for allowing himself to be 'manipulated' by the communists, and congratulated the people of Guatemala for freeing themselves from the hold of subversion. Ambassador Peurifoy, still armed at official receptions, told a reporter that the operation had run basically on schedule, 'maybe forty minutes late'.

As many Latin Americans watched in horrified trauma at the apparent ease with which the CIA had overthrown a popular government, Castillo Armas began to consolidate his less-than-legitimate rule. The sounds of firing squads produced the bodies of hundreds, perhaps thousands of militant union and peasant leaders. He also declared that the expropriated land would be returned to UFCO and the oligarchy. In the process of dislodging them from United Fruit's quarter of a million acres, the army and police killed as many as 3,000 peasants.

Once Washington's hand-picked man sat in the presidency, the concern over Guatemala ebbed and a period of thirty-seven years of military dictatorship – with an occasional civilian façade – began. The price, as the Americans saw it, was the cost of mounting the destabilization effort and the supplying of economic aid thereafter. For Guatemalans over the decades the toll ran into the many hundreds of thousands of dead and the imposition on their society of a clique of military monsters who would contuinue to rule with the blessing of the oligarchy into the 1990s.

## CUBA AND THE FIRST GUATEMALAN GUERILLAS

Castillo Armas was murdered by rivals in 1957 and Colonel Ydigoras Fuentes became president in an electoral farce. The following incident illustrates the mentality of the mustachioed new president. Fuentes met Father Tom Melville, an American priest working in Guatemala. The latter begged the colonel to consider keeping some of the dispossessed peasants on parcels of land. Ydigoras told the father that no land would be made available to them because peasants had no 'capital, and did not know how to work the land'. Ironically, United Fruit left its acreage uncultivated. Ydigoras and his successors undid the education and health reforms initiated under Arevalo and Arbenz aimed at making the population literate and starting provision of minimum medical care.

In the countryside suffering, caused by the reversal of reforms, increased. No land, no protection, no semblance of hope for education, health care, or opportunity – that was the reality of rural life for the majority of Guatemalans in the late 1950s. President Ydigoras, proud and cavalier in manner, remained obedient if not subservient to his real master: the CIA. But Ydigoras's eagerness to please the CIA brought him into conflict with other sectors of the military.

On 13 November 1960, Captains Luis Augusto Turcios Lima, Marco Antonio Yon Sosa and some forty-five other officers, members of the Child Jesus Fraternity, a secret military club, organized a revolt to protest the corruption in the military and the Ydigoras government, whose officials had pocketed unprecedented amounts of public money. But the protest had an additional dimension, deriving from a perceived insult from President Ydigoras Fuentes. As news reports revealed that Guatemala was the site for training CIA-backed Cuban exiles, the officer corps took umbrage. They had not authorized the president to invite the CIA to train a force in secret to invade Cuba. (The actual launching base for the Bay of Pigs expedition was Puerto Cabezas, on the northeast coast of Nicaragua, which Somoza generously provided for the CIA.) This was an issue of Guatemalan sovereignty! Indeed, the arrogant Ydigoras had not bothered to consult them.

The majority of the conspiring officers withdrew at the last minute, but enough remained to capture the staff headquarters in Guatemala City and seize large quantities of weapons and supplies. The members of the uprising then moved to the Zacapa barracks, two provinces to the east, where hundreds of peasants met the rebels and asked to join the armed revolt. The officers procrastinated and debated. Meanwhile, those officers loyal to Ydigoras staged a counterattack and the rebel officers, fighting until their ammunition ran out, dispersed into exile in El Salvador and Honduras. Within a year some accepted the government's liberal amnesty terms.

For Yon Sosa, Turcios Lima and a handful of others, the insurrection became a step in a process of turning them into revolutionaries. The two men had undergone counterinsurgency training, Turcios at Fort Benning, Georgia, Yon Sosa at Fort Gulick, Panama. Yet the example of Cuba was more compelling than the lessons of their Yankee teachers.

For these young officers Fidel Castro was not just a revolutionary, but a patriotic military strategist, who in two years masterminded the defeat of Fulgencio Batista's 50,000 man army with no more than perhaps 2,000 guerrillas. The writings of the Guevara, whose frustrating experience during the CIA takeover of Guatemala inspired him to legendary achievements as Castro's lieutenant, began to ignite the fuse of guerrilla revolution throughout the continent. The Cuban revolutionaries had thrown down the gauntlet. Unlike Arbenz, Castro had mobilized the people to defend their reforms and their sovereignty. And, by mid-1960, the Soviet Union had offered major help to a Latin American revolution – with weapons and oil shipped to Cuba.

The Cuba Revolution also loomed large to the Central American oligarchy and the military loyal to them as the most urgent threat by example to their continued rule. The CIA planners, in turn, hoped to put out the revolutionary fire by using a variation of their tested Guatemala method to overthrow the Castro regime, which by 1961 had taken on a clearly socialist character. Castro and Che Guevara were determined not to repeat Arbenz's mistake, which would allow the *gringos* to erase the revolution without a fight. When the right-wing Cuban exiles landed at the Bay of Pigs in mid-April 1961, Castro's forces, poorly trained and ill-equipped, nevertheless defeated them in seventy-two hours.

These facts were not lost on men like Yon Sosa and Turcios Lima. They declared revolutionary war against their former service and the oligarchs protected by it. In late 1960 Turcios led a group of former officers and NCOs, student leaders, workers and peasants to the Sierra de las Minas in northeastern Guatemala and opened a guerrilla *foco* – the strategy of basing the guerrillas in remote and defensible areas from which they could choose the time and place to attack vulnerable enemy outposts, popularized by Fidel Castro and Che Guevara in the Sierra Maestra of Cuba. Shortly thereafter Yon Sosa and more men opened another small front and were joined by student leader Cesar Montes with additional recruits.

Conditions seemed ripe for a successful guerrilla war. Unlike the Sandinistas, the Guatemalan leaders were not only military men, but were trained in counterinsurgency warfare. They had completed their 180° political turnabout from being army officers whose mission was to protect the property of the oligarchy and the foreign companies to becoming leftist guerrillas intent on overthrowing the government and converting the vast private estates into public property. Few people trained as officers had the courage and character to take such a risk. For Yon Sosa and Turcios the choice to become revolutionaries meant: victory or death.

Between early 1961 and the end of 1962 the revolutionaries began to stage their attacks on police stations and remote army outposts and barracks. They set traps and ambushes, carried off weapons and demoralized the poorly trained and poorly paid troops. The Guatemalan army fell far short of the kind of professionalism that Somoza had fashioned in Nicaragua. Officers tended to work for politicians, who, in turn, either owned large property or represented one of the oligarchs.

The Americans wanted to change this antiquated system and remake the Guatemalan force into an efficient instrument of repression, like the one in Nicaragua. As Yon Sosa and Turcios Lima realized, even before they led the military revolt against Ydigoras, the Guatemalan armed forces had nothing to do with defending the nation. Their only task was defense of the oligarchy and the foreign corporations.

As Americans instructed their new students in the basics of modern army routine, the guerrillas in the eastern mountains were trying to organize the peasantry as part of their revolutionary war strategy. The guerrilla patrol would avoid the army's better equipped and larger search units by using volunteer peasant spies and guides, who could track animals or people in the mountainous forests. Having established that the army was long gone from a village, the tattered warriors would enter the village and assemble the peasants.

'You have noticed that we have weapons,' Evaristo Aldana, the MR 13 (Movimiento Revolucionario named after the 13 November 1960 military uprising) patrol leader began his speech,

We have them so that we can struggle against the government and the landowners; against the capitalists that live off the toil of workers and peasants; and against the army that defends them and represses you. We are fighting for the land, so that each peasant shall have the land he tills.

Like guerrillas throughout Latin America in the early and mid-1960s, the Guatemalan revolutionaries were filled with optimism, thinking that the Cuban formula could be successfully implemented elsewhere – and especially under the conditions of gross racial and class exploitation that existed in Guatemala.

One of the factors the guerrillas undervalued in their optimism was the determination of the national security team in Washington to prevent any more 'Cubas' in the hemisphere. Another unanticipated obstacle to the success of the guerrillas was the opposition to armed struggle within the left, especially that of the Moscow-linked communist parties.

Men like Turcios Lima were ill prepared for the ideological wrangling between Trotskyists, Castroists and Moscow-linked communists. The communist line was that the Indian population was hopelessly backward and could not understand the revolutionary imperative. Other revolutionaries believed that organizing the indigenous population was the key to revolutionary victory. Turcios saw himself as a warrior for justice, but hardly an ideologue who could hold his own in debate with men who tossed around revolutionary phrases about immediate socialist insurrection, prolonged peasant wars and broad class coalitions that included national and petites bourgeoisies.

Turcios was a practical soldier, who knew how to elaborate a battle plan, establish a defense perimeter, train the men under him and keep their loyalty. Turcios had chosen the dry hills of the Sierra de las Minas as the ideal place for his battle scenario. His criteria did not take into account the ethnic makeup of the local population, which was predominantly *ladino* (people of mixed Spanish and Indian ancestry, or those who have abandoned Mayan symbols and religion). He ignored the ideological discussions and instead ordered his men to build well-concealed bases from which to ambush patrols and attack vulnerable army and police outposts. The political hair-splitting of the revolutionary ideologues confused Turcios. He did not know how to write a tract that combined military strategy with a political program. So he did what he knew best: he fought.

The dramatic successes of the guerrillas from 1963 to 1966 tended to overshadow their inability to formulate clear goals that coincided with strategy; nor did the military successes dampen the dogma being spewed forth by the various sects that vied for leadership. The men in Washington were not idle during this period; they had developed both a political and a military plan to coincide with the much heralded Alliance for Progress.

## MENDEZ MONTENEGRO AND THE 1966 ELECTION

Cooperating with Guatemalan military officials, some of whom were on CIA payroll, the Americans convinced the officer corps temporarily to set aside its lust for coups and direct military rule and allow for a relatively free election in 1966. The front running candidate, Julio Cesar Mendez Montenegro, a civilian lawyer turned politician, pledged reform and democracy. He held out the olive branch to the armed revolutionaries, offering a generous amnesty backed by his personal word. What Mendez Montenegro did not say was that the military clique had assented to the civilian presidency on the understanding that anti-guerrilla command be exclusively centered with the generals. In other words, the top brass allowed the civilian president to say anything he wanted to placate local and foreign public opinion, while the army pursued its own brutal war strategy.

The aura of normalcy, democracy and the semblance of civilian government lasted a few months, long enough to confuse some of the guerrillas and their supporters who believed that political space existed in which to operate. By 1967 they had seen the error of their ways as a counterinsurgency campaign began that virtually destroyed the guerrillas – and much of the civilian population that supported them.

The military showed little respect for Catholic priests and nuns who were operating in the guerrilla zones. Members of the Mary Knoll order, suspected of cooperating with the 'subversives', were expelled from Guatemala. The generals did not even ask Mendez Montenegro's permission. Fortunately for the guerrillas, not all of the newly radicalized priests were identified or expelled. Ultimately, guerrilla recruits did come from some of those remote Indian villages, where the revolutionary clergy worked at building consciousness.

US concern focused on the less-than-professional quality of the Guatemalan military. The Pentagon dispatched trainers and advisers and, by the late 1960s, working hand in glove with US Green Berets, the Guatemalan armed forces began to prove that they now possessed a killer elan – a will – that they had lacked in the humiliating days of Arbenz and Ydigoras Fuentes. The air force bombed guerrilla enclaves and dropped napalm on villages thought to harbor the revolutionaries; the ground forces began patrols that literally sought out any form of human life in a suspected guerrilla area and destroyed it.

Turcios Lima was unable to use his military acumen against the counterinsurgency. He died on 2 October 1966 in a most incongruous accident, when the sports car he was driving crashed and exploded. Turcios was the most feared of the guerrilla leaders and perhaps the least likely to have supported the reformist and electoral road encouraged by Mendez Montenegro. Without his presence the squabbling between groups increased, allowing for the counterattack to hurt badly.

Yon Sosa managed to evade the hunting patrols and in late 1969 turned himself into a Mexican military post. Thinking that the Mexican officers to whom he surrendered possessed the same code of honor he had learned and respected since attending military academy proved to be a fatal mistake. The Guatemalan generals, upon learning of Yon Sosa's successful evasion of their dragnet, offered large bribes to the Mexican officials. In early 1970 Yon Sosa and a few of the other remaining guerrillas were murdered in Mexican territory.

By 1969 the once proud and successful guerrilla movement of Guatemala was effectively reduced to a handful of ragged troops, desperately seeking refuge in the mountains. As many as 15,000 civilians were killed; scores of villages lay destroyed as testimony to the rebuilt spirit of the new Guatemalan army and air force. Under Mendez Montenegro Guatemalans also witnessed the emergence of death squads, a new phenomenon in Latin America.

Working with allies in the military and the police, Mano Blanco, as the killers called their organization, systematically assassinated labor leaders, radical professors, students and other 'traitors to the homeland'. Blaming the president for secretly allying himself with the guerrillas and their student supporters and criticizing the army for not being sufficiently diligent in dealing with the subversives, Mano Blanco began to terrorize the entire political sector of Guatemala from Christian Democrat to the left. Individuals suspected of harboring 'communist ideas' or engaging in 'subversive activities' would receive an announcement on their door: a white hand inside a red circle. Within a short period armed men in civilian clothes would arrive at the home of the accused and kidnap him. Inevitably, the mutilated, often tortured corpse of the victim would be found.

Before long, however, the fine line between ideological anti-communism and straight criminality eroded, and Mano Blanco members began to kidnap people whose families could pay ransom. When some of the band kidnapped the archbishop of Guatemala, in 1968, unsuccessfully trying to pin the crime on the left, the generals put their foot down and forced the Mano Blanco leaders, all military officers, into exile. The other members of the band fled or were shot.

Under the fig leaf of a civilian president, the formal counterinsurgency and the informal death squads had combined to defeat the revolutionaries. Except for a few surviving guerrillas hiding in mountains and jungles, the advocates of armed insurgency were either dead or in exile. Having celebrated its victory, the military disposed of the civilian façade and installed as president the man who had led the anti-guerrilla campaign in the late 1960s. General Carlos Arana Osorio, alias the 'Butcher of Zacapa', brought with him a new style of government. No longer would the generals rule to protect the property of the wealthy, but would carve out their own piece of the pie as well, insinuating themselves into the Guatemalan economy – as partners, or indeed *primus inter pares* with the old aristocracy.

Beginning with the civilian Mendez Montenegro regime in 1966, the army started to assume the role of the central agency of governance, while the civilian politicians of the right and the center right argued about how much political space to allow, and which kinds of reforms to adopt as a way of appealing to the poor and thereby undercutting the lure of revolution. For their part, the military had no interest in reform; with the death of Turcios and Yon Sosa, the rebel officer tradition was decisively ended, and the Guatemalan army was freed from insurrectionist tendencies in its own officer corps.

There were no Indians inside the military clique that ran the country. Yet, the indigenous population is the crucial element in Guatemalan life – for they comprise not only the majority but also the labor force and, as such, the sector that was assumed to be revolutionary, at least nascently so. The army's method was to eliminate not only the guerrillas, but also those Indians who might become guerrillas. The era of bloodshed was just beginning.

General Arana attacked the reformism of Mendez and expounded the virtue discipline instead. After his election, the death squads no longer sought camouflage; they were official agents of the government, not rogue elephants. Those who led them were publicly promoted and appointed to government posts. The army, Arana announced, was the only worthy institution in the country, and it alone would decide what kind of changes were needed and when.

What he devised was a form of colonization within Guatemala itself. The military intellectuals and their US counterparts began to construct a theory of how to combine repression with at least the appearance of social change, while ever enhancing the authority and legitimacy of the army itself.

Poverty and landlessness were the obvious issues, so they tackled them by offering government subsidies in both areas. The program called for the relocation of peasant families from overpopulated areas to non-populated areas. These so-called development poles, a version of the stategic hamlet idea in Vietnam, would relieve the political pressure on the one hand and allow the large estate owners to breathe easily on the other, since the new lands were those owned by the government and were located in remote and often barely arable sectors.

The army also offered a Salvation Army type operation whereby the very poor could find meager supplies of food and clothing at army outlet centers. Occasionally, an army doctor would come to a clinic and treat a few of the diseased poor. This program, as it developed over the decade, was declared to be a major reform, one by which the army was meeting the people's needs. In fact, the army was attempting to become the only institution in the country, one that provided for everything – to the extent that anything was provided. The peasants would see the two hands of the army, one holding the whip, the other the carrot. If the peasant refused the carrot, the army officers assured him he would receive the deadly whip.

In practice, of course, the program quickly fell into the hands of the corrupt, who usurped the lands for themselves and stole the food and other material intended for the poor. One piece of land on the Mexican border became known as 'The Generals' Zone', because they had not only seized the land under the law designed for the poor, but had used state funds to develop their 'investments'. The generals found willing partners in already established land barons and American companies who were anxious to reap profits from a situation in which they had an endless supply of cheap and docile labor and no taxes to pay.

And as if God had rewarded the bloodthirsty generals and the arrogant oligarchy, oil was discovered in Guatemala in 1970. The ruling cliques assumed that the Americans and the British would immediately finance the construction of refineries. But in the early 1970s money-laden entrepreneurs did not rush into Guatemala to refine the newly discovered 'black gold'.

## The 1970s

The discovery of oil only gave the Guatemalan generals one more reason to gloat. They ruled the country by force and secured the blessings of the Nixon administration, whose foreign policy officials appeared unconcerned about human rights violations. Military officers administered the newly oil-rich economy that was once the exclusive domain of the oligarchy and foreign companies. No longer were generals and colonels confined to the role of protecting the property of wealthy Guatemalans; by the late 1960s the military elite owned choice real estate, export agriculture, finance and even industry. The military exacted a sweet percentage for 'insuring' the oligarchy's property.

The guerrillas, the military elite announced, were permanently defeated. Should the ugly head of subversion raise itself anew, the generals declared, the army had shown its ability to deal with it ruthlessly. This was true. Indeed, the guerrilla leaders had underestimated the bestial capabilities of the armed forces and had allowed their modest military successes to overshadow the reality of their struggle. So the revolutionaries were unprepared when the government forces and US advisers delivered their lightning counter blows.

The remnants of the devastated guerrilla forces and their urban supporters, who had been forced to flee during the counterinsurgency or meet certain death, began to regroup in Mexico. From exile or remote mountain camps, the guerrilla leaders examined their mistakes, while fighting off the plagues of life in harsh conditions. Dysentery, respiratory ailments and scores of illnesses beset them; yet, as evidence of their dedication, they continued carefully to map out plans for a resurgence, while intermittently vomiting or suffering bouts of malarial fever. No longer would revolutionaries apply simplistic Marxist formulas to the task of winning state power through armed struggle. The *foco* had been a military strategy, not one that allowed a nation of different Indian groupings to be organized systematically. When villagers responded to the pleas of the guerrillas for support they were attacked mercilessly by the army, against whom they were defenseless. By attempting to apply Che Guevara's Cuban guerrilla war model to their country, the guerrillas failed to address the racial and ethnic complexities of Guatemala.

In the revised guerrilla strategy, the Indian population, previously ignored or dismissed as culturally backward, took on heightened importance. The Indians comprised the majority of the peasant and working class; they also were seen as key to a Guatemalan nationalism that was anti-colonial in its essence.

Instead of the *ladino*-dominated northeastern mountains of Izabel, the new guerrilla contingent chose the northwest jungles of El Quiche to launch the second round of insurgency. Blending revolutionary Marxism and Castroism with liberation theology and new forms of Indian race consciousness, the sixteen members of the Edgar Ibarra column agreed that the time had come to reignite the armed revolutionary struggle. This group formed the core of what became known as the Guerrilla Army of the Poor (EGP).

## THE GUERRILLA ARMY OF THE POOR

Secretly, they entered the northern border of Guatemala, across the Ixcan River from Mexico, on 19 January 1972. The guerrillas stormed the remote northern landing field, destroying two private planes whose owners had collaborated in the murder of Yon Sosa and disarming the few state employees at the strip. The group commandeered several motor boats, purchased supplies and set off down the Lacantun River; its members headed south with supplies and only a vague notion of the location of several villages marked on the map. The Guatemalan and Mexican armies both sent out patrols to search for the guerrillas, and choppers whirred overhead from dawn to dusk looking for plumes of smoke or some sign of the band's location.

To illustrate the arduous nature of guerrilla life Mario Payeras, one of the EGP leaders, wrote that the guerrillas dreamed about food. Tragi-comic incidents arose around the subject. One morning one of the *companeros* was reprimanded for licking the empty sugar sack instead of soaking it with water for making the morning coffee. The limited food supply imposed upon the small band 'disipline and rational planning'. The guerrillas used a hand grinder to make corn meal, reducing the amount they had to carry and the time it took to cook the corn. A few were hunters and 'except for the feathers, claws, and some of the cartilage, the entire animal was cooked and shared equally – including the bones'.

The guerrillas' column was made up of members of various Indian groups, former student revolutionaries, workers and ladino peasants. People from all parts of Guatemala marched daily through the jungle, sharing the discomforts and the natural beauties of the wild. After a month of existing on a few hundred calories a day they killed some deer and wild turkeys.

Hunger, admitted Payeras, had replaced revolution as the foremost thought on their minds, and they began to eat whatever raw food they could find, which, in turn, caused them to be racked with diarrhoea and cramps. The bone-thin, ragged column, pale from absence of sunlight in the jungle, reeking of thirty days of sweat that drenched their clothes, finally reached a village in the northern section of Ixcan, in the province of El Quiche.

Their first encounter with the peasants revived the guerrillas' zeal for their mission. The intense poverty of the hamlet was typical. The villagers possessed one radio, on which they had heard about the attack by the guerrilla band at the border. The peasants appeared eager to share their meager food supply with the men. But other villagers were less friendly and the Indians in the guerrilla troop did not know the dialects of the locals. In two years of life in the jungle, however, the guerrillas became experts in communicating with people of remote indigenous communities and on survival, part of which was avoiding the military patrols that tracked them.

Not everyone could endure the rigors of the mobile warrior's life in the steaming and perilous jungle. One guerrilla could no longer bear the daily grind and, using a wound in his foot as a good pretext, returned to his previous life as a store clerk. Another, Minche, an Indian who had served in the Guatemalan military, became paranoid. After painful discussions, the guerrilla leaders decided that he had to be executed, lest the future of the entire campaign become imperiled. The killing of Minche cast a pall on the small column, but gradually their relations with villagers improved. For two years the bearded, no longer emaciated rebel soldiers merged with the local population, although they gained only one recruit to their ranks.

In the cities students, veterans of the Arbenz era, labor leaders and professionals began to surface, defying the death squads and the formal repressive agencies controlled by the military. It did not take a genius to note that the fruits of the economic boom predicated on the country's positive growth statistics were not trickling downward to the majority. And people were angry – about the same old themes, the expropriation of the nation's wealth by the filthy rich and the repression by the military caste.

The 1974 election was a classic case of fraud and corruption. Two generals vied for the presidency. Arana's clique backed Kjell Langerud, a brute and a thief, against General Efrain Rios Montt, an evangelical Christian who spoke about reform and God in a strange syntax. Rios Montt clearly gleaned a majority of the diminished voting population, but the election was stolen from him. Criminality had become so institutionalized that the struggles over wealth and power were between factions of the same gang or rival military-led gangs.

The propertied classes were forced to ally directly or indirectly with the military factions just so that their wealth would have some protection. Those who tired of the gang warfare, in which rival death squads raided each other's lairs, were themselves subjected to the law of the death squad. Christian Democratic politicans who dared protest were gunned down, along with the suspected leftists, unearthed through the vast web of surveillance that blanketed urban Guatemala.

Between 1970 and 1975 the Committee for the Relatives of the Disappeared Persons calculated that more than fifteenth thousand Guatemalans vanished. That fact alone was sufficient to provide a chilling effect on all but the staunchest of political activists. During this period the United States maintained a steady level of military assistance to the repressive forces. People whose names had once been associated with even the mildest reform either disappeared or became mute, so terrorized was the populace.

## THE SENGARY IXCAN

In 1975 the tiny guerrilla band's shot rang throughout Guatemala if not through most of Latin America. The band's whereabouts had been unknown by the army and everyone else, except for a few contacts in Guatemala City and Mexico. Like their counterparts in the mountains of Cuba in the late 1950s, or those in Nicaraguan and El Salvador in later decades, they learned about military life the hard way. There was the guerrilla, the people, and the enemy – the nomenclature for all those who sided with the government, or wore its military uniform.

Luis Arenas Barrera was an old-fashioned villain, out of central casting. Rewarded for his role in the overthrow of the Arbenz government with a tract of land in Ixcan Province, Arenas came to epitomize the cruelty of the landed elite. He recruited Indian labor from the highlands to clear the jungle so that he could begin to farm and build a home – more like a fortified mansion when it was completed. With government help, including the use of military helicopters, he brought in the labor, exploited them to the nth degree, and even cheated them out of their wages. Because of the inhospitable jungle that surrounded his estate the Indians could not easily escape.

Arenas hired thugs to protect him and keep his labor force intimidated. He even built stocks for the 'unruly and rebellious' ones. He reduced those who lived near him to peonage by advancing them money on their coffee crops and then extracting usurious rates when time came to pay him back. Often he took his pay in coffee beans and mules on whose backs the crop was carried, guided by his gunmen through jungle paths to market.

Arenas earned the title 'Jaguar of Ixcan'. The vicious feline was the scourge of Ixcan, allegedly embodying the evil jungle spirit. It can supposedly grab several dogs in its jaws and leap over fences with them hanging from its mouth. Those who have come close to it swear that the fiersome jaws of the animal carry the stench of rotting meat. The peasants hated Arenas and feared him as they did the symbolic jaguar.

On 7 July 1975 a troop of guerrillas, dressed as laborers, entered Arenas's estate on pay day and lined up with the rest of the workers to receive the carefully counted money. Arenas himself oversaw the payment. Mario Payeras was with the guerrilla group. 'Looking like a bird of prey, the lord of the land was counting his coins and unfolding some crumpled bills.' Arenas reached for his gun when he noticed the strange men amidst the laborers, but the guerrillas fired, just as he cleared his revolver from his holster. The guerrillas explained to the startled onlookers the reasons for executing 'this enemy of the poor'. Before long, members of the crowd chimed in with the equivalents of 'Amen'. They watched in awe as the guerrillas made a ritual of scattering the payroll money onto the floor of the manager's office. Because they were not thieves, and because the warriors spoke the native dialect, they built the foundation of their reputation in the area.

The locals were grateful that the Jaguar of Ixcan was dead, but they had hardly finished celebrating his demise when the helicopters arrived, filled with troops trained in jungle combat to interrogate the villagers and comb the jungles for the 'subversives'. The guerrillas retreated to a point beyond the scope of the army. Within a few years other guerrilla groups sprang up in different parts of the country, also claiming the same heritage. Eventually, they cooperated. But the ideological infighting of the left prevented an early union of the revolutionary forces.

After the Jaguar's death, the anticipated military response took its toll – but not on the guerrillas. The military targeted the people whom it could find, rather than the elusive guerrilla units. Patrols entered the villages, routinely questioned the village elders, or went to the homes that informers had signaled to be those of guerrilla sympathizers to torture and murder. Some peasants were beaten to death others were dropped out of helicopters. But the army did not locate the EGP.

The revolutionaries continued to mount their offensive. They also took villages that had no or little defense, executed those identified as government agents and then engaged in 'armed propaganda'. The guerrillas would gather the villagers in the town center, explain to them the reasons for armed warfare against the government and then suggest measures for local self-defense against the army patrols. Unlike the behavior of the military units, the guerrillas treated the inhabitants respectfully, paying for all supplies and using only courteous forms of address in their dialogue. Recruiting began slowly, but by the end of the 1970s hundreds of Indian youth had swelled the ranks of the guerrilla army.

## COUNTERINSURGENCY

The impenetrable refuge that the first unit discovered in the thick jungle was no longer so safe by 1975. Counterinsurgency units, coached by Americans with years of Vietnam War experience, slashed their way through the thick growth. Sometimes helicopters hovered above the trees, men with binoculars peering down for traces of guerrilla movement. Other times, silent patrols tracked the guerrillas, each side stepping on poisonous snakes and risking fatal bites by malaria-carrying mosquitoes and other insects in the dense subtropical forest. When commanders grew frustrated they used another American Vietnam tactic: planes dropped napalm bombs over jungle areas.

The guerrilla leaders were united by a shared understanding of the political world. Despite differences in theory and tactics, they saw themselves as agents of history. Rigoberta Menchu, an Indian woman who became an articulate international advocate of the Guatemalan revolution talked of the need to realize the destiny of the indigenous people and of her own life's mission to redirect Guatemalan history toward its proper democratic and egalitarian course. The army, although paid and forced to obey orders, nevertheless had gained ground by the mid-1970s, thanks in part to the tutelage of US Special Forces personnel, who instructed them in how to become a team of mutually re-enforcing parts. It worked. The jungle units tracked the revolutionaries mercilessly, and although the guerrillas achieved the upper hand in the few combats that took place, they were soon deprived of the food and lodging that they had become accustomed to in late 1974 and early 1975.

During that period the revolutionaries built their reputation and lost few members in combat. The villages that had supported or were thought to support the EGP suffered heavy casualties. The guerrillas' answer to the vengeance exacted by the military was to establish village defenses. With a few weapons, the guerrillas contended, some villagers could stage ambushes while the others escaped to safety. But until these ideas were tested the guerrillas found themselves encumbered by ever larger numbers of refugees, whose only safety was in the protection of the small armed bands that roamed the northern provinces' least populated region. By August 1976, the army units began to withdraw from the regions where the guerrillas had gained the upper hand. The revolutionaries assessed their three years of survival in the jungle: they concluded with cautious optimism that the struggle was going forward.

One of the reasons for the revolutionaries' sense of progress was the inability of the military to widen its own political horizons. The passage of power in Guatemala City went from one murderous military clique to another, each represented by a general. In 1975 the military's sense of security in its own bailiwick was challenged, when two guerrillas disguised as shoemakers shot two officers known for taking special delight in torturing 'subversives'.

Such 'successes', however, did not alter the balance of real power. The spirit and combativeness of the rebels outweighed their abilities to achieve the desired changes. They engaged in lengthy and often dogma-laden debates and discussions about how to destroy the old and corrupt order and institute a new one, while maintaining collective leadership and egalitarianism of goods amongst themselves. The counterinsurgency, however, which possessed none of the revolutionaries' virtues or intellectual sophistication, did not become bogged down in ideological hairsplitting. Their goal was well defined: to destroy the oppostion. And they were amply supplied to achieve that end.

US and Israeli specialists taught new methods of scientific repression as well as the old-fashioned basics of rooting out guerrillas, skills they had acquired in counterinsurgency campaigns in Asia, Algeria and the Middle East. Israelis introduced computers in Guatemala City to 'test' for subversives. By reading the electric and water meters in several neighborhoods and registering houses whose consumption was significantly greater than the rest, the Israelis demonstrated to their Central American counterparts how to isolate the urban havens used by revolutionaries to hide from the police.

The revolutionaries, for example, needed electric mimeograph machines, which used more current than the homes of their neighbors. Also, groups of guerrillas frequented the few 'safe houses' to eat, rest and take showers, and these would logically use more water than 'normal households' for cooking, drinking and bathing. By analyzing the computerized data, the repressive authorities were able to select likely guerrilla targets for raids. Some of the homes belonged to citizens who had nothing to do with guerrillas or politics, but in Guatemala the police were little concerned with such 'mistakes'. The military's hold on power was based almost exclusively on their willingness to use violence. After killing thousands of peasants, whom they considered potential or actual subversives, they hardly cared about a few additional dead bodies.

The fishing expeditions paid off. Some important leaders and middle-level cadres were captured. Some resisted torture and died before talking; others could not hold out. The revolutionaries, in turn, believed that informers in their midst had tipped off the police. They developed tighter security, making their operations more cumbersome.

As scientific repression destroyed the underground organization, the revolutionaries revived open political activities. Despite the terrible consequences that resulted from holding public meetings or protests not sponsored by the ruling clique, Guatemalans, nevertheless, found the courage to begin to protest against the immediate conditions of their lives. Strikes broke out in the capital and other cities as workers reacted to the inflation that followed the discovery of oil in the early 1970s. Wages did not rise along with prices.

## Earthquake

Public-sector workers and even teachers had staged demonstrations in 1973 and 1974. Organizers, who had been quiet, re-emerged to lead protests against actions by the government that caused popular indignation. In late 1973 demonstrations took place to protest against increased public transportation costs. In the spring of 1973 fighting broke out in rural sectors between landless peasants and the government supporters who had usurped the land. None of these activities appeared to have direct links to the guerrilla war that was occurring simultaneously.

The government saw all opposition as part of one coordinated plan of subversion, emanating from Moscow and Havana. So, when Coca Cola bottling plant workers striked in 1975, the manager, an American right-winger who was a personal friend of the leading generals, assumed the strike was part of a larger communist conspiracy. He locked the workers out, ostensibly because they had formed an independent union. He then telephoned a friend at the Defense Ministry for help, and for the next two years death squads murdered union organizers, or forced others to flee the country. Some union members had their throats cut;

others suffered the removal of their tongues before they died. Yet, the workers maintained the strike for more than a year, while solidarity groups abroad championed their cause and made the Coca Cola strike into an internationally embarrassing incident by focusing international attention on the human rights abuses permitted or abetted by the Guatemalan government.

In 1976, compounding the difficulties of the poor, an earthquake that measured 7.5 on the Richter scale devastated the nation. The homes of the rich were well built and most of them had enough foundation support to withstand the shocks. The vast majority of the 25,000 who perished were rural poor. Over one million people were left homeless. Migration to Guatemala City by the scores of thousands began, to make an already squalid situation even worse. By 1977 there were more than three hundred thousand homeless that cluttered the outskirts of the capital.

The Guatemalan rulers, like Somoza in Nicaragua when the quake hit there in 1972, began to steal the relief money that poured in from abroad. Much of these funds never reached those who needed them. To dramatize the callousness shown by the rich toward the real victims of the quake, sick jokes abounded in elite society circles. One wit who frequented the fancy bars even invented the 'Earthquake Cocktail', guaranteed to 'shake you up'. This 'humor' reflected the feelings of the upper classes for the plight of the desperate Indian population.

By 1975, according to UN sources, the rich had grown considerably richer. Whereas in 1950 the wealthiest 5 per cent received 48 per cent of the total wealth of the nation, twenty-five years later this had increased to almost 60 per cent. The poorest 50 per cent of the country took 9 per cent of the income in 1950; by 1977 they received only 7 per cent. The number of poor had grown by over a million during that period.

Curable diseases, like gastroenteritis, bacterial infections, other poverty-related diseases and malnutrition were as well as responsible for 42 per cent of deaths in Guatemala. Even if they could afford a doctor, those in the rural sector had no medical facilities. In 1960 Guatemala had one doctor for each 4,644 inhabitants; by 1975 there was one physician for every 9,000 people. In 1976 over 60 per cent of Guatemalans were illiterate, yet between 1970 and 1980 the government reduced the education allocation from 16 per cent to under 9 per cent of the budget. The figures indicate more than inequitable distribution of the national treasury: in the eyes of the elite the poor of Guatemala had passed beyond the point of revitalization.

The natural disaster, combined with the government cutbacks of all supports for the poor and increases of prices for staples – including transportation – squeezed the populace to the point of desperation. They responded anew to the appeals of radical organizers, especially from the religious community. Priests and nuns helped organize the poor shanty-town residents to address the injustice of their situation and to begin to make demands on the authorities. More significantly, the organizers built alliances between the homeless and the working class.

One dramatic illustration of this cross-class alliance occurred when Ixtahuacan miners went on strike in late 1977. Their strategy moved beyond traditional picketing and into organizing on a national level. Columns of miners marched through towns and villages, soliciting support and solidarity from peasant and urban poor. As always, the generals reacted to political activity in their predictable fashion. By the end of 1977 political arrests and murders totalled well over a thousand. Among the death squad victims were some of Guatemala's best known lawyers, educators and politicians. Even though people from the humanitarian community of the world were watching, the government escalated the campaign of violence against all opposition without any sense of shame.

Revolutionary organizers went underground and from there continued to foment strikes and protests. By early 1978, in the capital, with the help of the militant religious community and the older radicals, some of whom resurfaced after years of hiding, some two hundred thousand people defied the terror apparatus and rallied to the miners' cause.

The military rulers, with the support of the wealthy sectors, reactivated the death squads, whose members began systematically to murder the organizers of the strikes and rallies, with the idea of cutting the leadership off from the newly formed mass organizations. In February 1978, a full-fledged riot exploded in Guatemala City – a direct confrontation with the power of the state. The military fired into the crowds, kidnapped selected individuals and assassinated those suspected of holding leadership positions.

By 1978 government politics meant terror and intimidation. Just as transference of power was done through *coup d'état* or through institutionalized agreement inside the military, so too did government politics descend to the theatrical level of French playwrite Alfred Jarry's King Ubu, the military man who becomes king and after eliminating all his opponents steals the nation's wealth. Even a decision on who should run in elections had to be cleared with the high command. In short, the citizens of Guatemala were effectively disconnected from all decisions made in their name by ruling officials – elected or appointed.

In 1978 the voters sent a clear message to the government. Two thirds of the eligible electorate abstained. Of those who did vote some purposely damaged their ballots; so, when the vote was counted no more than 15 per cent of Guatemalans had elected the new president, General Romeo Lucas Garcia, Langerud's defense minister and a man thought of even by his closest friends as a fiendish murderer.

When the alliance between the business and military elite was cemented in 1970, it meant that repression would be the everpresent instrument to thwart the masses. Middle-class or professional political groupings were either outlawed or so restricted that no meaningful civilian politics could develop; or, when a strong candidate appeared, like Vinicio Cerezo in the mid-1980s, he soon realized that the military had circumscribed political space to a negligible area.

The wars that commenced with the overthrow of Arbenz and led to the building of a self-conscious military continued unabated throughout the 1970s and 1980s because other than revolution there was no possibility for political expression. The very premise behind the Guatemalan military and their advisers from the Pentagon was the existence of permanent revolution. The military was the permanent counter-revolution. It protected Guatemalan property, US property and the supposed security interests of Washington as well.

Until Jimmy Carter's presidency, the Americans attempted to control the extent of the publicity of terror against the population, not the terror itself. In addition, American advisers tried to quash the violent bickering inside the officer corps. From the US vantage, Guatemala was important because revolution, if successful, could lead to another Cuba. And the aim of US policy throughout Latin America was to contain the Cuban Revolution. The insurgencies in Central America had to be destroyed, without the use of US troops on Latin American soil. Thus, the tactics of the Guatemalan military, ranging from the periodic use of death squads to the genocidal massacres of Indian villagers, all fell into the category of what was acceptable – in national security circles.

US military advisers constructed the Guatemalan army that roved the mountains of the north in the 1970s in search of guerillas. The Americans provided the guidance, if not the actual blueprints, for all the repression that was carried out in the country from the 1960s on. Until Carter took office in 1977, the Guatemalans and their Pentagon advisers had developed a perfect symbiosis. The Pentagon helped the Guatemalans to accomplish what both wanted done: destruction of the left and their source of recruitment, the Indian population.

Carter's human rights emphasis brought about a change of rhetoric from the government. Lucas called for a national dialogue as the hitmen were assassinating the very people with whom the conversation should have been held. In early 1979 the goon squads murdered Alberto Fuentes Mohr and Manuel Colom Argueta, two politicians who had advocated mild reforms and planned to run in the 1982 presidential elections.

Even before the election of Ronald Reagan in November 1980, the killers slew more than a hundred center political leaders; hundreds exiled themselves, but moved politically further toward coalition politics. Anti-military rule, anti-repression became the call of all the civilized people.

By 1979 there were three guerrilla bands operating in the northern sectors and the level of violence continued to escalate. A US army document reported that the guerrillas were thought to have the support of 60 per cent or more of the northern Ixil Indians. The number of armed revolutionaries throughout the country was estimated to be as high as 8,000. Intelligence officials in the United States concluded that as many as half a million Guatemalans belonged to some support network that offered vital collaboration to the rebel fighters. Almost all of the activity continued to take place in the northern highlands.

## The 1980s

By February 1982 the EGP linked its organization with those of the Organization of People in Arms (ORPA), the Rebel Armed Force (FAR) and the Guatemalan Workers Party (PGT) to form the Guatemalan National Revolutionary Unity (URNG.) The different groups brought with them varied military and political experiences. ORPA sprang up in 1979 as a guerrilla front. Its members, mostly splitting off from the rebel armed forces group, had fashioned a clandestine organization in 1971, until they had sufficient coherence to become public in the Indian areas of the southern highlands.

Throughout the northwest, center and southwestern parts of the country the guerrilla fronts began to attack the government forces and recruit people to their cause. In the north the Ho Chi Minh, Che Guevara and Yon Sosa fronts, in the center the Augusto Cesar Sandino and Otto Rene Castillo, in the south the Turcios Lima brigades declared themselves the foundation for overthrowing the old and instituting the new order. Before agreeing to unite under one military command, the leaders of the revolutionary factions debated the fine points of Marxist–Leninist–Castroist theory and dogma. Should the workers or peasants lead the revolution? Should the center of struggle be in cities or countryside? How to understand the Indian question inside the larger national question? How to think about the Cuban model of insurrection and revolution? And, while having these prolonged discussions of theory, strategy and tactics, always carefully covering their movements lest the police discover them.

By the mid-1970s the talking for most of the revolutionaries turned into action. From the fifteen-man column that executed the Jaguar, the northern-based guerrillas grew into a military unit that carried out ambushes, sabotaged provincial highways and cut communication links, which caused the army difficulties in sending reinforcements. In Guatemala City guerrilla units hit the headquarters of the Detective Squad, notorious for its savagery against suspected subversives, two police stations and the Air Force Command Center.

In the south the revolutionaries targeted large land owners known for their right-wing activities, destroying tractors and other pieces of machinery or burning crops about to be exported. After such attacks the guerrillas entered the surrounding villages and explained to the local Indian peasants and farm workers in their own language the nature of the revolutionary cause. In so doing they also demonstrated they could fight the government and the large estate owners and live to boast about it. The local populace, exploited to the core, tended to be sympathetic albeit frightened by the guerrilla methods. Teenagers proved ripe for recruitment because their seething indignation over the daily dose of injustice had primed them to absorb the guerrilla message.

The revolutionaries, however, were careful about bringing members into their units, because hating the oppressor was not sufficient basis to make a young man or woman into an effective guerrilla warrior. They chose those who could articulate not only the nature of their subjugation and the enmity they felt toward land owners, army officers and the major-domos who whipped them and cheated them out of their rightful wages, but could understand that all of this was part of a social and economic system, not just the evil of a few individuals.

One such man, whose *nom de guerre* was Simon Tic, was a plantation worker who, before joining the revolution, had received some education and could speak Spanish. He described how he began informally to organize other migrant field workers. 'I am an Indio, a legitimate Guatemalan. My ancestors were born here. My ancestors could not speak Spanish, but I have learned to distinguish....' Simon described the conditions on one estate, where the foreman felt free to demand that he and two others clean more than an acre of coffee land (several days' work) for one day's wage. He talked the others into staging the equivalent of a sitdown strike to protest the injustice. When the time for reckoning came Simon alone confronted the angry foreman, who screamed at him, threateningly:

'Boy, why did you quit work?'

'I am not an animal and will not be treated like one,' Simon replied.

He was willing to take the consequences, which on that occasion were fortuitous since the foreman desperately needed the area cleaned. On other occasions such an attitude begot whippings; others who stood up to authority were summarily murdered as an example to any who might conceive of such behavior.

The guerrilla force grew and by the end of 1981 they claimed credit for carrying out more than a thousand ambushes or attacks on barracks and other positions. The Yon Sosa front, based in the oil rich Alta Verapaz, inhabited by Kekcki Indians, turned the area into a major theater of operations. The government had moved ladino settlers on to lands there, pushing entire villages off their centuries' old plots, which provoked bitterness among the Indians. The Yon Sosa guerrillas took advantage of the discontent to recruit and set up support structures with which to harass and attack the enemy. The government responded with a vigorous and brutal counteroffensive. However, most often they could not locate the mobile and elusive revolutionaries.

So, they turned to the military intellectuals from the United States, Argentina and Israel to design, the counterinsurgency program. These experts calculated that before the guerrillas were defeated and 'social peace' restored in Guatemala, up to a hundred and fifty thousand civilians would have to die. Their estimate was low.

A collateral part of the US counter-guerrilla strategy was the removal of the urban support structure used by the revolutionaries. Relying on information gathered with the help of foreign intelligence advisers, the Lucas government's agents in the cities began to murder or kidnap (disappear) suspected opponents. An office of the Catholic Church estimated that in 1981 the repressive agencies eliminated more than fourteen thousand people. During the last three months of the year assassinations averaged twenty-five a day. The government ironically denied holding any political prisoners. This was technically true since suspected subversives were either killed or kidnapped, without any charge being leveled against them.

## LABORATORY FOR REPRESSION

Among the 1981 victims were seven Catholic priests and four Protestant ministers, as well as scores of lay preachers and Church-connected individuals. Guatemala was turned into a laboratory for repression. The international counterrevolutionary advisory corps from the United States, Argentina, Israel and Chile taught Guatemalan officials how to use techniques of torture that had worked against Montoneros, Palestinians and Chilean dissidents. Electric shocks to sensitive body parts left no marks – used in Brazil, Argentina and Chile in the 1970s. Water torture, administered by putting a hose with running water into the victim's nose and sealing his or her mouth – until they talked or drowned. Other tortures included tying the victim's hands and feet to two vehicles – horses in medieval days – each going in the opposite direction and moving slowly.

In the countryside the army simply murdered the population. The village of Rabinal, in Alta Verapaz, suffered a typical 'counter attack' – although the villagers had not been the attackers. Air force planes bombed the village. Troops then marched into the smoldering hamlet, torched the crops, looted the homes or what remained of them and raped the women in front of their husbands and children. Those who tried to resist were shot on the spot. On Good Friday 1981, forty-three Cakchiquel Indian peasants were summarily executed in a raid in the village of Chuabajito in Chalaltenango.

The 'retaliation' became so widespread that scarcely a village in Guatemala remained unaware of the price that would be paid for supporting the guerrillas. Supporting meant not only offering aid or recruits, but failing to inform the government authorities about any individual that might possibly have the remotest connections to the revolutionaries or their sympathizers. Routinely, after carrying out massacres in the countryside, the government would issue a press release declaring that it had won another military battle against the guerrillas.

The propaganda war accompanied the army offensive, but by 1983 the government's claims contained important grains of truth: the revolutionaries were badly hurt. Villagers did become intimidated by the rapacious brutality of the counteroffensive. Village chiefs and elders began to discuss the wisdom of collaborating with the guerrillas.

Inside the rebel organization the losses told. Once again, as they had in the mid-1970s, the roundups removed some of the staunchest comrades from action – and from life itself. Once captured, the 'subversives' were tortured, which worked sometimes to break the individual; and when it did yield valuable information, further arrests were made.

Hermeterio Toj Medrano, an Indian peasant who turned guerrilla fighter, told about his experience after an almost miraculous escape from an interrogation center. Toj described how Israeli, Argentine and Chilean intelligence officials attended torture sessions, gave advice and took notes about the effectiveness of various methods, ranging from electric shocks to mind altering drugs. Some comrades proved less able to resist the modern methods of inducing confessions, however.

When these stories leaked out to the media, the policy team in Washington shrugged their collective shoulders. This is war and war is rough. Indeed, the Pentagon anti-guerrilla specialists had drawn up a 'Program of Pacification and Eradication of Communism' for Guatemala and one of the reasons it had not been implemented was the Lucas regime's inability to administer a proper counterinsurgency. Lucas's generals had been so incompetent as to allow the human rights issue to arise and interfere with the smooth liaison between the Pentagon and the Guatemalan military. Even though President Reagan made known his disdain for human rights, Congressional restrictions on human rights abusing nations did not permit the Pentagon to pour aid and advice into the Guatemalan military. The guerrillas continued to dominate actual military encounters, so much so as to cause 'strategic concern' in Washington lest revolutionary governments spread from Nicaragua to El Salvador and Guatemala.

The Americans did not try to disguise themselves. Indeed, Indian villagers tried not to stare at a six-foot-two inch tall officer like Major George Maynes, as he stood, hands on hips, in front of military headquarters in Nebaj, where he was 'advising' on counter-guerrilla operations in the area. The presence of John Wayne types in Special Forces uniforms added to the intimidation of the villagers. The US officers were well aware of what the Guatemalan government was doing.

The Lucas government killed almost ten thousand civilians by mid 1981. The numbers tortured and displaced were far higher. But still the guerrillas attacked army units, blocked highways and cut telephone lines with relative impunity. The toll paid by the civilians, however, did force the revolutionaries to change their tactics.

## Genocide in the 1980s

By the middle of the 1980s the armed forces had won a strategic victory over the guerrilla forces. Even though the number of guerrilla dead in battle was relatively low, the revolutionaries lost their social base. The civilian population's losses, as estimated by UN sources, ranged as high as 150,000 dead; more than one million people were relocated and a quarter of a million refugees poured into Mexico alone. The revolutionaries had to retreat to remote corners of the country, to areas that were virtually impenetrable. The army set out to deprive the guerrillas of support and shelter by destroying the villages and relocating or killing the villagers.

One illustration of the method occurred in the Huehuetenango village of San Francisco, Nenton. The army company arrived in this hamlet that was suspected of collaborating with the guerrillas early in the morning and separated the village men from the women and children, who were herded together in the village church. Another squad found and slaughtered a bull, which was cut up and put over a fire. The soldiers then shot some of the women in front of their children; others were taken to their homes, interrogated, tortured – some were raped – and then killed with machetes. Some confessed before dying about the whereabouts of guerrillas or about which villagers collaborated.

The children, panicked over the shooting and the separation from their mothers, were left in the church. The soldiers returned after finishing with the women and systematically murdered every child, including the babies.

Then the company had lunch, eating the bull they had roasted. When sated they turned to the men and the village officials, who were locked inside the local court house. Their hands were tied as they were thrown on to the ground in the square. The soldiers then opened fire, riddling each body with rifle bullets. They then torched the courthouse. One survivor escaped to Mexico to tell the tale. The villagers of Huehuetenango watched army helicopter drop napalm on their jungle and dense forests, killing rare species of birds and animals, altering the rain patterns – and burning those people who lived inside of the wooded areas.

The difference between the Guatemalan struggle and those of El Salvador and Nicaragua was the overwhelming Indian presence in the country. Debates over how to appeal to the Indians, and what their class nature was had divided different sects of the Guatemalan left. By the 1980s the revolutionaries had woven the Indian population into the essence of their strategic fabric.

Revolution in Guatemala depended upon revolution on the land and the peasant population was predominantly Indian. The revolutionaries began to re-examine not only their own Guatemalan history, but the entire story of Latin America – including the periods before the Conquest. The Indian had always been the core of the labor force; ignoring Indian culture or referring to it as less developed missed the point. The Indian rose from being neglected by the Marxist revolutionaries to becoming the central focus in their plans.

As the revolutionaries began to recruit Indians of many tribes into their ranks and enlist the support of thousands of others throughout the country, the counterattack strategy of the government and its foreign advisers took shape. Whether planned or not, the revolutionary war of the 1980s permanently changed Guatemala. What held the Indians together were their traditions and institutions, their land and their language, and their way of doing things, ranging from how and what they planted to what they ate and wore and their methods of governance.

The US-designed counterattack destroyed not only over a hundred thousand people but a way of life that had survived the Conquest. The Guatemalan army shook the economic tree of the countryside. It 'freed' human labor, the potential to produce wealth, to contract itself to agribusiness or urban employers. It took away the Indians' poems and songs, forcing the population to become refugees and 'assimilating' them into the ladino culture.

The war, ultimately, turned into far more than a counterrevolutionary offensive: it became a genocidal effort to eliminate the essence of a people. The ruling elite's anti-communist justification for massacring their own countrymen and women rang hollow. In capitals throughout the world there was a growing disgust as people became aware of the extent of the killing. The already unpalatable scenario in Guatemala was made worse by the arrogance of the generals and the aristocrats. The scale of death and corruption increased to the point where the men at Foggy Bottom began to pressure the generals to clean up their image.

For that purpose, most of Latin America's military had learned, nothing succeeds like the spectacle of a free election. President Lucas assured the world that the 1982 presidential elections would be fair. No one believed him. The election results were obviously fraudulent and, when the losing parties protested, the demonstrators were dispersed by force. Lucas ordered the arrests of several opposition party leaders, all establishment types.

The repression against members of the political elite increased the already heavy concerns of some of the top army officers. Uppermost in their minds were the badly managed war and the incomparable levels of corruption. Added to this, the country's economic woes pushed the Guatemalan business and professional class to oppose Lucas. The Guatemalan economic slump, however, had little to do with bad management and corruption. Paralleling most Third World countries in the early 1980s, Guatemala was caught in a global squeeze, despite the discovery of oil in the 1970s, which some thought would yield economic security forever.

Because the country lacked refineries and neither foreign nor domestic capital appeared interested in building them, the oil find proved less than a bonanza. The Lucas government had to keep importing refined products while selling Guatemalan crude at a lower price. Dropping prices for coffee and cotton – the prize export crops – and the revolutionary war took their toll on agriculture. In addition, the guerrillas destroyed the crops of the large estate owners and they made tourism, another good dollar earner, into a dubious proposition. The State Department warned potential travelers to be cautious and not to visit certain parts of the country, enough to deter all but the most determined or ignorant.

Stagnation, inflation, a soaring foreign debt and the flight of capital – this was what Lucas's greedy and inefficient management had wrought, claimed his opponents. The almost total withdrawal of confidence on the part of the business community sparked discussion and then serious plotting inside the officer corps – at both senior and junior levels.

In fact there was a global recession, and all of Latin America and indeed Africa and much of Asia were suffering similar economic setbacks. But inside the junior officer clubs and homes provincialism reigned and Lucas, rather than a world system, was blamed for Guatemala's difficulties. Discussion tended to focus on Lucas's thug-like methods, his corruption, the bad name he had created for the army and for the country. Indeed, his overt brutality had led to the cut off of US military aid.

## RIOS MONTT AND THE CHURCH OF THE WORLD

Inside the army the discontent with the Lucas gang and their new heights of corruption had reached its apex. He and his brethren had looted the Treasury, mismanaged the economy and botched the most important task of their office: the holy war against communist subversion. By early 1982 the guerrillas and their support groups controlled significant sectors of Huehuetenango, El Quiche and San Marcos, had strong roots in other departments and marched virtually unopposed up and down the Pan American Highway, stopping crop-laden trucks and tourist buses. For members of the officer corps the most serious offense was the list of nearly sixty officers killed in 1981.

The defeats suffered by the army against 'the reds' were not only humiliating; they were unnecessary, given the methods available. Death squads gave Guatemala a bad name; they were old fashioned. To end the war, the officers learned from their American teachers, the military must turn itself into a death machine.

The majority of the officer corps organized a coup on 23 March 1982, which received support from the ruling oligarchy and the US government. With a coalition of other generals and colonels, and the support of the Christian Democratic and ultra right political parties, whose leaders were also fed up with the Lucas machinations, General Efrain Rios Montt assumed the presidency. Montt was a product of US counterinsurgency training, a student and teacher at the Interamerican Defense College in Washington, a man with a modern military outlook. He also promised to improve the human rights image, which could no longer be easily brushed aside when the time came each year for Congressional appropriations. Rios Montt was also a Born-again Fundamentalist Christian, who held a zealous attachment to the Church of the Word.

Under his command the army began a new style of counter offensive that delivered devastating blows to the guerrillas in most parts of the country. No longer was massacring entire villages sufficient to combat the guerrillas. The Rios Montt government forced the rural poor of Guatemala to choose political allegiance. Siding with the revolutionaries meant death. The government, borrowing an idea from US counterinsurgency experiences, offered its own program to the Indian peasant.

Rios Montt was no stranger to bloodshed and brutality. He presided over the 1973 massacres of peasants, when he was chief of staff under Arana Osorio. But in 1978 Rios Montt was 'born again'. He announced that he was retiring from the military to take up a career as an evangelical minister in the Christian Church of the Word. When he returned to the political–military sphere, he melded his newly found world of God with that of modern counterinsurgency.

Strangely, Rios Montt claimed that he never dropped his Roman Catholic affiliation. His brother was a bishop in the diocese of Esquintla. One of his admirers, the Archbishop of Guatemala, Mario Cardinal Casariego, told an interviewer in May 1982 of his affection for the military in general:

Thank God the young officers who graduated in 1958 are more religious [than the previous generation]. And they have more contact with the Church. ... I knew them when they were cadets. Now they are government ministers. One of them, the chief of the current junta, was captain of the company of cadets way back in 1958. And today he is chief of state.

The young officers did not share a similar esteem for the clergy. In 1982 the military commander of El Quiche, Colonel Roberto Matta, explained his approach to priests and nuns in his area: 'We make no distinction between the Catholic Church and the subversive communists.' The archbishop, imitating the proverbial three monkeys, ignoring the fact that priests and nuns had abandoned their parishes in Huehuetenango and Quiche, and refusing to acknowledge that the army was murdering, torturing and driving from their parishes members of the clergy, gave full support to the government. Indeed, even after the Bishop of Quiche, a native-born Guatemalan, was denied entrance into his own country upon his return from a visit to the Pope, in which he had pleaded with the Holy Father to intervene and stop the bloodshed in Guatemala, the archbishop declared: 'I don't believe there has been a real persecution in Guatemala.'

Rios Montt accepted support from the right wing of the Church, but he saw Roman Catholicism as less dynamic than the new evangelical churches. He attributed his evolution into leadership as a result of his born again experience. 'Do you know why I am a true political leader?' he asked rhetorically of his countrymen. 'Because I am here without your votes.'

With his comrades from Iglesia Cristiana Verbo advising him, Rios Montt announced that his government would not repress, but proposed a strategy to strengthen the development poles. *Fusiles y frijoles* (rifles and beans) he declared, was the path for his country to defeat communism and promote Christian values. Each week, following his assent to leadership, he appeared on Sunday evenings on Guatemalan television in civilian attire, and sermonized about the need for a national ideology, which, he declared, was 'communitarianism'. Taking his cue from the US-based Moral Majority, Rios Montt offered Guatemalans a return to the familiar authoritarian notion of obedience to the father as head of the traditional family and unquestioned obedience to the state. Rios Montt pledged that he would practice Christian morality as president. He pleaded with his people to pray as a way to stop violence. And he prayed before the TV audience.

There will be no more murdered people on the roadsides; anyone who acts against the law shall be executed. Let's not have any more murders. We want to respect human rights and defend them. It is the only way to live democratically.

Almost as he spoke, Guatemalan air force pilots were ferrying troops to remote parts of the country to 'search and destroy' the guerrillas. Mostly, however, they destroyed Indians and their villages. One teenage Indian woman was cut by a soldier's machete, raped by several of the young men and then forced to witness the execution of most of her family.

'Guatemala needs peace,' Rios Montt preached on 24 May 1982. 'Peace will not be created with weapons. Peace will not be created with police. Peace will not be created by all of the uniformed men. Peace will have to come from your heart.'

In June 1982, just after Rios Montt delivered his peace sermon, the Guatemalan army slaughtered over one hundred peasants in the village of Josefinas, in Peten; more than one hundred and sixty peasant families died in a massacre in Chisec, Alta Verapaz. On 9 June Rios Montt declared himself to be sole ruler of Guatemala, no longer a member of a three-man junta. Three weeks later he proclaimed a state of siege.

Rios Montt characterized his rule as the application of 'communitarianism', which became the only political theme permitted for discussion in the media. By June 1982 he had consolidated his power and declared that Guatemala was preparing to undergo a sea change at God's command, and that political discussion was too corrupt for the populace and was therefore banned. At the same time that Rios Montt saw visions he presided over a military that showed increased efficiency, which meant that the Indian population decreased in size. The army slaughtered scores of thousands by the mid-1980s and removed the Indians' cultural foundations: village, land, dress and language. By burning villages, the army forced the families to break away from the traditional bond; the men had to seek work in urban slums, or become migrant workers. Some of the peasants whose ancestors had farmed for a millennium drifted into a growing criminal class. Some, of course, became revolutionaries.

The new president, however, set out to make it impossible for the guerrilla movement to rise again. Backed primarily by junior officers with a strong sense of military elan and numbering not a few fundamentalists, Rios Montt sought and almost achieved dictatorial control. He appointed seven junior officers, known colloquially as the Seven Dwarfs because of their low rank, as special advisers. With their support he attempted to wipe out politics as it was known in Guatemala – or anywhere else. Just as Lucas and his gang had proven the ability of absolute power to corrupt absolutely, Rios Montt and his Dwarfs tried to demonstrate the reverse, that power need not taint its holders. Under his watch, he announced, government corruption would not be tolerated; and he would deal with those who had misbehaved in the past.

His objective was to mould the army into the single institution of the Guatemalan state, from which would flow peace, order and a proper spiritual life, laced with discipline, uncritical acceptance of authority and an end to discussion about how to guide society. Anti-communism was the watchword.

Rios Montt also attempted to heal the breach between the army and the United States, the country that symbolized near perfection for him. And he wanted to soothe the anger of the Guatemalan air force, unable to obtain spare parts for helicopters from the US manufacturers because of human rights violations. His backers saw Rios Montt as a man who might bring the political and military forces – unified in their anti-communism – into one patriotic effort to defeat the subversives. With primitive religion and modern counterinsurgency methods, the Rios Montt blend assuaged some of the anxieties of upper-class Guatemalans and restored confidence to a substantial part of the military as well. But his methods and rhetoric created new anxieties.

For the year plus of Rios Montt's leadership, Guatemala became one of the most bizarre places in the world. The brutal repression with modern techniques, the massacre of villagers, the ferreting out of 'subversives' in the cities all continued – only under the guise of preparation for the return of the Apocalypse. While having divine visions, Rios Montt also demonstrated an everyday pragmatism required to lead a military machine bent on destroying the basis of the Indian population.

The guerrilla leaders did not anticipate the use of mass murder as the means to cut off the revolutionaries from the population. The level of bestiality employed by the army and its foreign friends caused the guerrillas to suffer staggering blows. For a Guatemalan peasant any hint of connection to the 'subversives' could mean not only his family's death, but the eradication of an entire village.

As Rios Montt's soldiers bombed and burned their way through parts of the countryside, the guerrillas retreated to remote geographical positions, or went into exile in Mexico, where they could regroup and then return to Guatemala when conditions became more propitious. The theoretical differences that had existed before they unified their military commands re-emerged. Confronted with a strategy of genocide, the people who had organized around armed struggle as the route to popular power were faced with the dilemma of continuing the struggle and seeing the people themselves eliminated, or changing their basic strategic conceptions.

## Washington Responds to Rios Montt

The State Department greeted news of the March 1982 coup and Rios Montt's ascendancy with cautious optimism. The national security officials who lobbied Congress annually for military aid to Guatemala preferred the zealous evangelical preacher-cum-general to Lucas and his gangsters. What the Foggy Bottom crowd sought from the Guatemalan government was a change of image, which they thought would be sufficient to persuade Congress to release funds and military supplies.

They informed Congress of Rios Montt's promise to end human rights abuses and punish corrupt officials. The members liked what they heard. Rios Montt understood, however, that he could not simply purge corruption from a military apparatus that had grown used to rich perquisites of office; nor could he quickly compress the seemingly banal political differences amongst the elite into one unified package – at least not at the speed that he and his fervent supporters desired. So, he moved pragmatically, promising to punish, while simultaneously declaring an amnesty law that protected the very officers who had committed the greatest offenses during the Lucas period.

Over the ensuing post-coup months, he replaced Lucas followers when the appropriate pretext arose, without appearing to be plotting against them. He purged officers, but not just to appease the Americans. Rios Montt's vision of the perfect society involved the creation of a meshwork of organized and disciplined cells, integrated from the top downward for the purpose of cementing the cohesion of the family and the workforce to the source of social order: the army. The military was the dynamic, indeed the only force capable if not mandated from Heaven to perform this task of massive regimentation. In military thinking the command is the key to action, and obedience is the automatic response to orders.

Younger officers tended to see Rios Montt as clean, fervent, single-minded, a man willing to undergo suffering and sacrifice while disciplining the nation. He would head the team of military surgeons in excising the cancer of communism from Guatemala as the first step in restoring the nation to political health.

## Civil Defense Patrols and Modern Counterinsurgency

The human rights groups who monitored the counterinsurgency program under Rios Montt's tutelage called it genocide. The US advisers and some of their Guatemalan counterparts viewed the effort as a successful military campaign.

The plan had stages: first, break up as many Indian communities as possible by violence. Encourage those remaining to abandon their dress, language and customs and assume ladino identities. In community after community the army 'recruited' village men to 'defend' their village against the guerrillas. Allowing subversives to enter the village would mean terrible punishment for the members of the patrol – and their families.

Forcing natives to 'police' themselves was as old as colonialism. The more modern version employed by the Guatemalan armed forces came straight from US officers who told about the Phoenix Program in Vietnam. 'Sometimes,' remarked a US officer, in one of the most famous quotes from the Vietnam War, 'you have to destroy a village to save it.' In Guatemala, as in the war in Southeast Asia, villages identified as supporting the guerrillas were destroyed, the men interrogated, tortured and frequently killed; the women and children were relocated in strategic hamlets, or development poles, along with the few men who had 'turned' during questioning.

Those villages not in full support of the subversives underwent a different ordeal. Especially in the western highlands, in which the army suffered humiliating defeats in 1980 and 1981, the villagers were gathered together by troops, usually on market day. The screening of the population then took place as a masked informant pointed out the 'contaminated' element – those who collaborated with the subversives.

The army then set an example. The accused individual was placed in front of the assembled villagers and murdered. Company commanders employed their individual methods of intimidating the local populace: shooting, hanging, burning, beating, or hacking.

One pacification patrol entered El Quiche village on a market day in early 1983. A man with a green hood with holes cut for his eyes walked through the villagers indicating those who worked with the communists. The army then ordered the local civil defense patrol members to kill their fellow villagers. Faced with the threat of death for not complying with the orders, the members of the self-defense patrol hacked off the heads of their neighbors with machetes.

The policy makers in Washington showed little concern for the alarming death statistics from Guatemala. The fear that Guatemala, not El Salvador, would become the next Nicaragua, a domino that would fall on Mexico, governed their political thinking. Rios Montt's assumption of power eased their minds. CIA and DIA (Defense Intelligence Agency) reports agreed that the fanatic fundamentalist could not endure, but that as long as he remained in command the war would be prosecuted efficiently.

Rios Montt was a useful catalyst, a man who could pick up the threads of counterinsurgency and weave them together into a tangible policy. In national security circles there were no illusions that he would survive, because intelligence reports indicated the growing numbers of Guatemalan officers and members of the financial elite found him just too 'weird' to continue as president. He appealed to the far-right Reagan supporters, many of whom belonged to churches similar to the Christian Church of the Word. They appreciated strength, even if it was used in bloody fashion. Even the Ivy League Assistant Secretary of State Thomas Enders, who knew what destruction was occurring, cynically informed Congress that thanks to Rios Montt the death squad killings had virtually ceased and 'concrete measures have been taken against corruption. ...'

Just as the policy elite cared little for the fate of the Guatemalan people and nation when they overthrew Arbenz in 1954, so they were blasé about the consequences of the continuation of their anti-communist-driven foreign policy thirty years later. Like General Castillo Armas, the US instrument for change in 1954, their agent in 1982, General Rios Montt, fell a bit short of perfection.

He consolidated his power, but with each step he made enemies, some of them very powerful. The support from the archbishop not-withstanding, Rios Montt antagonized the Pope himself. Before His

Holiness visited Guatemala shortly after the coup the archbishop, pleaded with Rios Montt not to execute a group of political prisoners, whose trials had been less than open and fair. On the eve of John Paul's arrival, Rios Montt had the men killed. Then, to add injury to insult, he refused to release public funds for the Pope's visit, a violation of elementary protocol.

This incident helped galvanize support for the growing group of irate officers who saw the military primarily as a way to enrich themselves; he had also annoyed those who were passed over for promotion just because they had failed to perform even at minimum military standards. His Sunday sermons, at first a kind of joke among the ruling elite, began to grate on the sensibilities of the Guatemalan upper class. This man, they concluded, was a serious fanatic who could not be counted on to behave reasonably. He even talked about taxing the wealthy.

Like others whom the Americans considered puppets, Rios Montt proved less pliable over issues that he considered matters of national principle. When US officials informed him that they had a plan to resuscitate CONDECA, the moribund regional military alliance, Rios Montt protested and refused to authorize the use of Guatemalan armed forces to bully Nicaragua.

Rios Montt's 'weirdness' caused problems, however, only when it interfered with US policy objectives. He carried out the Pentagon's counterinsurgency policies with dispatch; he cleaned up the bad human rights image – not the reality. Official Washington did not deny the reports of Amnesty International and America's Watch, whose monitors counted the civilian war dead and reported on the genocidal activities of the Guatemalan military and their US counterparts. For the Pentagon, the war was going well, the guerrillas were on the run and areas once in enemy hands belonged anew to the government.

Congress allowed the Guatemalan air force to buy spare parts which worked out 'just fine' according to a sergeant advising a Guatemalan unit. What he meant was that the A—37 Dragonfly gunships could devastate a village or a guerrilla grouping with rocket and machine-gun fire. When two A—37s buzzed the presidential palace, on 8 August 1983, however, Rios Montt knew his time was up. The coup that leading generals had openly called for was upon him. His pledge to remove the Seven Dwarfs, and send his mystical advisers away from the presidential palace, rang on deaf ears. Rios Montt retreated into an obscure corner of the military establishment and into his religion. (In 1991 his name re-emerged as a candidate for president. He did not win.)

## Mejia Victores and the Continuation of Genocide

The new president was no stranger to the Pentagon. Or to brutality. Mejia Victores's assumption of power brought a wave of relief to the less than zealous members of the officer corps and to the Washington bureaucracy, which also felt uneasy in its dealings with a religious fanatic. The change in Guatemalan leadership, however, meant no relief for the majority of the population. By late 1983 the number of death squad victims had reached more than two hundred per month, almost double the average during Rios Montt's reign. The massacres in the countryside, under the guise of fighting the subversives, continued even though the guerrillas had been forced to leave.

Corruption, made more difficult by Rios Montt, reappeared in all of its previous forms, including the ability of one person to hire gun men to murder personal enemies, or possible lovers of wives and husbands – for $200 a hit. Sometimes the victims were labeled as communists, or guerrilla officials; in reality most of the death squad targets had little or nothing to do with politics.

The Reagan Central America team saw the transition from a 'kooky general' to a straight one as an opportunity to resume military aid, especially the provision of helicopter parts that would allow the Guatemalan army to ferry troops into 'suspected guerrilla territory' and to 'fire on enemy targets from the air'. In reality, the helicopters served to haul troops to villages suspected of cooperating with guerrillas so that the villages could be wiped out and the troops returned quickly to base. The helicopter gunships fired on unarmed peasants. By late 1983 the army controlled most of the rural areas.

Mejia Victores promised to pursue the war to its end, rid the presidential palace of religious zealots and evangelical rhetoric, and return to 'normalcy'. In practical terms this meant government by decree, issued by the commander of the armed forces acting as head of state. He consulted with other generals, announced the results to the nation and then had the armed forces carry them out.

The guerrillas by 1984 had evacuated most of the territory they had won in combat, and those not in exile hid in unpopulated difficult-to-reach areas. Nevertheless, Mejia Victores continued to pursue, not the elusive guerrillas, but the Indian population in the countryside. He warned that resumption of full-scale guerrilla war could occur at any moment. The army continued to commit routinely acts of terror that served as warnings to the remaining population that the army would be ever vigilant against 'subversion'.

In those provinces where activity had been high, the army destroyed most Indian villages systematically. The disoriented populace were placed in controlled villages, 'development poles', and forced to assume defense patrols against possible guerrilla activity. In return for carrying rifles, 'beans', as Rios Montt had called his tiny subsidy program, were given to the 'well-behaved' villagers. With these fascist versions of the Russian tsars' Potemkin villages in place, Mejia Victores proclaimed that major steps had been made in the battle against communism. The human rights monitoring groups reported a drop in the number of killings – down to about one hundred a month in 1985.

Some of the revolutionaries saw a sign of hope for their movement when Congress condemned the Lucas and Rios Montt governments for human rights violations and continued to withhold military aid. In fact, however, the real distance existed between Congress and those who ran the nation's foreign policy, in the CIA, and the Departments of State and Defense. As far as the national security apparatus was concerned there was no way that the United States was going to let Guatemala fall to Marxist guerrillas.

US policy was genocide, called by other names and justified as an anti-communist war strategy. In fact, if carried to its logical conclusion, the extermination of people suspected of being potential guerrillas due to their Indian blood and culture meant that racism was inherent in the policy. The US advisers knew only that their job was to prevent the communists from winning by any means necessary, and the murdering of young Indians insured against the reproduction of a guerrilla support system. To the ladino elite of Guatemala the Indians had always been somewhat less than human.

When Rios Montt and Mejia Victores were finished in their presiding roles over the slaughter, as many as 150,000 Indians had died. Some quarter of a million refugees had fled to Mexico. More than one million people had to relocate inside Guatemala. So horrendous were the casualties that some guerrilla leaders despaired over the prospect of armed struggle as the key to forcing change in Guatemala.

The political costs of military rule were paid by everyone. Guatemala had become a pariah nation thanks to the excesses of the thugs with general's epaulets who had governed the country since the overthrow of Arbenz. In addition, the military had to shoulder the blame for economic failures or inefficiencies in managing the bureaucracy. The

Guatemalan elite criticized them for every problem that arose from labor disputes to trade imbalances. Church officials heaped verbal abuse upon them and foreign critics of their rule abounded.

The media, that had virtually ignored the story, began to run features about the Guatemala slaughter, so that even the elite circles in the Reagan administration began to demand 'democracy' as a condition for clienthood. The prestigious nations demanded that Guatemala return to civilized forms, as if this would somehow obfuscate the brutal reality of life that Guatemalans had endured for thirty years.

By 1985 the military had so thoroughly entrenched itself, had so institutionalized its essence into the fabric of society that its leaders believed they had little to fear from civilian rule. A civilian president could not alter, no less abolish, the control mechanisms through which the army had 'pacified' the countryside. The military would enshrine its autonomy in law and declare an amnesty for its members, thereby exempting them from possible prosecution for the myriad of crimes they had committed against the population – from murder, torture, kidnapping and arson to the massive robbery of the country's patrimony. Finally, the military made it crystal clear that a civilian who challenged their authority would find himself summarily removed from office. With all these protections in place, the scene was set for the elections.

## The Guerrillas Reassess

The guerrilla leaders of the three groups met for lengthy strategic discussions after their retreat. Mario Payeras admitted that they had not anticipated the ferocity of the government attacks, nor the discipline with which the army behaved in its massacre-and-burn policies. At the same time, the guerrillas' headiness over their victories in the late 1970s and early 1980s had led them into a mood of overconfidence.

Poorly trained and poorly armed villagers could not defend themselves against the military. Nor could supporters of the guerrilla cause withstand the soldiers' brutality. Torture, mutilation and death coerced some of the staunchest peasants to reveal information about the location and identity of the rebels.

The guerrillas, having proclaimed certain territories 'liberated', found themselves unable to defend them against air attacks, followed by large ground units using armored attack vehicles. The rebel armed forces, however, could retreat, as they had been trained to do. The villagers were left with the consequences.

In the 1960s the guerrillas failed to establish a solid base of operations within urban and rural communities. And they negated the role of the Indian in the struggle. In the 1970s the regrouped organization took great care to construct a strategy that revolved around indigenous peoples – except for one omission. They did not anticipate the logical move that US advisers would dictate to the Guatemalan armed forces: adapt the Vietnam War model. Thus, when the villages were attacked there was no realistic defense plan, nor escape routes that might have allowed villagers to flee from the terror.

No matter how ideologically advanced some of the peasants had grown, the guerrillas had not prepared them for the onslaught of modern counterinsurgency. Much of the laborious organizing done during the 1970s was erased – by death and destruction of the village itself. The infrastructure that had developed in the urban areas, especially among working-class organizations, did not relate to the activities in the countryside because the revolutionaries had not figured out how to coordinate the two arms of struggle. Into the mid-1980s the guerrilla leaders discussed, argued, analyzed as the genocide continued.

The strategy that emerged by 1986 was dictated by the changing realities of Central America and Guatemala in particular: take advantage of any opening of political space; continue to engage in armed struggle where practical; and, in the spirit of Contadora and the larger Central American peace process, press for negotiations at the same time. The advent of civilian government forced on the Guatemalan elite by the excesses and brutality of the military changed the political equation.

## The Cerezo Years

Vinicio Cerezo appeared as the candidate acceptable to the world of public opinion and as a man whom the Guatemalan elite could abide. He claimed: 'I cannot advocate agrarian reform because the military would not tolerate it.' The ruling military circles appeared to like what they heard. Cerezo also declared just before election day in November 1985 that 'no one will be tried for past crimes'. For Cerezo 'the past must be forgotten'. The military assumed he was referring not only to the countless crimes carried out by its members, but to the attempted assassination of Cerezo himself, in 1979, which left the Christian Democrat wounded and frightened.

Throughout the world, he won the endorsement of liberals and conservatives alike. He appeared to be a man of democratic principle and personal courage, someone who could win enough internal and external prestige to bring the military brutes into line. All around Latin America dictatorships were falling; in Central America external pressures were forcing changes as well. 'Cerezo', said a Washington official, 'is the man who will be able to establish a set of rules to achieve social peace.'

What Cerezo and the Washington policy makers failed to realize was that nothing short of redistribution of wealth could serve the interests of stability and order. The key fact about Guatemalan politics lay in the very area that Arbenz was in the midst of addressing when he was ousted: almost 90 per cent of the population were desperately poor and just over 10 per cent had access to the better things of life.

The only way to govern the country without altering the balance of wealth was to institutionalize counterinsurgency, as the permanent form of governing. As one wit phrased it: 'In Guatemala, Clausewitz has been reversed; politics is an extension of war by other means. Cerezo enlarged the political space during his years in office. Freedom of expression grew, and with it, labor and other struggles took more overt forms.'

Side by side with counterinsurgency, pluralism developed from the mid through the late 1980s. But material life worsened, not because of Christian Democratic economic policies, but because the Guatemalan economy, like most other Third World structures, no longer possessed any independence. The prices of its exports and its imports were fixed by institutions far removed from Central America. Its creditors, ranging from private banks and foreign governments to the IMF and the World Bank, became collection agents. Guatemalan capital fled the country for more secure and lucrative investment centers. Technology continued to remove certain kinds of jobs from the labor force, with the result that the poor grew poorer, some middle-class families faced with Cerezo's enforced austerity measures dropped down to the level of poverty and the rich grew nervous.

The fragile balance between a republican form of government and a counterinsurgency state cannot withstand the pressures of constant, inherent social strife. Thus, President Cerezo's days were numbered, not by his own paralysis when confronted with threats by various and sundry military thugs, or by the bickering inside of the small civilian political space that existed. The façade of democracy also allowed the revolutionaries to re-enter the political domain, primarily in the labor and protest movements. (The military front continued at a very low level in the mid-1980s.) Cerezo realized that his position as titular head of state could not be used to resolve the issue of division of wealth.

To make matters worse he inherited a mismanaged economy whose leading indicators were pointing downward.

The owning class in Guatemala, like their counterparts in neighboring Central American republics, did not care about their country – at least as far as investing their money was concerned. Capital flowed out, poverty increased. The tax base needed to maintain the bare minimum of government services required that the rich pay a pittance to the government. This was, to the aristocracy, the equivalent of communism. It symbolized the vulnerability, not the strength, of wealth, and, like the United Fruit Company's fear of Arbenz's land reforms, the rich feared any tax on their assets.

In addition to the grumbling bourgeoisie and the arrogant officer corps, Cerezo had another master to serve as president: the International Monetary Fund. The generals had initiated the borrowing pattern, but under Cerezo the debt service grew painful and the fund directors imposed an austerity plan on him. Neither the military nor financial elite had any patience for explanations about why Guatemala could not simply continue as it had in the past; nor could Cerezo explain it to people with closed ears.

The revolutionaries also responded to the economic crisis by utilizing their newly found political space for protest and organizing. In the countryside guerrilla units surprised the over-confident military and slipped back into territory they once held. This time, maintaining a low profile, they waited for ideal opportunities and struck without warning at army patrols. They also destroyed economic targets.

As their American advisers taught them, successful counterinsurgency does not derive from military victories or terrorizing and relocating the population. A counterguerrilla campaign ends only when the ruling apparatus shows it can meet the bare needs of the population. Ironically, Rios Montt and his evangelical cohorts understood this notion, and were prepared to carry it out. But the majority in the oligarchy and the officer corps could not think in terms beyond their narrow self interests. Both deemed land reform unthinkable; without it, the majority had no basis for a decent life.

The revolutionaries stated their thesis simply. Since the military and economic elite would not consider sharing resources with the rest of the population, and since even under nominal democracy no redistribution took place, the population had to fight to get its share. The army had defeated insurgencies since the 1960s and, like the proverbial cat with nine lives, the rebels arose again.

Gradually, the guerrilla raids increased and, with them, the consequent retaliation through terror. But there were less people to terrorize and of those that remained in the villages many were at their wits end. Counterinsurgency, the American advisers began to relate to their bosses in the Pentagon, would be a permanent or at least a very long-term operation. Congress, reflecting the will of the public, could not stomach continued aid to brutal repressive forces in Central America.

As the Reagan period wound down US emphasis shifted from a victory strategy to one of negotiations with the revolutionaries. Some of the generals and the politicians acknowledged that the war could not be won; or, the cost was too great to continue indefinitely with a state of counterinsurgency alongside a slumping economy.

## THE MURDER OF MYRNA MACK

The guerrillas understood that US national security officials had decided to do whatever was necessary to prevent revolution from succeeding. The reward part of the strategy was missing. The development poles, the civil defense squads and the beans and rifles approach faded as the officer corps lost some of their enthusiasm for administration. Drug trafficking entered the Guatemalan equation and by the mid-1980s became a routine part of life for some members of the military.

As Central America moved from the top of the Reagan priority list down toward the bottom of the Bush agenda, the revolutionaries found new possibilities. In the countryside they harassed the army and the large plantation owners. With the onset of formal civilian government, they had re-established themselves inside of the civil society, in labor and professional, human rights and religious circles. The government's use of extra-legal means to curtail dissent resonated poorly by the late 1980s, especially in the ears of those who had become major creditors. IMF, World Bank and Inter American Development Bank officials had little patience for the human rights harangue that they received from outraged politicians and prestigious people throughout the world. They told the Guatemalan authorities to stop. President Cerezo, of course, was powerless to control the army and police. But the multilateral agencies' wishes were relayed to the generals and to the oligarchy.

Two incidents in late 1990 characterized the military's growing desperation over their inability to silence all of its critics by stopping the guerrillas permanently. Myrna Mack was a Guatemalan anthropologist who studied abroad and returned to her native land in the early

1980s to try to help the more than one million Indians who had been displaced by the army's war strategy. She publicized the existence of these impoverished people in academic circles, whence information spread to wider audiences. Her research included vast numbers of interviews with people of many tribes, all of which served as a massive indictment of the armed forces of the country.

In late August 1990, she noticed that several men were keeping her under surveillance, including two who rode motorcycles. Dr Mack told friends that she was convinced these men, judging from their body language and the way they dressed, worked for the military.

In the early evening of 11 September 1990 two men stabbed Dr Mack to death on the street as she left her downtown Guatemala City office. The police treated the case as a routine homicide, omitting from their report all testimony that identified the men watching Dr Mack as military intelligence agents. Myrna Mack's murder, the official report hinted, might have been linked to 'delinquents', who worked with her on 'black market' operations. President Cerezo remained non-committal when visiting Members of Congress quizzed him on the case.

The second event demonstrated to the military and their advisers that the old tactics would no longer work. It occurred on 2 December 1990, during Cerezo's final weeks as lame duck president. The army had stolen property from the people of Santiago, Astitlan. They had raped women and teenage girls, and beaten and stabbed village men until the villagers decided that enough was enough. Thousands from the region gathered, unarmed, in front of the army headquarters as a show of protest against the army's continued mistreatment of village residents. One of the officers, drunk according to some reports, ordered the men to open fire on the Indian peasants. When the noise and smoke from the volleys had cleared, more than thirty bodies lay on the ground, the majority children. There were fifteen dead. It appeared to be another routine massacre in the long era of bloodbath.

But the Indians who dispersed after the shooting immediately reorganized and began to collect signatures on a petition that demanded punishment for the murderers. In the document with thousands of signatures, some of them just an 'x', they also demanded that the army unit stationed in the village be moved.

The peasants did not win all their demands, but after several months the army unit was removed. Pressure from around the world finally began to dissipate the arrogant power of the third generation of military gangsters who had ruled the country since the capricious US-backed coup of 1954.

News spread quickly that unarmed people stood up to the intimidators after a massacre and refused to back down. In addition, peasants began to occupy land owned by the government. In the capital a wave of strikes spread and squatters took plots that were unoccupied. The new president, Jorge Serrano Elias, like Cerezo, could not control the armed forces and police, who assaulted the protesters. Serrano, however, understood that he had to include the masses in some form of concord if the government were to retain legitimacy. As long as land reform was inadmissible even for discussion the government had nothing but naked force on which to rely.

Like the Nicaraguan people at the end of the Somoza and the Sandinista periods, the peasants of Santiago, Astitlan, spoke for the majority. Resistance grew. So did repression again, the army responding like the clichéd Pavlovian dog. But the world was now in Guatemala, from the IMF representative to the United Nations observer who was to sit in on the scheduled talks between the guerrillas and the government forces. In Guatemala the remaining Indians clung to their heritage, making it clear that before they would give it up the bloodbath would have to continue.

The peace talks began in 1990 and continued in 1991. Like the FMLN in El Salvador, the Guatemalan revolutionaries tempered their demands as befitted the times and their military position. Although weakened over the decades they had proven their ability to revive and strike at the army and at the economic heights of the country. The war droned on – an ambush, a retaliatory massacre, a promise, and a wave of strikes and demonstrations.

The Bush administration pressed for settlement, as did international bankers and merchants. In the 1950s President Jacobo Arbenz had insisted that only through land reform could Guatemalans achieve a modicum of social peace. Nearly fifty years later the issue of land reform remained the pressing question. One State Department official, who served during the Carter years, bemoaned the day that President Eisenhower had made the decision to intervene and rudely and bloodily interrupt the dynamics of Guatemalan history. 'The tragedy', the official intoned, 'will endure for many decades more.'

The damage done to Guatemala cannot be calculated. It began in 1954 when under the guise of fighting communism the CIA toppled the

Arbenz government and the Pentagon subsequently fashioned a modern military strictly for internal repression. Behind the titular power of each elected Guatemalan president stood a gang of military guerrillas who maintained real power. And they reproduced like genetic clones of each other. The cost in human life over the four decades since Arbenz fled to Mexico came to almost one million people.

In Washington, State Department officials privately conceded that Guatemala 'is a human rights mess', but that as long as the lore of electoral government and political pluralism remain Guatemala will be considered a success story, not worthy of serious attention. The generals continue to kill and persecute the indigenous poor, but they tend to be obedient when Washington commands in other areas.

In January 1993 Guatemalan Army units waged yet another offensive against 'subversives' in several northern provinces. Human rights monitors reported that civilian casualties were high. In 1992, the revolutionary Rigoberta Menchu won the Nobel Peace Prize, and announced that she would return to Guatemala and promised to lead thousands of Guatemalan refugees in Mexico back to their native villages. A Guatemalan general was quoted in a newspaper saying that Ms Menchu's return would be dangerous for Guatemala and for Ms Menchu herself.

Like intervention in Nicaragua and El Salvador, US interference in Guatemala's destiny had little political or strategic meaning. Intervention in Central America in general and Guatemala in particular demonstrated two things: how the consequences of a *coup d'état* could endure for fifty years or more, and the extent to which imperial hubris dictated US policy, from 1954 through to 1992.

# 5
# CONCLUSION

In the late 1970s and early 1980s revolution appeared to carry the dynamics of the future as it spread in Central America and throughout the Third World. The romantic idealism of Sandinismo, the inspiring images of Farabundo Marti rebels and armed Guatemalan peasants became a source of hope for progressive idealists well beyond the developing world. In Europe and the United States, Australia and Canada, solidarity and support movements arose which, in turn, became part of the international political dynamic in the 1980s.

By the end of the decade, however, it was counterrevolution that prevailed. Even before the formal collapse of the Soviet Empire, and the disintegration of its internal parts, the age of revolution had waned. By late 1991, only Cuba clung to the orthodoxies of the past. In China, Vietnam and North Korea the ruling parties gave appropriate obeisance to the antiquated language of Marxism–Leninism, but the content of that ideology bore little resemblance to daily life.

Instead of inaugurating a new era of liberation, as revolutionaries believed, the uprisings of the 1970s and 1980s may well have symbolized the end of an historic era that had endured more than a century, one in which peoples aspired to nationhood, meaningful concepts of sovereignty and independence. By the 1990s, transnational corporations and multilateral lending institutions controlled the commanding economic heights of most poor nations.

Yet, in spite of the growing globalization of communication, transportation, production and distribution, nationalism continued to inspire people to act. Economic chaos threatened Central America, yet the leaders of the left continued to use a discourse which implied that there still was a path through which the majorities of El Salvador or Guatemala could realize themselves as a collective entity and enter the course of world history. As the socially necessary cost of labor was reduced throughout the world, the poor of regions like Central America became ever more an aggregate of cheap and mobile labor, a vast pool into which capital could dip when it needed.

The ugly fact of the 1980s was that an historic era characterized by the emergence of nation–states had run its course – and only a few Third World nations succeeded in winning their place in the mainstream of modern history. Nicaraguans emerged as historical players for the decade of the 1980s; the Guatemalan and Salvadoran guerrillas did not. The Cuban revolutionaries, after seeing their island nation play important roles for three decades in Africa, the Middle East and Latin America, clung desperately to maintain their version of the failed Soviet system. In the face of rapidly depleting Soviet support and energetic hostility from the United States, Cuba withdrew from its global role, attempting to maintain at home the gains of thirty years of struggle and to ward off the ever ambitious intentions of the United States, ninety miles away.

The Soviet Union ceded the territories it controlled directly and virtually abandoned those communist regimes such as Cuba and Vietnam that did not share its border. President Gorbachev admitted that the Soviet economic and social crises were so acute that it could no longer afford even a pretense of being a great power.

Nor could the Americans maintain the global empire they had amassed during the Cold War years. The United States ensured its military hegemony through displays of force in Panama in 1989 and Iraq in 1991, but lacked the economic means to convert victory into profits. In 1991 the United Fruit Company was no longer the monopoly that could dictate terms to Central American governments and take advantage of cheap land and labor there. Indeed, UFCO had broken apart from the 1960s on. New corporate systems took over the fruit business on a global scale. The old monopolies of the first half of the century were replaced by giant business entities, many of them centered in Japan and Europe. These conglomerates no longer needed protection from American marines; indeed, sophisticated corporate thinking tended to dismiss the Reagan administration's obsession with military spending as inefficient.

The IMF and the multilateral banks acted as collection and credit agencies for corporations and banks. Third World governments tended to be the caretakers for those who fifteen years earlier had eagerly offered them loans. By the early 1980s those who accepted the cash had become major debtors, and to maintain any status in the world trading scene they were forced to accept the dictates of World Bank and IMF technocrats, who designed their budgets. The meager services that governments offered in some poor countries were eliminated or greatly reduced.

As the geopolitical and economic order evolved in the 1980s, US interventionist behavior toward its traditional fiefdom in Central America remained unchanged. The flimsy Cold War pretext dissolved and the once formidable economic interests dissipated. Yet, decision-makers in the national security complex practised the same imperial hubris as had President Theodore Roosevelt in 1900, as if the urge to intervene was magically etched into the chairs of the Oval Office and the imperial impulse was osmotically transferred to whomever sat in them. Intervention was an outdated axiom posing as a coherent national policy.

The Third World state, with few exceptions, no longer provided education, health care, or basic services. By the 1990s most governments of the Third World did little more than maximize the mobilization of the national labor force and offer use of national resources for the benefit of foreign capital. Failure to run their states frugally meant a cut-off of IMF loans and withdrawal of their good housekeeping seal of approval.

In the 1980s President Reagan not only destabilized Central America but invaded the tiny Caribbean island of Grenada – ostensibly to rescue American medical students. Nearly a decade later the unemployment rate there was over 60 per cent. In late 1989, President Bush ordered the invasion of Panama, to capture one of his own agents. The campaign to get General Manuel Noriega, head of Panama's armed forces and long-time CIA and DEA agent, was the most expensive arrest in the history of the world. It cost as many as 1,000 lives and property damage exceeding $2 billion.

The war with Iraq in 1991 further demonstrated the extent to which the imperial impulse operated in US behavior. When it was over, the war turned out to be nothing more than a status quo conflict. Saddam

Hussein remained in power and the disco Arabs returned to their kingdom in Kuwait to persecute foreigners 'suspected of collaborating with Iraq'. The price of oil remained stable; the Middle East remained unstable.

The revolutionaries of Nicaragua, El Salvador and Guatemala were forced to adapt to global and regional changes. The Sandinistas, a 'loyal opposition' in 1991, maneuvered for position and property in Nicaragua. President Chamorro discovered that the country was virtually ungovernable without Sandinista cooperation. The United States went all out to back her candidacy but soon after she won the 1990 election she received little help from Washington. A decade of war following forty-five years of Somoza's looting of the country had left the economy destroyed, and there were no available funds forthcoming to rebuild it. So, as under Somoza, except without the presence of the National Guard as an additional irritant, Nicaraguans figure out individually and in families how to survive. Goods are once again available in the markets, but few Nicaraguans have money to buy them. *Playboy* and other US and European sex magazines have replaced the collected writings of Fidel Castro, Che Guevara and Kim il Sung on the newsstands. The bands and singers who toured Nicaragua and the world bringing revolutionary music to the masses are now playing commercial songs in discos. Violent street crime has increased, thanks in part to the number of demobilized soldiers and ex-Contras with weapons, and to the lack of available jobs in the country.

Disputes over land ownership, especially in Nicaragua's northern border regions, led to renewed fighting. The Sandinistas had not established a system by which clear title was held by those to whom land had been given since 1979, and some of the returning counter-revolutionaries were claiming their old property.

In El Salvador peace appeared close in late 1991. But many obstacles remained. The military clutched at the war because the war meant wealth. The generals and colonels who stayed in their plush quarters and vacation homes while battles raged still held forth the old communist bogey man in their attempt to intimidate the US Congress for one more dole of aid. The revolutionaries, however, learned and adapted to the changing times. They became reformers, but insisted on practical concessions from the government. They would be eligible to join a new police force, a UN agency would oversee a transition during which the army would be shrunk radically, a tacit recognition of the fact that its sole purpose was to combat internal opposition, not foreign aggressors.

Learning from the problems plaguing Nicaragua after the Sandinistas lost state power, the FMLN ensured that the Salvadoran accord included guarantees that the peasants who occupied lands in FMLN-controlled territory will hold exclusive title to them.

The telling statistics about the war in El Salvador were the 80,000 dead – imagine that many people dying in Wales (roughly equivalent in size and population) – and the one million Salvadorans who had moved to the United States. Washington, D. C., with a quarter of a million Salvadorans, many undocumented, had become one of the largest Salvadoran cities.

In Guatemala the UN observers began to play a greater role in talks between the guerrillas and the government. But no clear settlement was in sight. The slaughter continued even as the business establishment and indeed some of the officer class began to tire of the endless war. The government had defeated the guerrillas in the 1960s and again during the 1980s. Each time the revolutionaries re-emerged, as they do throughout history when injustice reaches intolerable levels.

Why were the wars fought? The guerrillas were possessed with the mission to bring about sovereignty and independence, along with social justice. The military and oligarchy partnership in all three countries had a parallel objective: to retain or increase their already lion-sized share of the national wealth. The populace continued to endure the daily assault by the oligarchy and the military on basic human sensibilities.

The United States interfered in the internal history of the nations to its south, to the terrible detriment of generations of Central Americans to come. Ronald Reagan's obsession with the specter of Soviet power in Central America became the justification for this new round of interventions. It was a fixation that he inherited from a century of presidents. The United States, ever the protector of the propertied class, intervened in the 1980s and into the 1990s because its leaders had acquired the habitual impulse to do so. Empire was a way of life; whether or not it translated into wealth, it certainly was a means to maintain institutionalized power and hegemony.

CIA analysts knew that the Soviets were uninterested in Central America, but their reports to that effect never reached policy levels. Instead, billions of dollars were poured into war-making endeavors in Central America in the name of combating a mortal US enemy. The US taxpayers received no security benefits from the money because there was no threat to begin with.

Once the decision was made, however, to fight the 'evil empire' in

Nicaragua, El Salvador and Guatemala, the local war lords were reluctant to let go of their financial angel. Under the guise of combating 'reds', the military cliques of El Salvador and Guatemala fattened their wallets at the expense of the US taxpayers. Meanwhile, their countrymen and women suffered.

Almost every aspect of Central American life declined for the majority of the people during the 1980s. Prospects for the 1990s looked even worse – in terms of economic development. Like much of the Third World, war was accompanied by deepening poverty, foreign debt, population displacement and serious environmental deterioration. The wars took their toll on the life of future generations as well. Added to the decades of uncontrolled spraying of pesticides and chemical fertilizers, and military governments turning a blind eye toward massive industrial pollution, came the contamination of war, of napalmed forests, the endless noise and exhausts of tanks, trucks and armored vehicles in once idyllic rural areas. War meant that meager budgets inadequate for peacetime development, would be dissipated for totally unproductive enterprise: the poor drafted into the armies, under orders from US-trained officers, killed the poor who joined the guerrillas, and tens of thousands of civilians suspected of supporting the revolutionaries – or who just got in the way of a bullet, a shell, or a bomb.

The policy makers in Washington continue to pay lip service to treaties pledging non-intervention and to the concept of sovereignty for smaller nations. In their actions they obey the more compelling dictates of an interventionist past. Presidents Reagan and Bush declared their devotion to the building of democracy in Central America, while supporting the very forces of plutocracy and violence that most oppose meaningful democracy.

Like the proverbial Bourbon kings of France the national security officials neither learn nor forget anything. If there is a certainty about the future of the Western Hemisphere it is that the United States will intervene again – against alleged radicals, drug traffickers, or terrorists.

Why, in light of the predictable American interventionist behavior, do Latin American radicals continue to resist? In 1920, when asked to comment on the significance of the Irish revolution, Sean O'Casey, the Irish playwrite, supposedly quipped: 'Never have so many died for so little.' It remains to be seen whether the hundreds of thousands of dead Central Americans will have perished for the betterment of their countries.

The likes of Carlos Fonseca, Roque Dalton and Myrna Mack live on in poetry and song. Their heroism forms part of a culture that perseveres in Central America and in the *barrios* of Los Angeles, Houston and New York. Their lives remain significant for new generations because Central American history and culture – unlike that of the northern colossus – remain inseparable.

When historians write the story of the 1980s they will mention Oliver North and the names of those major and minor players involved in the monumental Iran–Contra scandal, from CIA Chief William Casey to Eugene Hasenfus, who 'kicked' supplies from a CIA plane to the Contras before he was shot down and captured. These men brought death to the region in the name of fighting a mythical enemy. In fact, they were guided by the interventionist impulse that brought William Walker to Nicaragua in the 1850s and General Smedley Butler and his marines throughout the first two decades of the twentieth century.

# Further Reading

There exists a formidable literature on the military conflicts that have taken place in Central America in the modern era. The books suggested below are aimed at providing a balanced list for the general reader. Most contain their own bibliographies.

Christopher Dickey's account *With the Contras* (Simon & Schuster, New York, 1986) is an extraordinary piece of on-the-scene journalism. His profile of 'Bill', the CIA operator who arrived in Managua on the day of the Sandinista triumph, is also a classic piece of reporting. The details coincide perfectly with information the author gleaned from sources in Managua and Washington. Peter Kornbluh's *Nicaragua: The Price of Intervention* (Institute for Policy Studies, Washington, 1987) is a comprehensive account of the CIA's secret war on all of its fronts.

Piero Gleijeses' *Shattered Hope* (Princeton University Press, 1991), and Susanne Jonas' *The Battle for Guatemala: Rebels, Death Squads, and U.S. Power* (Westview Press, Boulder, 1991), both offer historical insights into Guatemala, as does Mario Payeras in his guerrilla journal, *Days in the Jungle* (Monthly Review Press, New York, 1983). Robert Armstrong and Janet Shenk's *El Salvador: The Face of Revolution* (South End Press, Boston, 1982) offers both the kind of information, analysis and passion that will help coming generations to understand the essence of that war in its early years.

For an overview, Gabriel Kolko's *Confronting the Third World: United States Foreign Policy 1945–1980* (Pantheon, New York, 1988) provides marvelous perceptions of contemporary American foreign policy thinking.

## Selected Books

Arnson, Cynthia J., *Crossroads: Congress, the Reagan Administration, and Central America*, Pantheon, New York, 1989.

Barry, Tom, and Deb Preusch, *The Soft War*, The Resource Center, Albuquerque, NM, 1986.

Berryman, Philip, *The Religious Roots of Rebellion: Christians in the Central American Revolutions*, Orbis Books, Philadelphia, 1984.

Blachman, Morris, William Leogrande and Kenneth Sharpe, *Confronting Revolutions: Security through Diplomacy in Central America*, Pantheon, New York, 1986.

Blum, William, *The CIA: A Forgotten History*, Zed Press, London, 1986.

Bonner, Raymond, *Weakness and Deceit: U.S. Policy and El Salvador*, Times Books, New York, 1984.

Booth, John A., and Thomas W. Walker, *Understanding Central America*, Westview Press, Boulder, 1989.

Cabezas, Omar, *Fire in the Mountains*, Simon & Schuster, New York, 1987.

Clements, Charles, *Witness to War*, Bantam, New York, 1984.

Fish, Joe, and Cristina Sganga, *El Salvador: Testament of Terror*, Olive Branch Press, New York, 1988.

Galeano, Eduardo, *Guatemala: Occupied Country*, Simon & Schuster, New York, 1967.

Gutman, Roy, *Banana Diplomacy: The Making of American Policy in Nicaragua, 1981–1987*, Simon & Schuster, New York, 1988.

Hamilton, Nora *et al.* eds, *Crisis in Central America: Regional Dynamics and U.S. Policy in the 1980s*, Westview Press, Boulder, 1988.

Herman, Edward S., and Frank Brodhead, *Demonstration Elections: U.S. Staged Elections in the Dominican Republic, Vietnam, and El Salvador*, South End Press, Boston, 1984.

Klare, Michael T., and Cynthia Arnson, *Supplying Repression: U.S. Support for Authoritarian Regimes Abroad*, Institute for Policy Studies, Washington, 1981.

Klare, Michael T., and Peter Kornbluh, eds, *Low Intensity Warfare: Counterinsurgency, Proinsurgency and Antiterrorism in the Eighties*, Pantheon, New York, 1988.

LaFeber, Walter, *Inevitable Revolutions: The United States in Central America*, W.W. Norton, New York, 1983.

Landau, Saul, *The Dangerous Doctrine: National Security and U.S. Foreign Policy*, Westview Press, Boulder, 1988.

Lawyer's Committee for International Human Rights, El Salvador: *Human Rights Dismissed*, New York, 1986.

McClintock, Michael, *The American Connection: State Terror and Popular Resistance in El Salvador*, Zed Press, London, 1985.

Montgomery, Tommie Sue, *Revolution in El Salvador*, Westview Press, Boulder, 1986.

North American Congress on Latin America, *1984 Report on Guatemala*, New York, 1984.

Pearce, Jenny, *Promised Land: Peasant Rebellion in Chalatenango*, Monthly Review Press, New–York, 1986

*The Report of the Bipartisan Commission on Central America, Chairman Henry Kissinger*, Government Printing Office, Washington, 1984.

Sundaram, Anjali, and George Gelber, eds, *A Decade of War: El Salvador Confronts the Future*, Monthly Review Press, London, 1991.

Thomson, Marilyn, *Women of El Salvador: The Price of Freedom*, Zed Press, London, 1986.

*Turcios Lima: Una Biografia*, Tricontinental, Havana, 1967.

Zimmerman, Marc, *El Salvador at War: A Collage Epic*, MEP Publications, Minneapolis, 1988.

# Appendix

## 'Political Parties and Paramilitary Groups in El Salvador'

### POLITICAL PARTIES

PDC      Christian Democratic Party
Founded November 1960. Based on principles of social Christianity and private property.

MNR      National Revolutionary Movement
Founded 1965. Social democratic party and member of the Socialist International.

UDN      National Democratic Union
Founded 1969. Operated as the legal arm of the outlawed Communist Party.

UNO      National Opposition Union
Coalition of PDC, MNR and UDN in both 1972 and 1977 presidential elections.

### PARAMILITARY GROUPS

ORDEN      Organizacion Democratica Nacionalista
Founded 1968. Civilian paramilitary network of 50,000–100,000 people under the direction of the President of the Republic.

### DEATH SQUADS

UGB      White Warriors Union
EM      Escuadron de la Muerte
Maximiliano Hernandez Brigades

FALANGE      Anti-Communist Armed Forces of Liberation-War of Extermination
Right-wing terror units emerging in the mid- to late-1970s, operating with the acquiescence if not direct collaboration of government and military forces.

### POPULAR ORGANIZATIONS AND LEFT COALITIONS

BPR      Popular Revolutionary Bloc
Founded 1975. Largest of the popular organizations. Coalition of peasants, workers, students, teachers and slum dwellers, including the two major peasant federations – Federation of Christian Peasants (FECCAS); and the Union of Rural Workers (UTC), and the national teachers organization ANDES, the Union of Urban Dwellers (UPT), the Union Coordinating

|  | Committee (CCS), and three university and secondary school federations (MERS, FUR, UR-19). Linked to FPL. |
|---|---|
| FAPU | United Popular Action Front<br>Founded 1974. Oldest of the popular organizations. Member organizations include two student unions (FUERSA and ARDES), one peasant union (MRC), one labor union (VP) and one teachers organization (DMR). Links with FARN. |
| LP–28 | Popular Leagues – 28th February<br>One of the smallest popular organizations, named after 1977 massacre of demonstrators protesting General Carlos Humberto Romero's fraudalent election. Primarily student dominated, but has one union affiliate (LPO), one peasant league (LPC), and one association of market workers (ASUTRAMES). Linked to ERP. |
| MLP | Popular Liberation Movement<br>Founded late 1979. Smallest of the popular organizations. Linked to PRTC. |
| CRM | Revolutionary Coordinating Council of the Masses<br>Founded January 1980. Executive committee of popular organizations and the UDN. |
| FD | Democratic Front<br>Alliance of union, professional and university groups as the Social Democrats and a splinter of the Christian Democrats. Formed in April 1980. |
| FDR | Revolutionary Democratic Front<br>Founded April 1980. Alliance of popular organizations represented in the CRM with the twelve groups of the Democratic Front. First President of the FDR was Enrique Alvarez Cordoba, killed November 1980, along with five other FDR leaders. |

## GUERILLA GROUPS

|  |  |
|---|---|
| FPL | Popular Forces of Liberation<br>Largest of the guerrilla forces, founded in 1970, headed by Salvador Cayetano Carpio, former member of the Communist party. |
| ERP | People's Revolutionary Army<br>Guerrilla group founded by students and a radicalized splinter of the Christian Democrats in 1971, headed by Joaquin Villalobos. |
| RN | National Resistance<br>Guerrilla group founded in 1975, out of a split with the ERP following the assassination of poet Roque Dalton. Headed by Ferman Cienfuegos. |
| PCES | Communist Party of El Salvador<br>Party founded in 1930 but outlawed virtually since its founding; armed wing headed by Shafik Jorge Handal. |
| PRTC | Revolutionary Party of Central American Workers<br>Small armed group founded in 1979, headed by Roberto Roca. |
| DRU | Unified Revolutionary Directorate<br>Policy and strategy committee for all five guerrilla groups, first established May 1980. |
| FMLN | Farabundo Marti Liberation Front<br>Coalition of all five guerrilla groups, formed October 1980. |

# Index

216